AMERICAN FAMILIES IN CRISIS

Selected Titles in ABC-CLIO's
CONTEMPORARY
WORLD ISSUES
Series

For a complete list of titles in this series, please visit
www.abc-clio.com.

Books in the Contemporary World Issues series address vital issues in today's society, such as genetic engineering, pollution, and biodiversity. Written by professional writers, scholars, and nonacademic experts, these books are authoritative, clearly written, up-to-date, and objective. They provide a good starting point for research by high school and college students, scholars, and general readers as well as by legislators, businesspeople, activists, and others.

Each book, carefully organized and easy to use, contains an overview of the subject, a detailed chronology, biographical sketches, facts and data and/or documents and other primary-source material, a directory of organizations and agencies, annotated lists of print and nonprint resources, and an index.

Readers of books in the Contemporary World Issues series will find the information they need to have a better understanding of the social, political, environmental, and economic issues facing the world today.

AMERICAN FAMILIES IN CRISIS

A Reference Handbook

Jeffrey S. Turner

CONTEMPORARY WORLD ISSUES

A B C   C L I O

Santa Barbara, California
Denver, Colorado
Oxford, England

Copyright 2009 by ABC-CLIO, Inc.

Library of Congress Cataloging-in-Publication Data
Turner, Jeffrey S.
   American families in crisis : a reference handbook / Jeffrey S. Turner.
     p. cm. — (Contemporary world issues)
   Includes bibliographical references and index.
   ISBN 978-1-59884-164-0 (hard copy : alk. paper) — ISBN 978-1-59884-165-7 (ebook)   1. Family—United States—Handbooks, manuals, etc.
I. Title.

   HQ536.T796 2009
   362.820973—dc22

                2008043888

13 12 11 10 09   1 2 3 4 5

This book is also available on the World Wide Web as an eBook.

Visit www.abc-clio.com for details.

ABC-CLIO, Inc.
130 Cremona Drive, P.O. Box 1911
Santa Barbara, California 93116-1911

This book is printed on acid-free paper ∞

Manufactured in the United States of America

Dedicated to the college students who have come and gone in my classroom and touched my life. All 12,000 of them.

Contents

List of Tables

List of Figures

Preface

We are living in an age of near-overwhelming change. To successfully adapt to change and the challenges it brings, families must embrace their past in order to live through the present and prepare for the future. For, contrary to that most popular of adages, while ignorance may well be bliss, knowledge of oneself and one's family is central to survival. To this end, *American Families in Crisis* is designed to encompass our current knowledge about that most central of human groups—the family—and stands as witness to its resiliency and durability in the wake of adversity and turmoil.

At one time or another, all families face troubled waters. A crisis can happen at a moment's notice and can penetrate the fabric of even the strongest families. Examples of family crises include unemployment, illness or disability, addictive behaviors, the loss of loved ones, caring for aging family members, or having to cope with a divorce. During these modern and uncertain times, other crises have added new dimensions to family disruption and disequilibrium and demand research attention: school shootings, natural disasters, deployed military families, and adolescent suicide. Any of these crises has the potential of creating a situation in which the family perceives a sudden loss of its ability to employ effective problem-solving and coping skills. Depending on the severity of the crisis, the signs and symptoms of domestic upheaval may last a few days, several weeks or months, or longer.

American Families in Crisis offers insight into how family crises can be identified, as well as how to prevent and respond to such challenges, in the process building family strength and resiliency. This reference manual begins with an introductory chapter exploring the conceptual components of family crises, including important concepts, themes, and theories widely used in the field today. Once this foundation has been established, the text explores 12 key problems plaguing modern-day families. In Chapter 2, readers will learn about the impact of the following on families:

- Addiction
- Adolescent runaways
- Unemployment
- Infidelity
- Divorce
- Chronic illness and disease
- Caring for aging family members

In Chapter 3, attention will be focused on five problems particularly prevalent in modern U.S. society:

- Domestic violence
- School violence
- Natural disasters
- Deployed military families
- Adolescent suicide

Throughout the book, an effort is made to integrate the key points explored in Chapter 1 into each of the above crises. This section, backed by hundreds of key reference sources (95 percent are post-2000) enables readers to explore the varieties of family crises that exist, including elements contributing to disharmony as well as intervention techniques designed to resolve them. A particular emphasis is placed on strategies and techniques for dealing with challenging or threatening family behaviors. The remaining chapters of the book present notable contributors to the field, important data and documents, and resources for further information.

Each chapter is designed to be engaging as well as informative, empirical as well as pragmatic. Everyday examples are used to show readers how the information can be applied to their lives. Strides have been taken to make the "facts" of the book interesting to the reader by revealing how other families deal with stress and crises and by offering ways for readers to apply the hard data of the book to their own families.

The volume is designed for a broad range of readers in college, high school, institutional, and public library settings. It makes a valuable reference source for high school courses focusing on marriage and family; troubled relationships, family stress, and crises; family development; parent-child relationships; and interpersonal relationships. At the college level, it has significant appeal to those students studying family systems, family therapy, guidance and counseling, crisis intervention, and conflict resolution.

American Families in Crisis exposes the reader to major crises impacting modern-day families. A thread weaving itself throughout the text is how a crisis in the life of one member affects other family members. Although it is made up of individuals, a family is a system, and what affects one member affects the others. A particular emphasis is placed on a preventive or proactive approach to family crisis intervention. Techniques for intervention, assessment of risk, and follow-up counseling are stressed. Intervention services designed to restabilize the family by providing the tools to improve family functioning and build connections to support networks in the community receive special attention.

Another key element throughout the book is the manner in which children are impacted by family stress and crises. We tend to think of childhood as a time of life free from pressures and worries. However, younger generations are not immune to the stresses surrounding them. On the contrary, children are sensitive to changes in routine and are often deeply affected when a crisis—a divorce, a natural disaster, a chronic illness of a loved one—touches their lives. Like adults, children encounter feelings of helplessness and lack of control that stress and crises bring forth. However, unlike adults, youngsters have little experience to help them place the current challenges into perspective. They are also less able to put their feelings into words. Complicating matters is that children are exposed to crisis events through television, radio, newspapers, magazines, and even adult conversations that they overhear. All of this may cause children to respond with a combination of worry and fear, which will inhibit their ability to cope.

This reference manual takes aim at such child-oriented issues and offers readers practical guidance and supportive assistance during times of family stress and crises. Although children respond differently to disasters—depending on their age, level of understanding, and maturity level—they need to be assured that resiliency and family equilibrium can be restored. They also need to know that loved ones are there to help them regain stability and support. Parents must recognize that when they assist children during times of domestic upheaval, they not only help youngsters handle their feelings but launch a recovery program of their own.

I would like to take this opportunity to thank those individuals who helped make this book a reality. At Mitchell College, appreciation is extended to Dr. Mary Ellen Jukoski and Dr. Gilbert J. Maffeo Jr., for their ongoing support of my research and writing. Dr. Catherine Wright, chair of the Behavioral Sciences Department, kept me sane as I neared the end of this project, often putting out numerous fires and protecting me from needy students who seemingly enjoy rattling the cages of those professors burning the midnight oil. Dr. Scott Horton and Dr. Nancy Levine of the Behavioral Sciences Department also provided needed support and encouragement, and their sense of humor lifted my spirits and added much-needed levity to my work. I wish to thank Lindsay Hollis for transcribing my often disjointed, hen-scratched notes and transforming them into a readable and fluid manuscript. My students also deserve praise and acknowledgment, for it was their very interest in family stress and crises that planted the seeds for my penning this reference manual.

I would also like to extend my appreciation to a truly wonderful team of professionals at ABC-CLIO. Mildred Vasan, acquisitions editor, saw the potential of this project early on and provided many helpful suggestions, encouraging me to push forward. *American Families in Crisis* is my fourth book with Mim, and for every title she has been a source of great inspiration and support. Holly Heinzer was a splendid managing editor, who proved invaluable with her knowledge, advice, and dedication. Holly is directly responsible for a number of additions, improvements, and refinements, and without her energy and ideas, this book would not exist. How Holly managed to maintain her upbeat, enthusiastic, and sunny disposition while working with a sometimes moody and cantankerous author remains, at least for me, one of life's greatest mysteries. I also wish to thank Kim Kennedy White, submissions editor, who brought spirited enthusiasm and vision to this project. Her editorial expertise was instrumental in transforming a rough manuscript into a readable and an engaging book. Appreciation is also extended to Joyce Dunne, copy editor, and to Christian Green, production editor.

Christian was responsible for orchestrating the completion of this title and keeping its production on schedule.

Finally, to my loved ones goes my deepest appreciation: my wife, Nancy, and sons Jeremy, Zachary, and Benjamin. Writing requires many personal and family sacrifices, and the patient understanding of those closest to my heart enabled me to devote the long hours necessary to complete this project successfully.

1

Background and History

Introduction

For the Greenwood family, the nagging problem was financial in scope. The Mattison household never seemed to recover from the accidental death of their nine-month-old son. Around-the-clock care for their aging parents placed the Thompson family in a continual state of sorrow and depression. And for Donna Rivera, the problem persisting for years was her alcoholic husband. (Names used in this book are fictitious unless otherwise noted.)

In this introductory chapter, the nature of family stress and crisis is explored, as is the concept of therapeutic intervention—be it individual counseling for the principally affected family member, the entire family unit, or some segments of it. This exploration is presented not only in terms of the traditional American family but also with full recognition that many variations in family systems exist today (e.g., single parents, cohabiting relationships, gay partnerships, grandparent-grandchild living arrangements).

Throughout the family life cycle, successful adjustment involves the mastery of tasks, challenges, and demands met along the way. For example, couples just starting out face such developmental tasks as establishing and maintaining intimacy, adjusting to parenthood, and launching careers. These are all life changes that bring along their share of change and challenge.

Other events persist into middle and late adulthood. In midlife, coping with the departure of grown children or caring for aging parents are but two examples of potentially stressful life situations. During late adulthood, adjusting to retirement,

1

adapting to lowered income, and dealing with the death of one's partner offer the potential for disruption and stress.

And throughout all of life, crises not limited to any developmental period of family life appear. They are sudden and abrupt, a "bolt from the blue." They are unexpected and capable of creating upheaval and disorganization: the deployment of an adolescent or a spouse to war, a school shooting, a natural disaster such as a hurricane or tornado, a family member's addiction to gambling, or an unfaithful spouse. These changes are especially difficult for families because they require the system to deal with many changes, often simultaneously (Nelson 2007; Kanel 2007; Patrick 2007).

As this book will reveal, some families are not able to rise to the challenge and instead experience suffering and defeat. Others, though, are flexible enough to make needed changes and are able to develop resiliency and higher levels of functioning. **Resiliency** is a family's ability to recover from disruptive change without being overwhelmed or acting in dysfunctional ways.

Stress: Basic Terminology and Concepts

Before the manner in which stress affects the family is explored, some basic terminology and concepts need to be defined. **Stress** is the common, nonspecific response of the body to any demand made upon it, be it psychological, sociological, or physiological. In effect, stress represents change. Demands made by the internal or external environment upset the balance of a person, heralding the need to restore internal stability.

From a family crisis point of view, stress is normal and often unavoidable. It needs to be recognized from the outset that stress in one family member impacts the system's overall functioning, all of the parts contributing to the whole. Necessary adjustments have to be made by the entire system. A **system**, then, refers to the family unit and the members comprising it. Although certain levels of stress accompanying life changes are minimal and can be easily handled, other levels are not so easily managed and can create a crisis situation (Miller and Cohen 2008; Greenberg 2008; Hattie, Myers, and Sweeney 2004).

It might prove worthwhile at this juncture to introduce two terms related to family functioning, particularly in relation to stress and crises. **Family equilibrium** refers to the ability of a system to function smoothly and demonstrate stability and balance, particularly in the face of challenge or change. **Family disequilibrium**, on the other hand, is a state marked by upheaval and instability. Usually, the family system loses its ability to utilize its resources in a way that controls and contains challenge or change.

A **stressor** is an external event or condition that affects the equilibrium of an organism. Stressors are thus situations that place the family in a stressful state. Examples of stressors include emotional turmoil, fear, disease, physical injury, and even fatigue. Everyday stressors may include domestic tensions, personal tensions, noise, interpersonal relationships, indecision or anxiety about work-related issues, and so forth. Obviously, stressors become very individualized. What is one person's stressor may be viewed with indifference by someone else (Catherall 2005; Goodrick, Kneuper, and Steinbauer 2005; Snyder 2001).

A number of stressors may work together at any one time and create disequilibrium. They may be big, small, nagging, or acute; some stressors remain uncategorized. In all, six major types of stressors have been identified. First are **social stressors**, such as noise or crowding. Second, **psychological stressors** include such elements as worry and anxiety. Third are **psychosocial stressors**, such as the loss of a job or the death of a friend. Fourth, **biochemical stressors** include heat, cold, injury, pollutants, toxicants, or poor nutrition. Fifth, **philosophical stressors** create value-system conflicts, lack of purpose, or lack of direction. Finally, **endemic stressors** are long term in scope and have become so prevalent that humans have learned to live with them, such as being afflicted with a chronic disease or illness (Blonna 2007; DiMatteo and Martin 2002).

Stressors are thus conditions producing some type of reactive change that triggers physical (e.g., increased pulse rate) and psychological (e.g., worry) reactions. But it should be pointed out that both good and bad circumstances can be stressors and thus can interfere with the body's balance or equilibrium and create a stressful state. For example, it does not matter whether you have won the lottery or are in the midst of moving into a multimillion dollar home, whether you have failed an important college exam or have just been reprimanded by your boss. A state of stress has been launched in each situation (Seaward 2005; DiMatteo and Martin 2002).

It is important to recognize, therefore, that stress has both positive and negative qualities. **Eustress**, or positive stress, occurs when the body's reactive change is put to productive use. For instance, athletes often use the anxiety and tension in their bodies before a game as a method of "psyching themselves up" for the competition. It may well be that humans function best at moderate levels of stress, or healthy tension. In fact, the lack of stress often creates a reaction known as "cabin-fever syndrome," where there is too little stimulation, variety, and challenge (Nevid and Rathus 2007).

Distress, on the other hand, is negative and unpleasant stress. It occurs when the body and mind are worn down from repeated exposure to an unpleasant situation (McGowan, Gardner, and Fletcher 2006). Stress of this nature can affect the body's overall immunity, nervous system, hormone levels, and metabolic rates. It can create anxiety and other forms of emotional upheaval and disorganization. Distress can also lead to real physical illnesses such as hypertension, headache, sleep disorders, peptic ulcers, and cardiovascular illness (Cormier and Hackney 2008; Greenberg 2008).

Primary and Secondary Stressors

Stressors can be either primary or secondary. A **primary stressor** is one that initiates the stress response. **Secondary stressors** are conditions that result from the first stressor and keep the stress response activated. Primary stressors are primary in the sense that they are the root origin of a series of other problematic life circumstances, the secondary stressors. Secondary stressors are not necessarily secondary in their potency and refer to the spillover of the primary stressor into other aspects of a person's life (O'Halloran and Linton 2000).

For example, suppose a person is suffering from drug addiction (primary stressor). The primary stressor in itself creates an altered state of consciousness through intoxication. But the stress response does not stop here. To illustrate, drug addictions also tend to upset the balance of family life and create turmoil and upheaval. Confrontation, embarrassment, fear, or abusive behaviors are not uncommon behaviors in homes dealing with an addicted family member. Extending beyond the family, the addict often faces employment difficulties, such as absenteeism and lowered work performance. All of these behaviors represent secondary stressors. Secondary stressors combine with the primary stressor, creating a self-destructive cycle.

Theories of Stress

Several noteworthy theories of stress have been proposed and are worthy of our attention. If the reader is to achieve a clear understanding of the many dynamics attached to family stress, an examination of how stress leaves its mark on the individual must be undertaken. This way, one will be able to better understand how the pieces of the system converge and affect the whole unit.

Han Selye's Theory

Han Selye (1982, 1980) developed the concept of the *general adaptation syndrome* to help explain the physiological changes that occur when prolonged physical or emotional stress is experienced. The general adaptation syndrome consists of three successive stages: alarm reaction, resistance, and exhaustion.

The *alarm reaction* stage occurs when the body's defenses prepare for the stressful situation. Hormones that arouse—for example, epinephrine (adrenaline)—are produced and the person switches from the *parasympathetic* nervous system (the system that controls internal organs on a day-to-day basis) to the *sympathetic* nervous system (the system that serves as a "backup" or "reserve" emergency system). For short spurts of energy, the backup nervous and hormonal (endocrine) systems are quite remarkable.

Should a family member remain under stress, the stage of *resistance* is encountered, wherein the body continues to produce huge amounts of energy. A person could remain in this stage for hours, days, months, or even years. Since the individual is in high metabolic gear, the wear and tear on the organism can be phenomenal. However, each of us experiences these two stages regularly with no significant impact on our health and well-being. This is because most stressors are encountered and removed with regularity. The trick is to not lapse into the third stage.

Exhaustion is the final stage of the general adaptation syndrome. Exhaustion hits us when a counterreaction of the nervous system occurs and the body's functions decrease to abnormal levels. Continued exposure to stress at this time may create stress-related diseases such as high blood pressure and ulcers, or even depression and death. Whether or not one reaches the stage of exhaustion depends on a number of factors, including the intensity of the stressor and the amount of time spent in the resistance stage.

Selye's three stages should be viewed as a cycle of adaptation. When used repeatedly, the human machine runs the risk of breakdown. Our reserves of adaptation energy can be compared to an inherited bank account from which withdrawals are made but to which deposits cannot be made. Following exhaustion from stressful activity, sleep can restore resistance and overall adaptation almost to previous levels, but total restoration is probably unlikely.

Karl Menninger's Theory

An interesting contrast to Selye's general adaptation syndrome is a stress theory developed by Karl Menninger (1963). Menninger proposes that stress introduces a psychological continuum that includes five levels of emotional response. Each level represents a progressive degree of emotional disorganization.

Level 1 disorganization is commonly called "nervousness," tension that is produced when an individual is experiencing stress management difficulties. Feelings of anxiety, fear, frustration, and even anger escalate. These feelings are also usually accompanied by psychosomatic disorders. Everyone at one time or another enters level 1.

Level 2 disorganization is characterized by neuroses such as phobias, hysteria, obsessions, and physical disorders. Individuals at this level typically withdraw by fainting or developing amnesia; they may become infantile, dependent on drugs, or hypochondriacs. Because of individual differences, an assortment of other debilitating or semidebilitating disorders may be present.

Level 3 disorganization often includes aggressive behavior (homicide, assault and battery, and other social offenses), often with little or no evidence of conscience. *Level 4 disorganization* often triggers psychotic behavior. That is, the person loses contact with reality, sometimes becoming paranoid and delusional. Finally, at *level 5 disorganization,* there is a loss of will to live, and the disorganized person at this level may become severely depressed, lethargic, or even suicidal. Physical death is not atypical at this level.

Meyer Friedman and Ray Rosenman's Theory

Why is it that some persons are more susceptible to stress than others? How can one person's pleasure be another person's poison? Again, individual differences account for wide variations in stress reactions. For instance, some persons can be classified as "hot reactors." Their psychological and physical makeup is such that stress causes disruption and a state of upheaval. Others react to the same situation without physical or psychological harm, or they react with only a brief disruption in their stability and well-being.

The *Type A and Type B stress theory* proposed by Meyer Friedman and Ray Rosenman (1974) helps to explain why stress reactions vary from person to person. More specifically, they suggest that the *Type A* personality is a stressful one and prone to cardiovascular disease. Individuals with a Type A personality are extremely competitive and impatient and always seem to strive to accomplish more than is feasible. They are always rushed and undertake multiple tasks on a regular basis. Type A behavior also includes difficulty in controlling anger and aggression, which usually persist beneath the surface and are expressed in the form of fist-clenching, facial grimaces, nervous tics, and tensing of muscles. Also, Type A traits include impulsivity, hurried speech, no compassion for other Type As, and feelings of guilt during periods of relaxation.

The *Type B* personality contrasts with Type A behavior. The Type B personality is characterized by a generally relaxed attitude toward life, no hostility, and competitiveness only when the situation demands it. Type B personality types have no sense of urgency about them and do not have free-floating hostility. Unlike Type A personalities, Type Bs have the ability to relax without guilt.

Research indicates that not only are Type A personalities more likely than Type Bs to suffer coronary heart disease but also fatal heart attacks occur almost twice as frequently in Type As. The relationship between Type A behavior and heart disease is reported to be especially significant for individuals in their thirties and forties, and it affects both males and females. Among women, the most prominent group of Type A personalities comprises those who have changed their lifestyle to fit executive careers. Research such as that conducted by Friedman and Rosenman illustrates that although cardiovascular disease is related to many factors, such as obesity and smoking, the role of the stressful personality cannot be overlooked.

In addition to the Type A and Type B personality types, a third has been recently recognized: the *Type C* personality. Type C personalities are individuals who sustain considerable stress but have learned to cope with it. Whether or not they are bothered by cardiovascular illness depends on how effectively they have learned to cope. Many of us tend to be in this category, since nearly all of us share, to a certain degree, some characteristics of the Type A personality. The more involved persons are with these characteristics, the more involved they are with stress and the more they need to learn about effective coping strategies.

Family Stress and Crises

Now that the nature of stress has been explored, including theoretical explanations, an application of this material to the family system is in order. As indicated at the outset, families rarely experience life without complication or strain. A **family crisis** occurs when the system encounters disruption to its everyday routines and experiences a state of disequilibrium or instability. Sometimes, day-to-day hassles can pile up and cause a stress overload. The crisis creates a turning point: things will either get better, or they will get worse (Nelson 2007).

Usually, the moment of crisis is followed by a period of disorganization and emotional upheaval, during which the family makes various attempts to resolve their problems and regain control. In the end, some adaptation is achieved for better or worse. This outcome is frequently governed by the way in which the family organizes itself and by its interaction during the crisis period (Goldenberg and Goldenberg 2008).

Developmental Crisis

A **developmental crisis** (also called a normative crisis) originates from predictable, developmental changes over the family life cycle. This crisis is related to the developmental tasks faced by the family at a given point in time, such as when the system moves from one transition to another. Developmental crises are regarded as normal, and therefore carry some element of predictability. Because of that predictability, intervention often includes anticipatory guidance, or the provision of information informing the family about what is going to occur.

If the crisis is handled advantageously, it is assumed that the result will be some kind of family achievement, maturation, or development. More important, the family regains its equilibrium. If the crisis is not handled well, new areas of conflict surface and disequilibrium results. In the next chapter, we explore the developmental crises of caring for aging parents. Notice how such a crisis for the most part represents an expected life transition and reflects a developmental, normative quality.

Situational Crisis

A **situational crisis** (also called a non-normative crisis) is neither predictable nor normal. Rather, this type of crisis is sudden and abrupt and can occur at any point in the family's development. Examples of situational crises include violent crime, the sudden loss of a child, hospitalization, or financial ruination. Because of the unpredictable and unforeseen nature of situational crises, families may not have the psychological, social, or material resources needed to manage the situation. Situational crises are often emotionally overwhelming and disabling.

Situational crises, similar to those of a developmental nature, require the family to find ways to restore equilibrium and stability, to develop new styles of coping. If successful, the system will grow through its adaptive strategies and no doubt enhance its resiliency (Myer and Moore 2006). If unsuccessful, the family may resort to ineffective strategies, and the suffering will most likely be long lasting. In addition, situational crises run the risk of never being resolved (Goldenberg and Goldenberg 2008; James 2008).

Traumatic Crisis

A traumatic crisis is an extreme variation of a situational crisis. A **traumatic crisis** is often life threatening and, due to the circumstances, gives survivors a feeling of extreme helplessness.

Traumatic crises are highly stressful events. In Chapter 3, "Special U.S. Issues," attention is focused on a number of such crises: domestic violence, school violence, natural disasters, deployed military families, and adolescent suicide.

One of the most important scholars in the field of trauma research is Charles Figley (Figley 2006; Figley and Barnes 2005; Barnes and Figley 2005; Figley 2002a, 2002b, 2002c; Figley, Figley, and Norman 2002). Figley observes that traumatic crises disrupt the lifestyle and routine of survivors, cause a sense of destruction and loss, and leave a permanent and detailed memory of the event that may be recalled voluntarily or involuntarily. From Figley's research some of the characteristics of traumatic crises that impact families can be identified. These are discussed below.

Limited Time to Prepare
Victims typically have little or no time to prepare because of the trauma's sudden onset. Because of this, the individual victim or family is prevented from planning and rehearsing a survival strategy.

Limited Sources of Guidance
Information is available on coping with family life situations, but these resources are usually geared toward developmental crises. Sources of guidance are limited for those families who must cope with such traumas as experiencing the World Trade Center terrorist attacks or sending loved ones off to war.

Experienced by Few
Families who are victims of trauma are relatively small in number and typically have limited access to one another. This situation underscores the need for families in similar situations to offer mutual support and guidance.

Slight Previous Experience
For most, the traumatic crisis is a new experience. For those who do have repeated exposure to the same type of crisis, the amount of stress experienced has a tendency to decline. For example, frequent flood and coastal storm victims demonstrate fewer stress symptoms than new inhabitants of these disaster-prone areas when natural crises occur.

Interminable Time in Crisis

Traumatic catastrophic crises may last days, months, and even years. Recovery is difficult and victims often feel that the worst is not yet over.

Lack of Control/Helplessness

Compared with families undergoing developmental crises, families trapped in traumatic crises are often unable to modulate the sources of stress and are powerless to remove or postpone them. Consequently, traumatic crisis victims experience a sense of being out of control and helpless.

Disruption and Destruction

Although developmental crises are disruptive, in the presence of change they usually bring new roles, routines, and responsibilities. Traumatic crises, on the other hand, have the potential of disrupting and destroying a family's entire lifestyle, including deep and permanent changes.

Sense of Loss

Loss as a result of traumatic stress can embody more than death. Indeed, a loss of time, loss of innocence, loss of a role or function, or loss of a sense of invulnerability can occur.

Emotional Impact

Developmental stressors are usually emotionally upsetting, but they tend to be acute for only limited durations. Catastrophic stressors often are acute as well as chronic.

Medical Problems

As mentioned, stress can create health problems. Such stress-induced disorders are found more frequently among victims of traumatic crises. The threat of physical harm or death causes the most intense of human reactions and leaves behind an emotional imprint, which may never go away.

At this juncture, it might prove useful to summarize the progress made so far in this introductory chapter. Most families encounter stress in their lives, and the stressors that trigger the need to adjust and adapt come in all shapes and sizes. In some cases, the stressors of family life are isolated and are resolved before a pileup of stress occurs. Should this be the case, disorganization and emotional upheaval often result. Our knowledge of the impact of stress has been heightened by the theories proposed by Selye, Menninger, and Friedman and Rosenman. Developmental, situational, and traumatic crises are variations of the disequilibrium that can result. Families may become disorganized in the face of a crisis and may not be able to effectively adjust to it.

History of Family Crisis Intervention

Family crisis intervention, an extension of family therapy, is a relatively new division of the helping professions. Its roots can be traced to the 1930s through the 1960s, to a number of key figures who began challenging conventional therapy by including whole families in their approach to helping troubled individuals. Although it is impossible in the confines of one chapter to trace the contributions of all family therapy pioneers, the reader is directed to Chapter 5 for background on some of the more notable figures—Milton Erickson, Jay Haley, Don Jackson, and Virginia Satir, among others.

At one time, maladaptive behavior was approached by individual treatment strategies. The therapeutic focus was placed squarely on the person creating family instability. Today, however, it is recognized that therapy should embrace the whole family, since domestic disequilibrium rarely exists in a vacuum. Rather, domestic problems are best understood when the practitioner examines the family as a system, including its roles, rules, and other processes of functioning. This treatment mode became known as **systems theory**, a school of thought proposing that individual behavior cannot be understood without reference to its past and present relationships, especially family interactions.

Michael Nichols and Richard Schwartz (2006) point out that unlike individual therapy, which is directed at a client's personal makeup, this new approach regarded the family as a whole as the unit of treatment. Treatment began to be viewed as most powerful and effective when it was applied directly to the entire family system. Family therapists began looking at families as not causing problems; rather, they became more interested in the family patterns of interactions that perpetuated and influenced problems. As this therapeutic approach took hold, all members of the family were encouraged to meet with the therapist, who in turn sought to analyze family dynamics as a whole. Early clinicians made an effort to help family members become more conscious of patterns or interactions and communication styles (Sexton, Weeks, and Robinson 2003; Sandoval 2002).

The family therapy movement took hold and gained a strong following. Proponents maintained that a systems approach shed more light on the many complexities of turmoil and instability. Therapists agreed that prompt, action-oriented intervention focusing on the crisis yielded great benefits for the entire system. A shift in therapeutic strategies thus emerged. Problems were treated by changing the way the system works rather than trying to "fix" a specific member. Family crisis therapists sought to help a distressed individual and his or her family by defining the crisis in terms of the system. Therapists utilized the family's combined coping skills to deal with the existing, as yet unresolved, situation (Goldenberg and Goldenberg 2008).

Since its inception in the 1930s, family therapy researchers have provided much insight into stress and crises. As the discipline evolved, each new theory built on what came before, and each provided a new perspective. Of particular importance to this volume are those theories aimed at how families adjust to disequilibrium and instability. Two theories in particular merit our attention—the ABCX and Double ABCX models. It is important for the reader to understand the importance of theories when investigating topics in the social sciences (or any discipline, for that matter). Theories are explanations that unify facts. Theories help us grasp the meaning of the facts being collected, thus enhancing our understanding of the topic at hand (White and Klein 2007). As family crises are explored in the next two chapters, reference is made to the various facets of the theories covered here.

The ABCX Model

Reuben Hill (1949) was one of the earliest researchers to explore the effects of stress on the family. His theory—referred to as the **ABCX model**—is an older, yet nonetheless relevant, contribution to the field of family studies. It is an excellent illustration of how a meaningful theory can withstand the test of time and still have contemporary application. Hill's model consists of four components, indicated by the letters ABCX:

The Stressor (A)
This part of the model refers to the stressor challenging the family. Recall that a stressor is a condition that usually triggers

change and brings the potential for instability and disharmony. Hill maintained that family stressors can be classified according to their impact: *dismemberment,* the loss of a family member (for example, death), which in turn affects the unit's social structure; *accession,* the addition of new family members (birth, adoption), which changes the family's structure; *loss of family morale and unity* (alcoholism, abuse); and *changed family structure and morale* (divorce, desertion). Note how all of these stressors can change many facets of family life, including roles and patterns of interaction.

The Resources (B)

This facet of the model represents the family's resources for dealing with the stressor. The successful application of these resources will provide resistance and, ultimately, prevent disequilibrium. Two primary forms of family resources have been identified: *integration* and *adaptability.* Family integration refers to unity and strength in such areas as affection, interests, and economic interdependence. Family adaptability embodies the concept of flexibility, that is, the family's ability to implement an assortment of problem-solving strategies as needs dictate.

The Family's Definition of the Stressor (C)

Here, the magnitude and severity of the stressor are assessed by the family. This assessment will be a subjective analysis of the stressor rather than the community's objective and cultural definition of it. The family typically explores the hardships that the stressor will bring, including sacrifices to be made and lifestyle changes to be implemented. Also affecting the family's overall assessment of the stressor will be how successfully it was dealing with the past changes and challenges or the presence of other stressors.

The Actual Crisis (X)

The last feature of Hill's model represents the amount of disequilibrium, instability, and disorganization that a crisis brings. Whether or not the stressor triggers a crisis depends on the preceding factors: the magnitude of the stressor, available family resources, and the ultimate definition given to the stressor. If a family is resilient and resourceful, stress may never reach this crisis point. Should this not be the case, the family will not be able to maintain equilibrium.

The Double ABCX Model

Stimulated by Hill's work, Hamilton McCubbin and Joan Patterson (1983) developed a theory that complements and expands the ABCX model. It is distinguished from Hill's model by its emphasis on the additional life stressors influencing the family's resiliency and adaptation ability. The **Double ABCX** model also describes those psychological and social factors families use in managing crises, the processes families engage in to attain satisfactory resolution, and the eventual outcome of these efforts. The Double ABCX model can be broken down as follows:

1. The *pileup of family demands (aA factor)* is the first component of the model. More than likely, families are not dealing with a single stressor (e.g., an economically disadvantaged family is forced to deal with a natural disaster). Rather, there is a pileup of stressors and strains, referred to as the aA factor in this model. These demands or strains may result from individual family members, the family system, and/or the community. A variety of stressors and strains contributing to a pileup can be identified as follows:

   • *The stressor and its hardships.* The stressor brings hardships that often increase and intensify as the situation persists or remains unresolved. When hardships such as anxiety, insecurity, or frustration persist, they become additional sources of strain contributing to family distress.
   • *Developmental crises.* Occurring simultaneously but independently of the initial stressor, these crises are developmental or normative. Recall that such crises are normal and can be expected (e.g., adult children caring for aging parents), but their presence along with other stress adds to the demands placed on the family.
   • *Prior strains.* Many families carry some residue of strain, often the result of some unresolved demands from earlier stressors or transitions. When a new stressor is introduced, these prior strains usually complicate the situation by adding to the pileup of demands.
   • *Consequences of family efforts to cope.* Separate stressors and strain can evolve from the coping behaviors employed by the family. Suppose, for example, that in a household facing financial hardship one partner takes a

second job. Although this type of coping will reduce the financial difficulties, the second job might create others: loneliness of the other partner, disruption of lifestyle, physical and psychological demands placed on the doubly employed partner, and so on.

- *Intrafamily and social ambiguity.* Every stressor embodies ambiguity because change creates uncertainty about the future. Within the internal framework, the family may feel uncertainty about its structure. This uncertainty is particularly evident with such situations as the death of a family member, the military deployment of a loved one, or a divorce.

2. The second component of the Double ABCX model is labeled *family adaptive resources (bB factor).* Resources are an integral part of the family's ability to meet demands. Resources include characteristics of individual members, the overall system, the family unit, and the community. In response to a crisis situation over time, two general types of resources evolve: existing resources and expanded family resources.

- *Existing resources.* Such resources are already in place and will typically minimize the impact of the initial stressor. Moreover, existing stressors will reduce the probability that the family will enter into a crisis. Examples of existing family resources include togetherness, conflict resolution skills, role flexibility, and shared values.
- *Expanded family resources.* These include new resources (individual, family, and community) strengthened or developed in response to the strain and demands. Examples include the reallocation of family roles and responsibilities, or the seeking of community resources. The authors emphasize that one of the most important resources comprising the bB factor is social support. Those families able to gain support through friends, relatives, community resource specialists, and the like tend to be more resistant to major crises and better able to regain equilibrium.

3. The third component of the model is called *family definition and meaning (cC factor).* The cC factor represents the

meaning given to the *total* crisis situation, including the stressor believed to have initiated it, the added stressors and strains, old and new resources, and estimates of what needs to be accomplished to restore balance and stability. All of these elements require considerable work to resolve: clarifying the hardships and issues so that they are more manageable and responsive to problem-solving strategies, decreasing the intensity of the emotional burdens accompanying the crisis, and encouraging the system to continue with its task of promoting each member's social and emotional development. Also, family coping and eventual adaptation are often facilitated when members view crisis situations as a challenge or an opportunity for growth.

4. The fourth component is termed *family adaptation balancing (xX factor)*. As stated, adaptive resources emerge from individual family members, the family system, and the community. Each of these elements has both capabilities and demands. Family adaptation occurs through reciprocal relationships, that is, demands of one of these elements met by the capabilities of another. When this reciprocity is accomplished, a simultaneous balance is achieved at two primary levels of interaction. In relation to this concept, consider the following forms of balance:

- *Balance of member to family.* The balance sought here is between individual family members and the family system. Family stress often emerges when a demand-capability imbalance exists at this level of family functioning. More precisely, the demands an individual member places on the family may exceed the family's ability to meet these demands, thus creating the imbalance. To cite an example, the stressor of a rebellious adolescent may create an imbalance because of the family's rigid rules and inability to alter expectations, which would allow for the autonomy a teenager often needs for personal development. To remedy this imbalance, a new "balance" between the individual member and the family system is needed.
- *Balance of family to community.* A "fit" must also exist between the family and the community of which it is a

part. McCubbin and Patterson (1983) observe that two in-stitutions in particular—the family and the work community—compete for the involvement and commit-ment of family members. Often, this competition creates a demand-capability imbalance, which in turn produces stress. As an illustration, the stressor of a mother return-ing to work may create an imbalance if the family de-mands that she make a priority commitment to her husband and children. To resolve this imbalance, the fam-ily must reestablish and achieve a balance between its de-mands and capabilities and those of the work community.

The concept of family adaptation is regarded as the central concept in the Double ABCX model. It is used to describe a con-tinuum of outcomes that reflect family efforts to achieve a bal-ance fit at the member-to-family and the family-to-community levels. The positive side to the continuum of family adaptation is labeled *bonadaptation* and is characterized by a balance at both levels of functioning. This results in the maintenance or strength-ening of family integrity, the continued promotion of member de-velopment, and the maintenance of family independence and its sense of control over environmental influences. At the negative end of the continuum is family *maladaptation,* which is character-ized by a continued imbalance at either level of family function-ing or the achievement of a balance at both levels. Maladaption comes at a price in terms of a deterioration in family integrity, a curtailment or deterioration in the personal health and develop-ment of a member or the well-being of the family unit, or a loss or decline in family independence.

Examples of Prevention and Enrichment Programs

Over the years, family therapists have developed prevention and enrichment programs to deal with stress and crises. Such thera-peutic intervention has gained increasing popularity and is ex-panding rapidly in terms of the number, scope, and type.

A distinction exists between prevention programs and en-richment programs. Bernard Guerney and his associates (1985) point out that prevention is concerned with dealing with prob-lems on a community-wide basis rather than an individual basis.

Prevention does not, however, mean that one works only with people of families who have no stress or difficulties. Early and efficient treatment programs and programs dealing with aftermath problems also fall into the category of prevention programs. Whether it is before, during, or after a crisis arises, effective prevention programs are designed so that they are applicable to large numbers of people. Their impact must also be broad enough to make a substantial difference when the rate of the problems on a community-wide basis is examined.

Enrichment programs, on the other hand, are typically targeted to strengthen families not at risk. However, as Guerney and associates point out, in the wake of such crises as divorce, addiction, and natural disasters today, it seems fair to say that all families are at risk. Because of this prevalence of risk, enrichment programs should not be sharply distinguished from prevention programs. Rather, enrichment programs should be viewed as belonging at the lower end of the at-risk continuum, not off the continuum entirely. Therapeutic interventions need not be sharply segregated with respect to whether they are prevention versus enrichment. Instead, any particular program may define as its target population families anywhere or everywhere on a continuum of risk or on a continuum of strength or resiliency. Additionally, all intervention programs (whether they be preventive or enrichment) should be viewed as having a common purpose: improving the family system and improving the psychosocial well-being of each member of that family system.

Examples of Family Intervention Programs

It will prove useful at this juncture to identify and briefly discuss several representative intervention programs. Guerney, Guerney, and Cooney (1985) offer the following descriptions:

Family-Structured Enrichment

The goals of family-structured enrichment programs are to build personal skills into daily family life. Couples and families participating in this approach receive programmed instruction from a group leader and participate in structured exercises on a wide range of topics. Depending on issues relevant to the family seeking assistance, the specificity of the program may vary. For example, it could include such topics as problem-solving and conflict resolution skills or more specific areas such as intimate partner violence, infidelity, loss of a family member, or unemployment. In general, the program focuses on family development and its transitions, family needs, and the needs of special families, such as those facing military deployment or those dealing with the aftermath of divorce.

Family Relationship Enhancement
The family relationship enhancement program can be used by individual family members, a subsystem from a family (e.g., siblings), an entire family system, or groups consisting of any of these combinations from different families. The primary teaching techniques are skill training and practice. Among the skills taught are those designed to enhance family adaptation and adjustment, particularly in the face of adversity; problem-solving skills; utilization of family resources; communication effectiveness; and heightened awareness of others. Also, families are taught how to maintain these desired behaviors.

Marriage Encounter
Originally conceived by the Roman Catholic Church, Marriage Encounter has been altered to fit both Protestant and Jewish faiths. The program is designed as a retreat that typically involves large numbers of couples. Usually beginning on a Friday evening and ending on a Sunday afternoon, it covers a wide range of topics designed to enhance the marital arrangement and prevent stress: self-disclosure skills, empathy, self-awareness, tolerance, and marital unity. Typically a religious ceremony and a renewal of marriage vows conclude the weekend.

Minnesota Couples Communication Program
This marital enrichment program is widely used and is based on a theory of growth-oriented systems. That is, the marital or family system is seen as having a number of potential patterns and structures. Couples receive training on how to develop strategies that will enable them to experience various levels of interactions and deal with stressful life circumstances. Emphasis is placed on such areas as accurate self-perception, improvement of communication skills, flexibility in interactional styles, and adjustment to threatening and potentially damaging domestic situations.

Special Considerations for Children

As the next two chapters reveal, family stress and crises are no strangers to the lives of children. On the contrary, Alice Honig (2003, 1986) writes that some degree is to be expected throughout the entire course of child and adolescent development. She maintains that an assortment of situations throughout life produce stress reactions, including physical illness; pain; concentration; anxious anticipations of failure due to overly strict or high parental expectations; fear and tension originating from domestic violence or divorce; rejection from being teased and bullied; fear of abandonment through loss or separation; living through the unpredictability and danger of a natural disaster or school shooting; or experiencing the uncertainties and insecurities that often accompany unemployment.

Honig points out that childhood stress surfaces for identifiable reasons. For example, stress can originate from *internal* factors. It can develop from a chronic illness or disability or from the painful stomachaches of a young child lying in bed and listening each night to parents' violent quarreling in the next room. Stress can also emerge from *external* factors. For example, a kindergarten child from a military family, forced by a recent family move to attend a new school, finds walking the new route alone a terrifying experience. The youngster may arrive home with soiled pants because bowel or urinary control has been lost.

Stress can also be *acute* as well as *chronic*. Acute stresses arise suddenly, they are usually isolated episodes, and their impact may not last long. Some acute stressors, such as a single hospitalization for a child, are often associated with short-term emotional disturbance, but not with long-term upset or imbalance years later. Chronic stressors, on the other hand, may be cumulative even for the most well-adjusted child and can lead to long-term disturbances. An alcoholic or an unpredictably abusive parent are examples of chronic stressors that may impair even the psychologically sturdiest child functioning. The chapters that follow supply more specific information on the potential impact of chronic stressors.

Lorraine Stern (1986, 1985) feels that a certain amount of stress in a child's life is not necessarily bad. Coping with stress and the changes it brings helps a youngster learn to overcome obstacles and develop into a flexible, adaptable person. But too much stress or poorly handled stress can undermine a child's emotional and perhaps even physical health. The following suggestions are designed to help parents and significant others reduce the stress in children's lives:

Set Aside Plenty of Quiet Time with the Child
Children and caregivers need time just to be together. Any uninterrupted period is important, and affection is good therapy for the day-to-day stressors the youngster faces.

Adults Need to Be a Source of Support for the Youngster
A child under stress or experiencing a crisis needs more than the usual amount of warmth and closeness. Children are not spoiled by being held and comforted at times of need.

Treat the Child's Distress as Real, Even if It Seems Inappropriate from an Adult Perspective
Sometimes children have traumatic—and dramatic—reactions to seemingly minor experiences. This is perfectly normal, and the best way for an adult to respond is to treat such a reaction as legitimate and intercede accordingly.

Keep Discussions of Adult Uncertainties Out of the Youngster's Hearing
A discouraged remark about not having enough money or the inevitability of a divorce can severely upset a child. Children not only take these problems to heart but often feel responsible for them as well. If a child does overhear a disturbing conversation, give immediate, optimistic reassurance that the problem can be solved.

If Possible, Prepare the Youngster for Future Stressful Experiences
Sometimes an adult can soothe fears and correct misconceptions about a coming event in a concrete, developmentally appropriate fashion. Most hospitals, for example, have special programs that use tours, games, or books to prepare children for hospitalization. Adults can use children's books to ease the impact of other upcoming events.

Do Not Hesitate to Seek Outside Supportive Assistance
As indicated, acute stressful life stressors alone rarely cause long-term problems. Rather, stress leads to trouble or pressure when it is present in the midst of ongoing difficulties such as poor self-

image or pressure to perform in school. Early therapeutic intervention can not only solve an immediate problem but also strengthen the youngster's future coping capacities.

Adults Need to Examine Their Own Stress Management Skills

How a caregiver handles and controls stress has a lot to do with how a child fares. Adults need to examine whether they have an optimistic attitude or feel overwhelmed by circumstances. If adults are ineffective with their coping strategies, they can help both themselves and their children by obtaining professional help in stress management.

Characteristics of Strong and Resilient Families

As this chapter draws to a close, it would not be surprising if you spent a moment or two reflecting on your own family, perhaps recognizing its strengths or reflecting on areas needing attention. Maybe you have thought about how your family has weathered past family crises, perhaps analyzing what it did right or how it might have done things differently.

Numerous researchers have examined characteristics of stress-effective families and the skills used to improve their health, well-being, and resiliency (e.g., James 2008; Kilpatrick 2006; Vangelisti 2004; Walsh 2003; Greenstone and Leviton 2002). All families, including single parent–led families, blended families, working couples, and older families, can survive stress and grow closer. But how do they do it? Suzanna Smith (2005) and Dolores Curran (1985) have isolated the commonalities of stress-effective couples and identified certain attitudes and characteristics that shed light on strong and resilient families, those systems that learn to meet daily pressures and manage life's changes. The reader might want to keep these qualities in mind as the various crises are presented in the next two chapters. The characteristics are:

Recognition of Stress as a Normal Part of Family Life

Healthy couples do not equate family life with perfection. Indeed, their goals and expectations are frequently lower than those of other families. These families also do not correct problems with self-failure. Rather, they anticipate stresses like children's behaviors and occasional disagreements over money as a normal facet of family life. Furthermore, they tend to develop ways of coping that are both traditional and unique, which will end up being invaluable when dealing with normative and non-normative crises.

Commitment

Commitment is the expectation that the family system will be together forever, in good times and bad. Committed families feel a sense of trust, belonging, and unity. They solve problems together and look toward the future, giving the family purpose and direction. Commitment is marked by giving time and energy to each other on a daily basis and by developing family interests. Strong families make choices about what activities are important to them. Commitment does not mean the family overtakes the individual, creating enmeshment. Strong families know that family members will grow and develop individual identities. They affirm and appreciate positive qualities and encourage and support each other.

Family Wellness

Research shows that individual wellness helps a person manage daily pressures, and this ability has a positive impact on family equilibrium. Family wellness also means that all family members have a healthy lifestyle that includes proper nutrition, regular exercise, adequate rest, and relaxation. Family wellness goes beyond just physical health. It is a holistic way of living that nurtures and develops the body, mind, and spirit. Wellness also means looking outside the self and tuning in to the feelings, needs, and welfare of others.

Effective Communication

Effective family communication maintains positive, healthy relationships, helps solve problems, and lowers stress. Effective family communication also means family members are specific about what they need or expect from others, as well as sharing their own feelings, thoughts, and experiences. Strong families deal with conflict quickly and directly by using effective communication and problem-solving skills (Turner and West 2006; Segrin and Flora 2005; LePoire 2005; Day 2003). Moreover, healthy families rely on the importance of honesty and sincerity. They employ nonthreatening techniques that enable them to get in touch with their own feelings and those of others within the system. Parenting partners share ideas, activities, and emotions without the feeling of being owned or judged.

Conflict Resolution Skills and Creative Coping Skills

Related to the last point, the families best able to deal with everyday stresses are those who develop workable ways of solving their disagreements and an assortment of coping skills. Conflict resolution skills depend largely on communication, while coping skills depend on creativity, ingenuity, and perseverance. Among parents, self-esteem is usually equal, with neither partner allowing himself or herself to be manipulated or pushed around by the other. In this respect, healthy communicating partners rarely exhibit a boss-employer relationship. In addition, they utilize compromise to resolve conflict and practice collaboration, exploring underlying issues and arriving at solutions that best meet the needs of the family.

Adaptability

Stress-effective families are adaptable and flexible. They see relatives, friends, and community as valuable supports in dealing with stresses and therefore turn to them when the need arises. On the other hand, highly stressed families view such support systems as their own inability to deal with conflict and turmoil. Healthy partners also adapt and borrow each other's techniques in resolving conflict and dealing with stress. When confronted with a stressor, they are able to modify attitudes and habits to best meet it. These types of behaviors reflect the flexibility that healthy families possess, a skill that enables them to cope with the many stresses and demands that life presents.

Appreciation

Stress-effective family members genuinely care about each other. This caring can be demonstrated in a number of different ways. First, a person's good qualities can be accented and positive words used to describe that family member. Second, caring is conveyed through both words and deeds. Finally, appreciation is accepted by those who extend it. Although accepting appreciation is difficult for some people, it is important because it establishes trust and goodwill between people as well as builds self-esteem.

Family Time Together

Stress-resilient families spend meaningful time together on a regular basis. Time together gives the family an identity and a sense of unity. Time with supportive people nurtures positive self-identity in family members and reduces feelings of isolation. Research consistently shows that strong families eat, play, work, and share outside activities together. Strong families celebrate traditions that enrich family life and build memories for the future.

Summary

Successful adjustment over the family life cycle involves the mastery of tasks, challenges, and stresses that life brings. In this chapter, the topics of stress and crises, and how they both affect the family system, were examined. Stress is defined as the common, nonspecific response of the body to any demand made on it, be it psychological, sociological, or physiological. Stress can have both positive (eustress) and negative (distress) dimensions. Stress is a response to stimuli called stressors, which may range from fear and fatigue to physical injury and emotional conflict.

This chapter also explores how a variety of stressors can be working together at one time. Stressors can be social, psychological, psychosocial, biochemical, philosophical, and endemic. A distinction has to be made between primary stressors, responsible for initiating the stress response, and secondary stressors, the behaviors that result from the primary stressor and keep the stress response activated. Our knowledge of the manner in which stress impacts individual behavior has been heightened by the research of Selye (the general adaptation syndrome), Menninger (levels of emotional disorganization), and Friedman and Rosenman (Type A and Type B personalities).

A family crisis occurs when the system encounters disruption to its everyday routines and experiences a state of disequilibrium or instability. Usually, the moment of crisis is followed by a period of disorganization and emotional upheaval, during which the family makes various attempts to solve its problems. A developmental (normative) crisis originates from predictable changes over the course of the family life cycle. A situational (non-normative) crisis is not predictable, but instead, sudden and abrupt. A traumatic crisis is often life threatening and, due to the circumstances, gives survivors a feeling of helplessness.

In addition to tracing the historical roots of family crisis intervention, the chapter describes two of the more prominent theories of family stress and crisis. Reuben Hill's ABCX model consists of four components: the stressor (A), resources (B), family definition of the stressor (C), and actual crisis (X). The Double ABCX model, developed by Hamilton McCubbin and Joan Patterson, expands upon Hill's earlier work. It consists of four components: the pileup of family demands (aA), family adaptive resources (bB), family definition and meaning (cC), and family adaptation (xX).

The family's depletion of resources and the inability to perform basic functions usually mean that therapeutic intervention is needed. Systems theory is the preferred mode of therapeutic intervention, which operates on a belief that individual behavior cannot be understood without reference to its past and present relationships, especially family interactions.

Intervention is viewed as most effective when it is applied directly to the entire family system, which means the therapist does not look at families as causing problems, but rather at the family patterns of interactions as perpetuating and influencing problems. Several varieties of family prevention and enrichment programs are described: family-structured enrichment, family relationship enhancement, Marriage Encounter, and the Minnesota Couples Communication Program. The chapter concludes with a discussion of stress-effective families and the qualities they possess: recognition of stress as a normal part of family life, commitment, family wellness, effective communication, conflict resolution skills and creative coping skills, adaptability, appreciation, and togetherness.

References

Barnes, M., and C. R. Figley. 2005. "Family Therapy: Working with Traumatized Families." In *Handbook of Clinical Family Therapy,* edited by J. Lebow. New York: John Wiley and Sons.

Becvar, D. S., and R. J. Becvar. 2006. *Family Therapy: A Systematic Integration,* 6th ed. Boston: Allyn and Bacon.

Beels, C. 2002. "Notes for a Cultural History of Family Therapy." *Family Process* 41 (1): 67–82.

Blonna, R. 2007. *Coping with Stress in a Changing World,* 4th ed. New York: McGraw-Hill.

Catherall, D. R., ed. 2005. *Family Stressors: Interventions for Stress and Trauma.* New York: Brunner-Routledge.

Cormier, S., and H. L. Hackney. 2008. *Counseling Strategies and Interventions.* Boston: Allyn and Bacon.

Curran, D. 1985. *Stress and the Healthy Family.* Minneapolis: Winston Press.

Day, R. D., ed. 2003. *Introduction to Family Processes.* Mahwah, NJ: Lawrence Erlbaum Associates.

DiMatteo, M. R., and L. R. Martin. 2002. *Health Psychology.* Boston: Allyn and Bacon.

Figley, C. R. 2002a. *Brief Treatments for the Traumatized: A Project for the Green Cross Foundation.* Westport, CT: Greenwood Press.

Figley, C. R. 2002b. "Theory-Informed Brief Treatments." In *Brief Treatments for the Traumatized: A Project of the Green Cross Foundation,* edited by C. R. Figley. Westport, CT: Greenwood Press.

Figley, C. R. 2002c. "Introduction." In *Treating Compassion Fatigue,* edited by C. R. Figley. New York: Brunner-Routledge.

Figley, C. R., ed. 2006. *Mapping the Wake of Trauma: Autobiographical Essays by the Pioneers of Trauma Research.* New York: Routledge.

Figley, C. R., and M. Barnes. 2005. "External Trauma and Families." In *Families and Change,* 3rd ed., edited by P. C. McKenry and S. J. Price. Los Angeles: Sage.

Figley, C. R., K. R. Figley, and J. Norman. 2002. "Tuesday Morning September 11, 2001: The Green Cross Projects' Role as a Case Study in Community-Based Traumatology Services." In *Trauma Practice in the Wake of September 11, 2001,* edited by S. N. Gold and J. Faust. New York: Haworth.

Friedman, M., and R. H. Rosenman. 1974. *Type A Behavior and Your Heart.* New York: Knopf.

Goldenberg, H., and I. Goldenberg. 2008. *Family Therapy: An Overview,* 7th ed. Belmont, CA: Thomson Learning.

Goodrick, G. K., S. Kneuper, and J. R. Steinbauer. 2005. "Stress Perceptions in Community Clinic: A Pilot Survey of Patients and Physicians." *Journal of Community Health* 30 (2): 75–93.

Greenberg, J. S. 2008. *Comprehensive Stress Management,* 10th ed. New York: McGraw-Hill.

Greenstone, J. L., and S. C. Leviton. 2002. *Elements of Crisis Intervention: Crises and How to Respond to Them.* Belmont, CA: Thomson Learning.

Guerney, B., L. Guerney, and T. Cooney. 1985. "Marital and Family Prevention and Enrichment Programs." In *Handbook of Family Psychology and Therapy,* edited by L. l'Abate. Homewood, IL: Dorsey Press.

Hattie, J. A., J. E. Myers, and T. J. Sweeney. 2004. "A Factor Structure of Wellness: Theory, Assessment, Analysis, and Practice." *Journal of Counseling and Development* 82 (3): 354–371.

Hill, R. 1949. *Families under Stress.* New York: Harper and Row.

Honig, A. 1986. "Stress and Coping in Children." *Young Children* 41 (4): 50–63.

Honig, A. S. 2003. *Love and Learn: Positive Guidance for Young Children.* Washington, DC: National Association for the Education of Young Children.

James, R. K. 2008. *Crisis Intervention Strategies,* 6th ed. Belmont, CA: Thomson Learning.

Kanel, K. 2007. *A Guide to Crisis Intervention,* 3rd ed. Belmont, CA: Thomson Learning.

Kilpatrick, A. C. 2006. *Working with Families: An Integrative Model by Level of Need,* 4th ed. Boston: Allyn and Bacon.

LePoire, B. A. 2005. *Family Communication: Nurturing and Control in a Changing World.* Thousand Oaks, CA: Sage.

McCubbin, J. M., and J. M. Patterson. 1983. "The Family Stress Process: The Double ABCX Model of Adjustment and Adaptation." In *Social Stress and the Family,* edited by H. I. McCubbin, M. B. Sussman, and J. M. Patterson. New York: Haworth.

McGowan, J., D. Gardner, and R. Fletcher. 2006. "Positive and Negative Affective Outcomes of Occupational Stress." *New Zealand Journal of Psychology* 35 (2): 95–104.

Menninger, K. 1963. *The Vital Balance.* New York: Viking.

Miller, G., and C. Cohen. 2008. *Current Directions in Health Psychology.* Boston: Allyn and Bacon.

Myer, R. A., and H. B. Moore. 2006. "Crisis in Context Theory: An Ecological Model." *Journal of Counseling and Development* 84 (2): 139–144.

Nelson, P. T. 2007. "Surviving a Family Crisis." [Online article; retrieved 8/9/07.] http://ag.udel.edu/extension/fam/FM/issue/survivecrisis.htm.

Nevid, J. S., and S. A. Rathus. 2007. *Psychology and the Challenges of Life: Adjustment to the New Millennium,* 10th ed. New York: Wiley.

Nichols, M. P., and R. C. Schwartz. 2006. *The Essentials of Family Therapy,* 3rd ed. Upper Saddle River, NJ: Prentice Hall.

O'Halloran, T. M., and J. M. Linton. 2000. "Stress on the Job: Self-Care Resources for Counselors." *Journal of Mental Health Counseling* 22 (4): 354–362.

Patrick, P. K. 2007. *Contemporary Issues in Counseling.* Boston: Allyn and Bacon.

Sandoval, J., ed. 2002. *Handbook of Crisis Counseling, Intervention, and Prevention in the Schools,* 2nd ed. Mahwah, NJ: Lawrence Erlbaum Associates.

Seaward, B. L. 2005. *Managing Stress: Principles and Strategies for Health and Well-being.* Sudbury, MA: Jones and Bartlett.

Segrin, C., and J. Flora. 2005. *Family Communication.* Mahwah, NJ: Lawrence Erlbaum Associates.

Selye, H. 1980. *Selye's Guide to Stress Research.* New York: Van Nostrand.

Selye, H. 1982. "History and Present Status of the Stress Concept." In *Handbook of Stress,* edited by L. Goldberger and S. Breznitz. New York: Free Press.

Sexton, T. L., G. R. Weeks, and M. S. Robbins, eds. 2003. *Handbook of Family Therapy: The Science and Practice of Working with Families and Couples.* New York: Brunner-Routledge.

Smith, S. 2005. "Building a Strong and Resilient Family." [Online article; retrieved 8/11/07.] http://edis.ifas.ufl.edu/HE326#FOOTNOTE_2.

Snyder, C. R., ed. 2001. *Coping with Stress: Effective People and Processes.* New York: Oxford University Press.

Stern, L. 1985. *Off to a Great Start: How to Relax and Enjoy Your Baby.* New York: Free Press.

Stern, L. 1986. "How to Help Your Child Handle Stress." *Your Child's Health* 8:20–21.

Turner, L. H., and R. L. West, eds. 2006. *The Family Communication Sourcebook.* Thousand Oaks, CA: Sage.

Vangelisti, A. L., ed. 2004. *Handbook of Family Communication.* Mahwah, NJ: Lawrence Erlbaum Associates.

Walsh, F., ed. 2003. *Normal Family Processes: Growing Diversity and Complexity,* 3rd ed. New York: Guilford Press.

White, J. M., and D. M. Klein. 2007. *Family Theories,* 3rd ed. Thousand Oaks, CA: Sage.

2

Problems, Controversies, and Solutions

Introduction

As we learned in the last chapter, a family crisis occurs when stress disrupts the stability of the household and causes disequilibrium. When a system is in crisis, family resources or possibly outside intervention is needed to weather the storm. Many families find strength in the face of adversity and recover within relatively short periods of time. Other families, though, are unable to repair the damage and experience a state of helplessness and even hopelessness.

Family crises vary in intensity, duration, and severity, and our task in the next two chapters is to better understand the many sides to stressor events and the challenges they pose. In this chapter, we examine a representative number of situational and developmental crises: addiction, adolescent runaways, unemployment, infidelity, divorce, chronic illness and disease, and caring for aging parents. These crises alter family equilibrium, but some form of control and confidence is usually restored. In Chapter 3, our focus is on traumatic crises, overwhelming life events that pose complicated coping and adjustment processes: domestic violence, school violence, natural disasters, deployed military families, and adolescent suicide. Here, the lives of survivors run the risk of never returning to normal—recovery is especially difficult and can take months, years, or sometimes an entire lifetime.

This in no way means that the family crises covered in this chapter are easily overcome or should be treated lightly. The reader is reminded that families react differently to stressor events and that any of the crises explored here bring the potential for more serious consequences and added stressors (e.g., divorce unleashing self-destructive behaviors or caregiving for aging parents bringing out the potential for elder abuse). Also, it must be kept in mind that a family's resiliency and recovery hinge on its equilibrium at the time of the crisis. The family dealing with multiple stressors is susceptible to even greater vulnerability and more extreme crisis reactions.

In this chapter and the next, background material on each crisis is presented along with important terminology, implications for family life, and intervention efforts. Later chapters are designed to complement the material in this section of the book, such as notable historical events (Chapter 4) and contributions to the study of family stress and crises (Chapter 5).

Addiction

Brian Southworth is a highly touted junior executive in a prestigious account firm in Boston. He is the husband of Jessica and father of two elementary school-age children, Janna and Molly, and lives in an affluent, upscale neighborhood in nearby Cambridge. He is proud of his accomplishments and pleased with the way his life has been unfolding.

Brian is also a problem drinker, although he did not know it at first. His consumption of alcohol started innocently enough—an occasional beer or cocktail with partners at the firm after work, a glass of wine with Jessica, a beer or two watching the Red Sox on the weekends. Soon, though, his drinking pattern changed. Pressures from work and some marital friction with Jessica intensified Brian's thirst. He began having several drinks in the afternoon, then a few more with dinner, a nightcap or two before turning in. He became friendly with hangovers in the morning.

As his consumption increased, Brian rationalized that booze was becoming his best friend, a means to help him relax and get him through the day. He also convinced himself that he was only hitting a small speed bump. But losing a huge account at work and further squabbling with Jessica over financial matters did little to still the waters. He started spending less time with his family and more time pulling away. Brian was falling deeper and deeper into a black hole.

It was only a matter of time before Brian's tolerance increased, the curtain of relief demanding a higher price. The bracers during the day became more frequent, sometimes beginning early in the morning. The glasses got bigger, trips to the liquor store more frequent. Brian upgraded proofs for greater potency. He kept a wary eye on the liquor cabinet so that he would not run dry, especially on weekends.

Problem drinking creeps up on most people, with denial often cloaking the damage and concealing the truth. Brian convinced himself he was not a problem drinker and manufactured lie after lie to justify his dependence. He told himself he had every right to drink, that he deserved to imbibe, given the pressures he was under. He continued to tell himself that his drinking was temporary, and that he would cut back as soon as things settled down.

These were fairly convincing rationalizations, but his behaviors painted a different portrait, a man clearly in trouble. He became secretive and dishonest, doing whatever was necessary to cover his tracks. He hid empties in the garbage, wrapping them in separate plastic bags or newspapers, sometimes tossing them in public trash bins to avoid detection. He lied to his wife about cash withdrawals from the bank. He blamed hangovers on lingering colds or other imagined illnesses.

Cutting back was easier said than done. Brian remembered one particular morning being shocked at the amount of vodka he had consumed the previous night. He told himself he needed to get the upper hand. He refrained from drinking for a little while and began to feel better, confident that he had regained control of his life. Brian began brimming with optimism and was convinced that he could have a glass of wine or a short cocktail at the end of the day. Of course, this plan failed. He would have the one drink and the cycle would start all over again.

Brian Southworth was fighting alcohol addiction, and without proper treatment would no doubt lose the battle. An **addiction** is defined as a dependence on a behavior or substance that a person is powerless to stop. The dependence becomes a dominant preoccupation in a person's life. Beyond this preoccupation, additional symptoms are shared by addicts like Brian Southworth: loss of willpower and control, harmful consequences to oneself and others, an unmanageable lifestyle, escalation of use, and withdrawal symptoms upon quitting. An addiction is also a progressive syndrome, which means that it increases in severity over time unless it is treated (Brown 2004; Center for Substance Abuse Treatment 2004; Khantzian 2001).

As we will see, addictive behaviors also cause a wide range of secondary stressors, including the breakdown of families. Alcohol addiction and domestic violence often go hand in hand, with alcohol intensifying the abuser's feelings of anger, aggression, and hostility (Bell et al. 2006; Kaysen et al. 2006; Wekerle and Wall 2001). Also, children who grow up in surroundings where drugs and alcohol are openly available and misused are more at risk to succumbing to addictive patterns of behavior (Russell 2007; Asenjo 2007). Figures 6.1, 6.2, and 6.3 in Chapter 6 provide a statistical glimpse at the use of illicit drugs in the United States, including variations by gender.

At one time, the term *addiction* was used almost exclusively for substance addiction, such as dependency on alcohol or cocaine. Today, though, addiction also includes mood-altering behaviors or activities. This shift has led to the creation of two addiction categories: *substance addictions* (e.g., alcoholism and other forms of substance abuse) and *process addictions* (e.g., gambling, Internet addiction). Millions of American families know firsthand the headaches and heartaches of addiction, and millions of others are at risk. It is impossible within the parameters of this chapter to discuss the many kinds of addiction that exist, but the following brief statements may help illuminate the kinds mentioned to highlight their magnitude.

Alcohol Addiction

Alcohol is a depressant of the central nervous system that, when consumed in moderation, induces relaxation and eases inhibitions. Responsible drinking is accepted in everyday life in most societies around the world. In excessive amounts, though, alcohol can severely impair judgment and coordination and create physical and psychological dependence. Alcohol addiction impairs work performance as well as family equilibrium and has been linked to liver damage, peptic ulcers, and other health problems. Approximately 14 million people in the United States are addicted to alcohol, and millions more display symptoms of abuse, including binge drinking (National Institute on Alcoholism and Alcohol Abuse 2007; Russell 2007; Asenjo 2007). The reader is directed to Chapter 6, especially Figures 6.4 and 6.5, for alcohol abuse information. Table 6.1 in that chapter provides information regarding substance abuse among the elderly population.

Gambling Addiction

This addiction, similar to all others, is characterized by a desire to escape from reality and a distortion of normalcy. It is marked by an increased preoccupation and obsession with gambling, resulting in the destruction of a person's life—family, work, and friends. Gambling dominates the addict's life and exerts profound control, evidenced by an increasing desire to bet more money frequently, even in the face of mounting serious consequences. Denial typically clouds the addict's ability to see damages inflicted on oneself and others. The National Institute of Mental Health (2007) estimates that 4.2 million Americans are addicted to gambling. Of this total, 60 percent have annual incomes under $25,000 (Black et al. 2006; Toneatto and Ferguson 2003; Sellman et al. 2002; Hodgins, Makarchuk, and Peden 2002; Clarke and Dempsey 2001; Petry 2000).

Internet Addiction

Once again, this addiction is characterized by a desire to escape from daily life or personal problems. In this case, the anonymity of the Internet provides the means for escape. It is estimated that more than 85 million Americans are online, with that number expected to increase by 12 million in the next year. The latest studies suggest that nearly 6 percent, or 11 million, online users suffer from Internet addiction (Young 2007). **Internet addiction** refers to excess use of the Internet that causes psychological, social, and physical problems for the user. It includes a number of different activities: chat rooms, online pornography, Internet gaming, or compulsive surfing and data collection. The obsessive use of cell phones and text messaging, known as **contact addiction,** is an extension of Internet addiction. In addition to creating family disharmony, Internet addiction has the potential for creating a disregard for health and appearance, sleep deprivation, and decreased physical activity and social interaction with others (Young 2007; Chou and Belland 2005; Griffiths 2003; Shaffer 2002; Jones and Minatrea 2001; Oravec 2000). Particular concern has been directed to the number of children and teenagers engaged in Internet use and abuse (see Turner 2003).

According to Asenjo (2007), all addictions are extremely costly public health problems in the United States and cripple millions of families. Addiction is a progressive disorder, which means that it increases in severity over time unless successfully treated. Addiction is characterized by frequent **relapse**, or return to the abused substance or behavioral pattern. Addicts often make repeated attempts to quit before they are successful.

The National Institute of Drug Abuse and Addiction (2007) points out that many people incorrectly view addiction as strictly a social problem. Parents, adolescents, older adults, and other members of the community tend to characterize addicts as morally weak or as having criminal tendencies. They believe that addicts should be able to stop taking drugs or engaging in other addictive behaviors if they are willing to change. These myths have stereotyped not only those with addictive behaviors but also their families, their communities, and the health care professionals who work with them. Addictions comprise a major public health problem that has wide-ranging social consequences (Dawson et al. 2005).

Implications for Family Life

People with addictions usually realize they are increasingly isolated from their families. A growing body of literature suggests that addictions have distinct effects on different family structures. We recognize today that the effects of substance abuse frequently extend beyond the nuclear family. Extended family members may experience feelings of embarrassment, resentment, or fear, or they may wish to ignore or cut ties with the addict. This removal of social support is a good example of family maladaptation discussed in Chapter 1.

According to the Substance Abuse and Mental Health Services Administration (2004), various treatment issues surface depending on the family structure that includes a person with an addiction. The following family structures illustrate the complexities that might arise:

- *Client who lives alone or with a partner.* Here, both partners need help. The treatment of either partner often affects both. When one partner experiences addiction and the other does not, issues of codependency might arise. **Codependency** refers to a relationship in which a person exhibits too much, and often inappropriate, caring for addicts who depend on him or her.

- *Client who lives with a spouse (or partner) and minor children.* As pointed out earlier in the chapter, the enduring effects of parental addiction on children suggest that a parent's problem often has a detrimental effect on youngsters (see Andreas, O'Farrell, and Fals-Stewart 2006; Chalder, Elgar, and Bennett 2006; Kroll 2004; Fitzgerald, Lester, and Zuckerman 2000). The spouse of an addict is apt to protect the children and assume the parenting duties not fulfilled by the addict. If both parents are fighting addictions, the effect on children worsens.
- *Client who is part of a blended family.* Blended families pose special challenges under normal circumstances (see Turner 2002), but an addiction can intensify problems and become a threat to the family's equilibrium. (A **blended family** is a family that results when a divorced parent with custody of children remarries.) Those offering help and assistance need to be aware of the familial dynamics of blended families and recognize that special considerations may be required.
- *Older client who has grown children.* An older adult with an addiction can affect everyone in a household. Additional family resources may be needed to treat the older adult's addiction.
- *Client is an adolescent and lives with family of origin.* When a teenager is dealing with an addiction, siblings in the family may find their needs and concerns are ignored or minimized by parents or caregivers. In many families that include adolescent addicts, at least one parent also faces an addiction. This unfortunate modeling can create a combination of potentially dangerous physical and emotional problems.
- *Someone not identified as the client having an addiction.* When someone in the family other than the person with presenting symptoms is involved with addictive behaviors, issues of blame, responsibility, and causation often surface. The family needs to refrain from blaming but still be encouraged to reveal and repair family interactions that create the conditions for continued addiction.

Approaches to Therapy

Addictive behaviors will not go away on their own. On the contrary, therapeutic intervention and the addict's commitment to change are needed to conquer such problems (Kesten 2004; Deegan 2003; Lemanski 2001). The Substance Abuse and Mental Health Services Administration (2004) acknowledges that the dual forces of addiction treatment and family therapy are the preferred paths to recovery.

The fields of addiction therapy and family therapy share many commonalities, but they differ in ways that impact treatment approaches and goals. Although treatment for an addiction is generally more uniform in its approach than is family therapy, overlap exists. We take a brief look at each.

Many addiction therapists base their understanding of a family's relation to an intoxicant on what is called the *disease model* of addiction (see DiClemente 2003; Graham, Schulz, and Wilford 2003; White, Boyle, and Loveland 2002; Heyman 2001). For example, this is the stance taken by the American Medical Association (AMA 2006). Alcoholism is viewed as a primary, chronic disease with genetic, psychosocial, and environmental factors influencing its development. The AMA maintains that no cure exists for alcoholism, but effective treatments are available, such as the social support offered by Alcoholics Anonymous and Al-Anon.

Family therapists, on the other hand, utilize a *family systems* approach to intervention (see Chapter 1). The systems model conceptualizes addiction as a symptom of dysfunction within the family. Addiction experienced by one family member affects all components. It is this focus on the entire family system that defines this type of therapeutic intervention.

But while different in focus, the fields of addiction treatment and family therapy are compatible and complementary. For example, while family therapists focus on intrafamily relationships, addiction therapists concentrate on helping clients achieve and maintain abstinence. Also, while addiction therapists see as their primary goal arresting a client's abuse, family therapists see the family system as an integral component of the addiction. Finally, addiction therapists regard the individual with the dependence as the primary person requiring treatment. Family therapists, on the other hand, might assume that if long-term change is to occur, the entire family must be treated as a unit. In this sense, the family as a whole constitutes the client (Substance Abuse and Mental Health Administration 2004).

Adolescent Runaways

Kevin Gaston had been an abused child for as long as he could remember. His stepfather would physically beat him, often with his mother looking on. When Kevin turned 13, he packed what few belongings he owned and snuck away in the middle of the night. Despite extensive searches, he was never found.

Fourteen-year-old Maria Rodriguez stunned her parents and neighbors alike when she left home unannounced and stayed away for six days. When found, Maria said she had met someone online six months ago while chatting on the Internet, a charming young man she claimed she loved. When he asked her to run away so that they could meet and spend time together, Maria felt like it was a romance come true and left home the next day.

Paul Margolis, age 16, became a runaway when he decided to "get away from all the hassles at home." He did not get along with his parents, had few friends, and hated school. Paul was also bullied on a regular basis by a group of senior athletes, adding to his desire to leave it all behind. He left his Connecticut home in April and turned up six months later in California.

Each of these episodes involves a **teenage runaway**, defined as a person under 18 who is away from home or place of legal residence at least one night without the permission of parents, guardians, or custodial authorities. The above incidents are hardly remote occurrences. Indeed, the problem of teenage runaways has reached such magnitude in recent years that social scientists are labeling it one of the key family life issues in the United States today. According to the National Runaway Switchboard (2006), between 1.3 and 2.8 million teenagers in the United States run away or are forced out of parental homes each year.

When teenagers decide to run away, the emotions experienced by parents are immense and, in many instances, beyond description. Sleepless nights and endless days are spent worrying about the health, safety, and welfare of their teenagers. Such concerns are not only legitimate but also realistic. Many runaways end up working as prostitutes; others fall victim to drug pushers and hardened criminals. Without adequate protection, shelter, and food, runaways are prey not only to the dangers of the street but also to a wide range of other risks: malnutrition, emotional and conduct disorders, sexually transmitted diseases, unwanted pregnancies, criminal behavior, substance abuse disorders, and sexual and physical assault (Tyler and Johnson 2006; Halcon and Lifson 2004; Van Leeuwen et al. 2004; Baer, Ginzler, and Peterson 2003; McMorris et al. 2002; Tyler et al. 2000; Cauce et al. 2000).

Characteristics of Runaways

Through the years, we have gathered a considerable amount of information on runaways. For example, we know that runaways come from the full range of American families: white, black, Latino, Native American, and Asian; single-parent and two-parent households; and privileged, middle-class, working-class, low-income, and homeless families. It is important to note that runaways do not always run away from "home." Teenagers also run from foster care, shelters, group homes, and residential treatment facilities (Schaffner 1998).

Just as many females run away from home as males, although females are more likely to seek help through shelters and hotlines. The average age of a runaway is 14, but it is not unusual to see 11- to 13-year-olds choosing to flee. One study (Whitbeck and Hoyt 1999) exploring age differentials involved more than 600 adolescent runaways between the ages of 12 and 22 years. Both males and females first ran at age 13.5 years. Very few ran prior to age 10. The majority (80 percent) had run by 16 years of age. All were on their own by age 19. Few differences were seen between adolescent males and females throughout the years studied. The researchers noted that the timing of the first runaway climbs very steeply from about age 11 through 17 years, indicating that the cycle often begins prior to becoming a teenager. It was also speculated that the greater the number of family structural changes (e.g., divorce, separation) and geographic changes (changing residency), the earlier the first run.

Sometimes, adolescents run away from home because of peer group pressure or because they are drawn to the glitter of a big city. Some leave seeking fame and fortune; others wish to rejoin friends who had moved away. Still others choose to flee because they feel as though they have an "unshareable" problem, such as not wanting to divulge a crime they have committed or, in the case of females, an unintended pregnancy. For many teenagers, running away is seen as a solution to their problems, as they believe that no other options exist for them (Thompson and Pillai 2006; Son 2002).

Sadly, some teenagers are *throwaways,* dubbed so because their parents have encouraged—or told them—to leave home. One source (National Runaway Switchboard 2006) found that more than 50 percent of youth in shelters and on the streets reported that their parents either told them to leave or knew they were leaving but did not care. Such parents did not want their adolescents to ever return, and some teenagers were even physically forced out of the home.

Most throwaway adolescents are likely older, usually between the ages of 15 and 17 years. At these ages, adolescents are often more independent, tend to resist parental authority more than during earlier years, are more likely to become involved in activities that bring them into conflict with their caretakers, and are often viewed by their caretakers as being capable of living on their own. All these factors increase the likelihood of throwaway episodes (RunawayTeens.org 2007).

Intervention for Teenage Runaways

Beyond family therapy, treatment programs for adolescent runaways often include individual or group therapy. Other interventions include community programming aimed at topics and problems unique to adolescence, such as substance abuse, inappropriate sexual behavior, or strained parent-teenager relationships. Runaways often need help in developing effective communication abilities, including assertiveness training and conflict resolution skills. Self-esteem issues are also addressed. Additionally, programming is directed at parents of teenage runaways, including school programs, conferences, training sessions, literature, and support groups (Fest 2003).

Social service advocates generally acknowledge that more voluntary agencies are needed to help adolescents around the clock, as well as the establishment of central youth boards, the creation of shelter homes, and the development of community recreation facilities that are easily accessible to teenagers. Most experts (e.g., Thompson and Pollio 2006; Van Leeuwen et al. 2004; Baker et al. 2003) advocate more federal funding to support programs designed to combat the growing runaway problem. Many feel that if federal funding does not keep pace with the problem, needed assistance for runaways becomes unpredictable. This means that the safety and welfare of our adolescent population will succumb to institutional restraint.

The growing abundance of research that has been gathered on teenage runaways is indicative of widespread societal concern over this situational family crisis. The runaway problem is one that has been with us for ages, whether it be in the form of the fictional characters Huckleberry Finn, leaving his home to seek adventure along the Mississippi River, or Dick Whittington, striking out on his own to discover fortune in England. Yet today's runaways, whose numbers are increasing dramatically each year, face far more complications, hazards, and dangers than those choosing similar routes years ago.

Parents must strive to openly communicate with their teenagers and work on being able to detect problems before they develop. If such efforts are effectively undertaken, perhaps we can begin to curb this family crisis. More important, perhaps we can convey to adolescents that staying at home to work through problems or getting social service assistance in the community is far more effective than running away from one's problems. It is the obligation of parents and guardians everywhere to convince teenagers that, compared with striking out on one's own at a young age and facing the turmoil, insecurities, and threatening conditions of the outside world, the home will always be the source of love, care, and affection, especially during the challenges of the adolescent years.

Unemployment

Sharonda Beck was in shock when the news was delivered. An account executive and a single parent for eight years, Sharonda assumed she would always have her job in corporate America. But she found out last month that she was a casualty of downsizing and learned firsthand the stark reality that no one is really assured of job security during tough economic times. With her oldest daughter a senior in high school and looking at colleges, and a son in middle school, Sharonda suddenly found herself jobless.

Downsized. Laid off. Let go. Pink slipped. It does not matter how you refer to it. Regardless of what a person does, no matter what the job performance, he or she may someday find himself or herself unexpectedly out of work, and that is just the beginning. As Sari Harrar and Rita DeMaria (2006) observe, whether you are downsized or flat-out fired, the financial stress and embarrassment of being unemployed, plus the anger, worry, and lowered self-esteem that can go with it, can strain even the most solid families. Money is tight. Household routines change. Expectations shift.

When unemployment hits home, the family is confronted by a situational crisis. The primary stressor of unemployment creates a variety of secondary stressors. The strain of being unemployed is reflected not only through the financial challenges of paying regular ongoing bills but also through increases in alcohol and drug abuse, marital problems, and criminal activity among those who are unemployed. Researchers have also found that lengthy periods of unemployment can lead to depression, and even suicidal behavior. Many unemployed persons experience such symptoms as migraine headaches, high blood pressure, and stomach ailments. Those working with the unemployed need to be sensitive to the many consequences of job loss, including how it often triggers financial desperation, negative self-appraisals, and physiological complications (National Council on Economic Education 2008; Alleyne, Egodigwe, and Holmes 2004; Foston 2003).

Trends and Patterns of Unemployment

Numerous factors affect America's rate of unemployment. For example, an overabundance of workers in a selected career, instability of the economy, automation, and the demise of old industries take their toll on unemployment rates. Technological change, including a series of product and process innovations, has and will continue to exert profound influences on the labor force. Being affected the most are those factory workers having limited job skills. In 2006, more than 7 million people were out of work, nearly one in five jobless for more than six months (U.S. Department of Labor 2008; Harrar and DeMaria 2006). (Table 6.2 in Chapter 6 charts projections of occupations with the largest job declines from 2004 to 2014.)

According to the National Council on Economic Education (2008), there are three types of unemployment, each of which describes the particular circumstances of the individual and his or her employment situation.

Frictional Unemployment

Frictional unemployment refers to temporary unemployment originating from the normal and routine job search process. This type of unemployment helps the economy function more efficiently, as it simply refers to those individuals who are in search of better or more convenient jobs and those who are graduating and just entering the job market. Some degree of frictional unemployment exists in any economy.

Structural Unemployment

Structural unemployment refers to changes in the economy caused by technological progress and shifts in the demand for goods and services. Structural changes eliminate some jobs in certain sectors of the economy and create new jobs in faster-growing areas. Persons who are structurally unemployed do not have marketable job skills and may face prolonged periods of unemployment, as they must often be retrained or relocate in order to find employment.

Cyclical Unemployment

Cyclical unemployment is unemployment caused by a drop in economic activity. This type of unemployment can hit many different industries and is caused by a general downturn in the business cycle.

Unemployment does not affect all segments of the population equally. As of July 2007, the number of unemployed persons in the United States stood at 7.1 million and the unemployment rate was 4.6 percent. (The **unemployment rate** is the percentage of the U.S. labor force that is unemployed. It is calculated by dividing the number of unemployed individuals by the sum of the number of people unemployed and the number of people employed.) Rates are invariably higher among nonwhite segments of the population. African American adults are about twice as likely to be unemployed as white adults (8.5 percent and 4.0 percent, respectively). The unemployment rate of Hispanics hovers at 5.8 percent. Overall, minorities also have fewer job opportunities and lower levels of pay when they achieve employment, illustrating the inequality that exists between whites and nonwhites in the vocational arena. Teenagers are more apt to be unemployed than any other population segment (U.S. Department of Labor 2008; U.S. Census Bureau 2007; Gnuschke and Alvarado 2007).

As David Kessler (2007) sees it, losing a job is a personal loss. It is not like losing a loved one, but similarities can be drawn. For better or worse, in our society we tend to identify ourselves by our jobs, and when one's workplace is taken away, sadness and emptiness are often felt. Many displaced workers go through a grieving period, making it difficult for coworkers and friends to find the right things to say. Telling displaced workers that it is not their fault (which might or might not be true) or that they will recover may seem logical, but it probably will not be helpful, at least not in the early going. When someone has been wounded this way and may have withdrawn from the people who are close, being logical or trying to raise his or her spirits may be unwelcome. The wounded party probably is not ready for these words yet.

Implications for Family Life

In addition to managing the feelings that accompany unemployment, the displaced worker must also cope with managing his or her family life. This can be highly stressful for everyone, especially as financial pressures mount. We remind the reader that the family is a system, and all members of the family are affected by a crisis such as job loss. Jeri Miller (2007) writes that unemployment brings the system a multitude of challenges, including day-to-day issues and emotional ups and downs. She identifies some of the major tasks at hand, as follows.

Financial Worries

Unemployment is a primary stressor and financial worries are a secondary stressor. Even if the employed person has received a severance package and unemployment compensation, concerns about money create tension and financial instability. It is important for couples to review their financial commitments and spending priorities, which means they need to analyze their income, assets, and liabilities. For some, this may mean worrying less about image and lifestyle and focusing instead on managing their money wisely.

Daily Routines and Domestic Duties

We established in Chapter 1 that a family crisis brings about a disruption of routines, which in turn creates household instability. If the unemployed person is conducting a job search from home, domestic routines may be disturbed. Even if the other spouse is working, getting in each other's way is commonplace. Unemployed professionals and their spouses must negotiate other issues as well, such as the division of domestic labor. Many partners believe the unemployed person is now available for all kinds of tasks throughout the day, from chauffeuring to laundry. Obviously, couples need to acknowledge the adjustments and expectations that must be made and be respectful and supportive of each other.

Managing Emotions and Blame Issues

We mentioned earlier that the unemployed person experiences a wide range of emotions: denial, anger, doubt, and even relief. The family can be an important source of trust and support when combating these feelings. More specifically, the unemployed person needs to overcome obsessive thoughts, such as dwelling on past choices and missed opportunities. It must be recognized, too, that the unemployed person being blamed for a job loss by one's partner accomplishes nothing. If the partner of the unemployed sees job loss as a reflection of his or her inadequacy, more depression and hopelessness are likely. The family needs to recognize that blaming and criticism will not help a person regain self-worth.

Changing Values

Unemployment can evoke a sense of relief, especially if the person was not happy or was under extreme stress at work. The unemployed person may enjoy the freedom to reexamine his or her values, priorities, and career goals. However, if one's partner is not comfortable with the other's changing values, the potential for conflict arises. Some partners may feel the displaced worker should just take a job to restore the household income. An unexpected change in career direction may also threaten or cause jealousy in one's spouse.

Issues Involving Children and Teenagers

Many parents avoid telling children about a job loss for fear they will worry or because the parent is embarrassed. However, children can sense when something is wrong. If they feel parents are not giving them important information, they may become mistrustful or feel that something is being hidden. Helene King (2007) echoes this sentiment and adds that it is usually futile to try to keep information from children. Without knowing the source of adult unhappiness, a child might feel responsible for the sadness or anger. It is important for all members of the family to talk together and help each other while a parent is between jobs. Children can be understanding and supportive when they know they are not to blame.

In conclusion, a job loss does not have to damage or derail family relationships. Some family systems actually grow stronger because spouses learn how to support each other during a situational crisis such as this. Indeed, the family can be a source of needed support and understanding during unemployment. The key is being able to communicate and compromise with other family members and face the practical and emotional issues surrounding job loss. It is the resilient family that digs in its heels after a pink slip is delivered, offering mutual support and understanding while navigating the pitfalls of unemployment (Harrar and DeMaria 2006). Robert Fetsch (2006) concurs with this assessment and adds that one of the most important characteristics of resilient families who cope well with unemployment is the meaning they attach to the unemployment. When individuals and families see unemployment as manageable, it becomes less stressful. The more positive the meaning, the better people adapt to the change.

Infidelity

Another situational crisis warranting our attention in this chapter is infidelity. **Infidelity**, also called adultery, an affair, or a nonconsensual extramarital relationship, is sexual activity with another person without the consent of one's spouse. There are different types of affairs, depending on the form of involvement and the escalation of the relationship. Of these, the *isolated affair* is the most common. This relationship, often referred to as a "one-night stand," is defined as sexual activity without emotional commitment or future involvement. The less common *intense affair* is characterized not only by regular sexual activity but also by emotional involvement with the partner and the escalation of attachment.

Although estimates vary on how many men and women engage in affairs, there is fair agreement that about 40 percent of women and 60 percent of men have an affair at one time or another. These figures may be on the low side, though, since some respondents are probably reluctant to admit to such behavior. For this reason, it is likely that affairs, initiated by either the husband or wife—or both—occur in a majority of marriages (Peluso 2007; Manette 2005).

What kinds of people are more likely to become involved in a nonconsensual extramarital relationship? Although most people who have affairs are somewhat dissatisfied, sexually and otherwise, within their marriages, some of those who stray are actually content with their spouses and their marriage. Still, married people who have affairs have certain predictable qualities: They tend to be liberated and also to have a high need for sexual intimacy and a low level of emotional dependency on their marriage partners (Peluso 2007; Spring and Spring 2005; Temple 2004; Mitchell 2001; Sponaugle 1989).

In recent years, incidences of affairs among women have been growing. Cassandra Black (2007) points to a number of reasons for this upswing. For example, the large number of working women today must now take into account the social lives beyond the confines of home. The job, business lunches, work-related travel, and the Internet are all breeding grounds for infidelity in a shaky marriage. Also, infidelity carries a lesser risk financially than it did years ago. Many women make just as much or more money than their spouses and do not depend on them for survival. And many women today are choosing to have children later, or not at all, and do not have youngsters to consider if they decide to test the waters outside of a stale marriage.

Interestingly, Black (2007) acknowledges that sex is often not the driving force behind infidelity. Rather, many women seek to fill emotional voids rather than sexual voids in their extramarital relationships. If a wife does not feel valued or respected, or feels taken for granted, she may turn to someone who can fill these emotional craters and help her feel better about herself. In this respect, unfaithful wives are sharing their bodies and, more important, their hearts.

Whether the affair is initiated by husband or wife, deceit and dishonesty come to characterize the relationship. Excuses must be fabricated to make up for absences and time away from home, and sometimes to explain changes in mood or dress. Often, lies must be spun to keep the affair out of sight, not only from one's partner and other loved ones but also from work associates and even friends and acquaintances.

Extramarital affairs clearly complicate people's lives. Additionally, serious negative consequences result from affairs for the couple's children and family, the extramarital sex partner, and that partner's family. The consequences for the adulterous spouse can be equally serious: the breaking of trust; guilt, anger, and regret; lost respect and love; the disruption of a career and the loss of reputation; sexually transmitted diseases; sexual conflicts and dysfunctions; and sometimes even suicide or homicide. Such consequences provide another good example of how a primary stressor has the potential of unleashing multiple secondary stressors.

Online Infidelity: Cheating on the Internet

To say that the Internet has revolutionized the computer and communications world would be an understatement. Designed in the 1960s as a network to link university and government researchers, the Internet has become an information infrastructure that now spans the globe and allows people to electronically interact without regard for geographic location. Although originally a network of technical communications, the Internet today provides a variety of services and activities, including electronic commerce, information access, communication, and entertainment (Borgman 2003; Gleick 2003; Neville 2002).

An extensive review of the literature (Hertlein and Piercy 2006) indicates that formulating a definition of Internet infidelity is difficult, although one component constantly surfacing among researchers is its secrecy. In cases of Internet infidelity, the unfaithful spouse can carry on the relationship in secrecy by rapidly closing chat windows being used, deleting transcripts, and purging e-mail boxes. In addition, what might appear as someone typically working in his or her cubicle or on a home PC may actually be a spouse secretly engaging in online infidelity. Most researchers also mention sexual chemistry in their definition of Internet infidelity. That is, most participants feel sexual in a medium that makes it relatively easy to flirt or share sexual fantasies online. Internet affairs are often discovered because the trace (or trail) of e-mails and chat room conversations is discovered by suspicious partners.

Deborah Corley (2007) points out that online chatting or e-mailing can begin simply as a distraction from boredom or emotional malcontent. Behaviors considered off limits in a face-to-face situation with strangers are suddenly available through the powers of the Internet. Those persons seeking to connect with a potential partner via the Internet can present themselves in any way they choose and can omit information they do not want others to know. What started innocently can easily move toward a real-life emotional and/or physical extramarital affair. But even if the behavior never advances to meeting in person, many partners view cyber-sex chatting and/or pornography viewing as a form of infidelity, a threat to the marriage, and just as emotionally distressing as a "live" affair. Notice how such perceptions of online infidelity are a reflection of the third component of the Double ABCX model, defining and attaching meaning to the family crisis.

Anthony Bradley (2006) believes that the anonymity provided by chat rooms allows users to share their intimate feelings without becoming embarrassed. Initial chat conversations may be fairly innocent, but when a partner receives a sympathetic response from a fellow chatter, this response can translate into a deep emotional attachment to him or her. The messages often then become intensely personal and can lead to an online affair. Even if it stays on a nonphysical plane, it can still be devastating for a wife or husband to discover that a partner has been indulging in emotional infidelity with someone who is relatively unknown (Underwood and Findlay 2004). The initiator may believe that it is all harmless escapism and that he or she is doing nothing wrong, but the spouse may feel a deep sense of betrayal, knowing that one's partner has been discussing intimate details with a virtual stranger (Bradley 2006).

Thus, online relationships may not reach the legal definition of infidelity, but they can lead to a breakdown of a marriage if not kept in check. The injured spouse may feel a definite alienation of affection, which is indeed grounds for a trial separation or even divorce. Truly innocent chatting online with others who share an interest or a hobby is clearly not infidelity, but the amount of time spent away from a spouse in pursuit of those chats can lead to serious intimacy issues (Pollick 2002).

Divorce

For Bill and Laura Tucker, it started out as a match made in heaven. They fell in love in high school and dated steadily throughout their formal schooling. Shortly thereafter, they married and, in time, started their own family. Over the next 12 years, the Tuckers brought up three children in what neighbors called a happy and loving household. That is why it came as a total surprise when Bill and Laura first filed for a legal separation and, six months later, obtained a divorce.

The marriage of Darnell and Myisha Cummings did not even last that long. The two conceived a child before they completed high school and reluctantly agreed to get married. Without a high school education, Darnell had to settle for tedious and low-paying jobs while Myisha became a full-time teenage mother. Mounting bills created financial pressure, which did not help the marital strife that had begun to appear on a regular basis. As the conflicts escalated, both Darnell and Myisha knew their relationship was going nowhere. Within two years, they called it quits and obtained a divorce. Darnell has since moved away, while Myisha—still in her teens—has custody of their child.

The dissolution of a family by divorce can occur at any stage of marriage and can be a major crisis for all its members. However, contrary to the thoughts of many, the divorce rate is declining in the United States. The divorce rate per thousand people actually peaked in 1981 and has been moving downward ever since. The divorce rate in 2004—3.7 divorces per thousand people—was at its lowest level since 1970 (see Table 6.3 in Chapter 6). But it needs to be recognized that the number of people entering marriage, as a proportion of the population, has also been falling for the past 25 years. The current marriage rate in the United States is at its lowest point in recorded history. Marriage rates rose as the divorce rate rose, but reached an earlier peak in 1972 (U.S. Census Bureau 2007; Brentano 2007; Willis 2007; Murphy 2007).

This trend prompts researchers like Andrew Cherlin (2005, 2004a, 2004b, 2003) to remark that marriage as an institution is here to stay, but we need to acknowledge that its present form differs from its past. This conclusion is due at least in part to changes in marrying, divorcing, and remarrying. He observes that a smaller proportion of families today than in the 1950s resemble the two-biological-parents-with-children family that has been the norm in the United States. Rather, a larger proportion consists of single parents and their children or families formed by remarriage after divorce. The common assumption that a family occupies one household is also increasingly incorrect. Although separation and divorce sever the ties between father and mother, the ties between children and parents tend to remain intact (Andrews 2007).

Because of these trends, an increasing number of families extend across two or three or more households, linked by the continuing ties between parents and children who live apart. Thus, kinship ties are more complex and far reaching than in families formed by first marriages. Also, even the definition of a family can become problematic. For example, a child whose mother and father have divorced and remarried may define the members of his or her family differently from either of his or her parents.

It may well be, then, that how one views America's divorce rate depends on how one views the role of marriage and family in society—this is how Leonard Cargan (Cargan 2007a, 2007b; Cargan and Ballantine 2006) approaches the matter. Those who view the nuclear family as the norm regard the U.S. divorce rate as an indicator of the breakdown of the social structure and a sign of moral decay. However, those who perceive marriage as a choice for personal fulfillment may see the divorce increase as an indication that this goal is being better met.

Cargan proposes that it is expectations, then, that determine what is acceptable and desirable in marriage. As indicated above, these expectations are changing toward an emphasis on self-fulfillment, personal happiness, personal growth, and sexual satisfaction. Couple this with our immense romantic expectations of marriage, along with our lack of preparation for it, and it is not surprising that few anticipate the conflicts that occur, not to mention being ill-prepared to resolve them. It is thus conceivable that many turn to divorce, not because they regard marriage so little, but rather because they expect so much of it—affection, companionship, empathy, and self-actualization, to name but a few areas.

Implications for Family Life

Divorce is a difficult situational crisis to deal with largely because couples and families must confront a number of diverse processes and mentally taxing decisions. Internationally renowned family studies researcher, therapist, and consultant Constance Ahrons (Ahrons 2007, 2004a, 2004b, 2004c, 1998; Ahrons and Tanner 2003) has supplied considerable insight into the family changes that accompany divorce. She regards divorce as a family transition that consists of five stages. These five stages represent a process through which family members acquire new roles and the family itself takes on a new definition. Her stages represent an interesting parallel to the four components of family crises captured by the Double ABCX model discussed in Chapter 1.

Individual Cognition

During the **individual cognition stage**, there is an awareness that something is wrong in the marital relationship. Individual reactions vary in the early phases of this stage: blaming one's partner, anger, depression, or even denial of the problem. Any resolution chosen at this stage depends on the couple's history of coping strategies. Some couples may decide to stay in the marriage until the children are grown. Others may decide to spend time and energy on interests outside the family while attempting to maintain the facade of an intact marriage. This process of emotional divorce, the withdrawal of emotional investment in the marital relationship, is self-protective and may have some positive benefits for the individual. However, this withdrawal will have implications for the entire family system.

How long this stage lasts hinges on the coping behaviors used and other factors related to the family's vulnerability to stress. Equilibrium in the family is usually maintained, although precariously, during this transition. Role patterns may remain stable even in the midst of the growing family tension. Families may deal with internal stress by assigning one member the role of family scapegoat, and he or she is then blamed for any trouble. Thus, the coping strategies families use to alleviate feelings about the parents' marital difficulties often elevate family stress in other ways. Note the interplay here between primary and secondary stressors.

Family Metacognition

In the **family metacognition stage**, the entire family begins to realize that the marriage is deteriorating, and the family system begins to change in recognition of the problem. The problem is typically discussed by the family and the dialogue often sums up each member's anxieties. This is also a time for potential solutions and consequences of the problem to be discussed.

If the family has not demonstrated adequate and rational problem solving in past crisis situations, it is not apt to do so at this time, and for many families, this stage marks the time of greatest disequilibrium. Wife and husband roles are fading, and new ones (divorced coparents) have yet to develop. The future seems uncertain and ambiguous, and the family often searches for role models. For example, old rules and rituals may be sought by the family to preserve stability, but these usually fail to provide unity or comfort. Or children may begin to seek information about divorce by looking for friends who have experienced this crisis.

Separation

The third transition proposed by Ahrons is the **separation stage**. During this stage, one parent moves out of the home and away from the family. The family system is in a state of flux, and family members often express more doubt in regard to family roles and boundaries. For example, a youngster may wonder if his or her parents are both still part of the family.

The typical separation involves the father moving out while the mother and children remain as a system. Ahrons feels that the mother-headed household faces a difficult situation—should it reorganize and fill roles once enacted by the now absent father, or should it maintain his psychological presence in the system by not reorganizing? If the system attempts to reassign roles, the father's return is usually met with resistance. Or if they deal with the father as psychologically present, they perpetuate family disequilibrium characterized by the father's intermittent exit and return. Referring back to the Double ABCX model of family crisis, the system thus experiences imbalance and instability.

The family typically faces stress at this time, even if it has successfully coped with earlier stages. However, it may not experience serious disruption if its coping strategies are successful. Also during this transition, the family typically shares its marital separation with extended family, friends, and the community as it begins the tasks of the economic and legal divorce. Ahrons believes these mediating factors can help and/or hinder the transitional process. The family typically encounters the legal system now and faces secondary stressors in confronting the realities of economic hardships (that is, splitting money, selling the home) and child-focused issues of custody and care. All of these factors may heighten the intensity of this situational crisis.

Family Reorganization

During earlier stages, the lack of clear boundaries caused much of the family's confusion and stress, but in the **family reorganization stage,** the clarification of boundaries itself creates distress.

One of the most stressful chores confronting divorcing parents is that of redefining their coparental relationship, the relationship that permits them to continue their child-rearing obligations and responsibilities after divorce. Ahrons takes this a step further by saying this task requires them to separate their spousal roles from their parental roles, terminating the former while redefining the latter. This complex process of ceasing to be husband and wife while still continuing to be mother and father creates the foundation for divorced family reorganization.

For family adaptation to occur, divorcing spouses need to form new rules to redefine their continued relationship. For example, the divorced family needs to develop new structural rules that will guide its patterns of transactions (who relates to whom, when, and under what conditions). This type of arrangement can help clarify responsibilities and, by eliminating possible disagreements, minimize conflict between ex-spouses. Such rules are also critical to the child's understanding and to the stabilization of his or her relationship with each parent. How divorced parents define the ways in which they will share parenting can be critical to the child's psychological adjustment. Without a clear understanding of the relational rules, the child may become a victim in unresolved spousal or parental conflicts, yet another secondary stressor (Steadman 2007; Bailey 2007; Hansen 2007).

Family Redefinition

Ahrons feels that the outcome of the **family redefinition stage** depends on the relationship between the divorced parents. Although a continued and cooperative relationship between divorced parents reduces the crisis potential associated with divorce, its dynamics remain largely unexplored. As already indicated, the growing debate about custody rights reveals the general lack of knowledge about the time-honored concept "best interests of the child" and brings the custom of sole custody into serious question. Shared custody and coparenting represent an alternative and would thus play a role in family redefinition.

A major feature of the redefinitional process appears to be the parents' ability to maintain a child-centered relationship. For some this includes maintaining a continuing friendship. For others, though, the relationship becomes less intimate and more task oriented. Finally, components of this stage include the processes of remarriage and the introduction of stepparents into the postdivorce family, situations requiring further adjustments and adaptations. It is beyond the scope of this chapter to explore the dynamics of re-marriages and blended families, although in Chapter 6, various trends and statistics are made available to the reader.

To sum up, the research of Ahrons enables us to see the in-dividual and family factors involved in divorce. None of her identified processes or transitions exist in a vacuum, though, nor are they independent or mutually exclusive of one another. Also, since reactions to divorce are highly individualized, variations of the identified stages are more than likely. They should not be taken as precise and rigid blueprints that everyone follows. Nonetheless, her theory is useful in helping us to understand the changes that people face when negotiating this painful situa-tional crisis. Her theory also succeeds in capturing how divorce represents a complex and multifaceted experience.

Effects of Divorce on Children

One and one half million of our nation's children—about 20 percent—will experience the divorce of their parents this year. Often, these children suffer needlessly when their parents at-tempt to punish each other. Some children feel personally re-sponsible for the divorce. Many are persuaded to take sides by their parents. Others may bear the brunt of displaced parental aggression. Coping with the divorce may also spill over to other aspects of the child's life and create additional problems, such as in schoolwork. And children may exhibit a wide range of emo-tional reactions, such as anger, sadness, irritability, distractibility, and rejection (Baksh and Murphy 2007; Grabenstein 2007).

One of the most extensive and comprehensive investigations focusing on the effects of divorce on children was undertaken by Judith Wallerstein and a team of researchers (Wallerstein, Lewis, and Blakeslee 2000). Wallerstein, who launched her research in 1971, identified and tracked the lives of 60 families in which the parents had separated and filed for divorce in California. Over the course of time, Wallerstein and her colleagues discovered that the children of divorce—now in their twenties, thirties, and forties—still suffer from the fallout of their parents' split. Many of the adult children reported fears of betrayal, feelings of pow-erlessness, unrealistic ideas about love and partnership, and shy-ing away from intimacy altogether.

It should be pointed out, though, that many children of di-vorce show remarkable resiliency in the face of domestic turmoil.

Resiliency as a response to divorce tends to be enhanced by open and honest family communication, not placing the blame on the child and not trapping the child in the middle of a divorce cross-fire. Resilient children also tend to have access to a meaningful support system, such as the presence and reassurance of other family members, friends, and teachers (Smoke 2007; Baksh and Murphy 2007).

Chronic Disease and Illness

First comes the shock: emergency treatment for a stroke or heart attack, for example. Or perhaps it is the diagnosis and treatment of cancer. Or test results that reveal the presence of a chronic medical condition that will be with the person and the family forever, such as chronic pain, diabetes, or arthritis. Next comes the long haul. When a health condition travels home with a patient from the hospital or the doctor's office, it takes up residence in the family bedroom and kitchen, on the family calendar and in everyone's daily lives, and in everyone's heart and mind. The script of the family system has been changed: money, work, fun—they are all different now. Family members discover that managing the way an illness impacts the system is just as important as keeping up with medications and doctor's appointments and treatments. Compounding matters is the fact that most chronic illnesses today are not short-term; they are processes that go on and on (Harrar and DeMaria 2006).

Good health is something that many of us simply take for granted. We often feel that we are immune and invincible, cloaked in a suit of armor that protects us from conditions threatening our health and well-being. Indeed, we never fully appreciate our health until we have to face the fact that we have a condition or illness that will not go away (Conway 2007; Davis 2007). For a statistical analysis of chronic health conditions in the United States among the young as well as the old, we direct the reader to Chapter 6 and Figures 6.6, 6.7, 6.8, and 6.9.

We need to be reminded that we are mortal beings and that we live in a world marked by potential risk and accident. One false step on a staircase, a heart attack, or an automobile accident can forever change our lives. Whether it be a baby born into the family with a developmental illness or a marriage partner contracting cancer, challenging health conditions such as these often make family members dependent on others for the simplest tasks and alter family dynamics. The most pressing issue is whether the family system can regain equilibrium in the wake of instability and strain (Szinovacz 2007; Wills 2007; Bouvard 2007).

In this section, we focus on physical disability and chronic illness and the impact they usually have on the person and the family. We do so because of the widespread nature of these health conditions in the United States, the special challenges that afflicted persons must face, and the various family adjustments that usually have to be made. Regarding the last point, disabilities and chronic illnesses exert an influence on the system in a wide range of interactions, such as work-family dynamics, parent-child relations, sibling interactions, and caring for elderly parents. We also include the topics of disabilities and chronic illnesses because of the huge challenges they pose for individuals, health care professionals, and policy makers.

Before exploring the manner in which physical disability and chronic illness impact family life, the terms *physical disability* and *chronic illness* need to be clarified. A **physical disability**, such as cerebral palsy or a spinal cord injury, is an impairment of body structure and function, including mobility impairments, amputations, skeletal deformities, and disfigurements. An individual is considered to have a disability if he or she has difficulty executing certain activities (e.g., talking, walking, seeing, hearing), has difficulty performing activities of daily living (e.g., bathing, toileting, eating), or has difficulty with certain social roles (e.g., working at a job). An individual who is unable to execute one or more activities, who uses an assistive device to move from location to location, or who needs assistance from another individual to execute basic activities is considered to have a severe disability.

Disabilities are widespread in the United States. An estimated one in five Americans has some kind of disability, a proportion translating into an estimated 50 million noninstitutionalized persons. About 1 in 10 Americans has a severe disability, which accounts for approximately 24 million persons. And with the population aging and the likelihood of having a disability increasing with age, the growth in the number of individuals with disabilities is expected to accelerate in the future. Currently, about one in two seniors 65 years of age and older has a physical disability (Centers for Disease Control and Prevention and the Merck Foundation 2007; U.S. Department of Health and Human Services 2007).

Improved medical care and prevention efforts have contributed to dramatic increases in life expectancy in the United States during the past century. However, they also have produced a major shift in the leading causes of death for all age groups, including older adults, from infectious diseases and acute illnesses to chronic diseases and degenerative illnesses. In 2002, the top three causes of death for U.S. adults age 65 or older were heart disease (32 percent of all deaths), cancer (22 percent), and stroke (8 percent). These causes accounted for 61 percent of all deaths in this age group (Centers for Disease Control and Prevention and the Merck Foundation 2007).

A **chronic illness**, such as diabetes or arthritis, is a progressive disorder caused by a nonreversible condition that often leaves the person with some type of disability. Chronic illness is thus a long-term or permanent condition, one that often results in the need for rehabilitation or continuous care. Although chronic illness cannot be cured, it can often be controlled by carefully following dietary, exercise, and medication regimens. More than 90 million Americans are estimated to live with chronic illnesses; of this figure, about 57 million have two or more chronic diseases. Currently, more than two-thirds of health care costs are spent treating chronic illnesses; among older Americans, almost 95 percent of health care expenditures are for chronic diseases. The cost of providing health care for one person age 65 or older is three to five times greater than the cost for someone younger than 65 (Centers for Disease Control and Prevention and the Merck Foundation 2007; U.S. Department of Health and Human Services 2007).

According to the Centers for Disease Control and Prevention (2007), chronic diseases—such as heart disease, cancer, and diabetes—are the leading causes of death and disability in the United States. Chronic diseases account for 70 percent of all deaths in the United States, which is 1.7 million each year. These diseases also cause major limitations in daily living for almost 1 out of 10 Americans, or about 25 million people. Although chronic diseases are among the most common and costly health problems, they are also among the most preventable. Adopting healthy behaviors such as eating nutritious foods, being physically active, and avoiding tobacco use can prevent or control the devastating effects of these diseases.

While advancing age increases the risk of contracting both a physical disability and chronic illness, racial disparities also need to be considered. The health status of racial and ethnic minorities of all ages lags far behind that of nonminority populations. For a variety of reasons, older minority adults may experience the effects of health disparities more dramatically than any other population group. First, older adults are more likely to have chronic illness and require frequent contact with the health care system. Second, many live in poverty, making access to health care a challenge. The care of older adults who are chronically ill, poor, and members of an ethnic community is an increasingly urgent health priority (Centers for Disease Control and Prevention and the Merck Foundation 2007; U.S. Department of Health and Human Services 2007).

It is beyond the scope and focus of this book to present a descriptive, medically oriented discussion on the chronic illnesses and diseases that exist today. Rather, our efforts will continue to focus on how stressor events impact family life. The reader seeking more information is directed to Martz and Livneh (2007), Natelson (2007), Thomas (2007), Schwartz (2007), Schulz (2006), and Putnam (2006).

Implications for Family Life

Whether being born with a lifelong disability such as cerebral palsy or being afflicted in midlife with cardiovascular disease, adjusting to a long-term health impairment is difficult for the person as well as the family system. We must continually remind ourselves of the interplay that exists between the two. Although the afflicted individual certainly shoulders the burden of the illness, the family system is also influenced by the changes in the health of a loved one. The resulting interaction can be found at all stages of the family life cycle.

Although disabilities and chronic illnesses are considered separate medical conditions, they do share certain characteristics. For example, both are usually permanent conditions that pose an assortment of limitations. Both can dramatically alter a person's life. Also, a physical disability can create a chronic illness and vice versa.

As indicated above, chronic disease and illness influences the lives of everyone in the family system. The demands of caregiving must be negotiated and stress levels addressed. Family members' emotions may be on a continuous roller-coaster ride. Sacrifices need to be made, and the workload of caregiving seems never-ending. On the other hand, families may come together and grow closer, bolstering their resiliency. Their lives may take on new meaning. They may find rewards they had not expected on their journey through illness. The only certain thing is that chronic illness is a family experience, one that is shared by the entire family system (Seaburn 2001).

In addition to playing a vital role in reducing the discomfort of the chronically ill and disabled, the family can do much to help the chronically ill maintain a sense of dignity and self-worth. As we discovered in Chapter 1, the family can draw from existing and expanded resources to weather this situational crisis. The most resilient chronically ill are those who have strong support from within and who communicate effectively with those who care. Regarding the latter, it is not uncommon for the chronically ill to pull away, even from family members. Many do not seek the company of others, let alone ask for help. Experts agree that working through one's feelings with others helps to combat the loneliness that is prevalent following the early stages of a prolonged illness.

Open and clear communication is especially important as family roles and responsibilities change with the illness. Relatives outside the immediate family or friends may be so uncomfortable with the situation that they may deny the illness. They may feel overwhelmed and cut off communication at a time when they really need each other's support. If the strains are too great, a family member might shut down, feeling hopeless, isolated, and trapped. Sometimes relatives fret over minor issues while holding back painful news, angry feelings, or resentments (ElderCare Advocates 2007; Bumagin 2006; Burbank 2006).

Family caregivers also need to get in touch with their own insecurities and fears (e.g., loss of income, loss of a spouse or parent, death of a loved one). By doing so, they are less likely to express them inappropriately or take them out on others. The stressor of chronic illness will likely produce a wide variety of secondary stressors. For example, parents usually express a variety of reactions when they learn that their child is health impaired: shock, denial, sadness, fear, and anger. Many parents also believe that the child's disability was their fault. Some reason that the disability is punishment for a sin or wrongdoing. The extra care and special accommodations often required by health-impaired family members often alters how parents and siblings interact with the person, as well as with one another. The difficulty of living normally while relating to and caring for a disabled person often unleashes anxiety, confusion, and despair. Even the most competent and balanced family units can feel overwhelmed. Yet parents and siblings usually adjust to the reality of the disability in diverse and unique ways and establish family equilibrium. Indeed, many families discover that living with a health-impaired person promotes family cohesion and resiliency (Jackson 2001).

As this section winds down, a few concluding comments are in order. Millions of Americans, young and old, are limited in their daily functioning because of a chronic mental health or physical health condition. According to David Seaburn (2001), for the vast majority of these individuals, family is their first line of health care. Whether the family member is a child with cystic fibrosis, an adolescent with diabetes, a parent with multiple sclerosis, or a grandparent with Alzheimer's disease, it is the family, first and foremost, that cares for an ill loved one.

Caring for Aging Family Members

Eighty-three-year-old Marion Thorpe lost her husband 10 years ago and has been living with her son Bob ever since. A number of factors prompted the move, including lingering depression from her loss and financial hardships. Although Marion remains in fairly good health, Bob and his wife, Christine, must prepare her meals every day as well as tend to an assortment of her personal needs.

A medical crisis within the family changed the lives of Roberta and Frank Cummings. Tests revealed that Roberta's 78-year-old father, Carl, was in the early stages of Alzheimer's disease. Because he was living alone and needed day-to-day assistance, Carl moved in with his daughter shortly after the prognosis was made. This move postponed institutional care, something the entire family wanted to avoid for as long as possible. In the meantime, Carl receives medical attention each week while Roberta and Frank provide as much loving care as possible.

For Carla Davidson, a middle-aged tax accountant, the plan needing to be implemented was an obvious one. Her elderly parents still lived independently in their own home, but they were finding daily chores increasingly difficult. The oldest of three children and the one living nearest to her parents, Carla took it upon herself to provide the needed assistance. She regularly visits her parents during the week and on Saturdays and faithfully tends to the cleaning and laundering.

These scenarios are illustrative of the growing numbers of adult children caring for their aging parents, an example of a developmental or normative family crisis. Among adults over age 50, more than 1 in 10 is providing assistance with basic everyday activities to his or her parent(s). Such assistance includes providing direct physical and medical care to parents every day and tending to daily living needs, including financial support, household chores, shopping, and transportation.

All indicators suggest that such involvement will increase in the years to come. Projections show that a larger proportion of adult children are likely to become caregivers as the 65 years and over population continues to grow at a faster rate than the population under age 65. The growth in the number and proportion of older adults is unprecedented in the history of the United States. Two factors—longer life spans and aging baby boomers—will combine to double the population of Americans age 65 and older during the next 25 years. By 2030, 71 million older adult Americans will account for roughly 20 percent of the U.S. population (Centers for Disease Control and Prevention and the Merck Foundation 2007; Center on an Aging Society 2005; Szinovacz 2007; U.S. Census Bureau 2006). See Figure 6.10 for projections of the elderly population.

The majority of today's caregivers are female. Women are the primary caregivers of young children, and as our society ages, an increasing number will find themselves back on this job for their parents. Women are presumed to be responsible for the well-being of their family members. Until quite recently, the care and well-being of the family was the only occupation of a large percentage of women in the United States. For those who also worked outside the home, including many lower-income women, family caregiving was an additional responsibility (Szinovacz 2007).

However, the numbers of male caregivers today are growing. This trend is already occurring for spouses, but we may even see more sons begin to help caregiving daughters and daughters-in-law in the care of elderly parents. Also, the gender differences in caregiving for others, which have been pronounced in the child-raising years because of occupational and family structures, do not seem as prevalent in the later years with retirement.

Large differences are not found between male and female caregivers in the later years. Whether the number of younger male caregivers will increase and whether younger male and female caregivers will adapt similarly to their caregiving remain uncertain.

In analyzing patterns of female intergenerational care, Marcia Ory (2006, 1985) believes that certain demographic and social trends will affect the quantity and quality of services rendered. For example, she believes that changing gender roles, coupled with increased labor force participation among middle-aged women, may place an additional burden on already strained family resources. Further, an important question to ask is whether assistance to the aged will decline as more women enter the workplace. Women traditionally have spent many hours in support of the aged in their families and in their communities. With escalating proportions of females in the labor force, assistance may not be as readily available in the future.

The fact that we are living longer than ever before means that a new wrinkle in caregiving patterns will become evident: the old helping the old. Indeed, in years to come we will see the existence of more four- and five-generation families. This trend means that older impaired parents needing assistance will be getting it from their offspring, who are themselves aging. In this fashion, it will become increasingly common for 85-year-old parents to be cared for by their 60-year-old children (Schaie 2007; Moody 2006; Gibson 2002). See Chapter 6 (Table 6.4 and Figure 6.11) for more information on the elderly population.

The notion that most younger generations want to help their aging parents was borne out in the research of Elaine Brody (2006). Exploring intergenerational attitudes about familial closeness and care, she found that young women in particular were just as committed to caring for aged relatives as were their middle-aged mothers and their grandparents. Most of the women she studied also reported that they sincerely wanted to care for aging family members, not because they were obliged to do so nor because it was their "duty." In addition, aging parents reported that they wanted to be cared for by their offspring if it was at all possible for their children.

But not all adult children have the flexibility to provide extensive care. For example, many adult children have to settle for less intensive involvement because of family and/or vocational obligations, or the presence of a personal crisis. Along these lines, little research has been conducted on the impact of an adult child's divorce on the relationship with elderly parents; clearly, however, a loss of a spouse with his or her attendant pressures may cause such a drain on the divorced child's resources and available time that the child may never be able to establish a solid basis from which to provide affectional and supportive relationships to elderly parents. Thus, the stressor of caring for aging parents might be compounded by a pileup of other pressures and strains.

Implications for Family Life

The care of aging parents brings many changes, including ones affecting the underlying family system. Often, the assistance received prompts parents to reflect on the past while looking ahead to the future, causing many to rethink earlier relationships. Many experts (e.g., Haber 2007; Bumagin 2006) point out that most family relations prior to the point at which they are in need of assistance are characterized by regular contact, affection, and a desire to help in time of need. But when the obligation and/or need to help becomes the dominant element in the family system, trouble often brews. Problems may even begin when actual aid enters into the relationship because it has the potential for weakening the enjoyable aspects of it. Thus, realignment of care from the parent to the offspring may create problems because it represents something that neither system is accustomed to.

Caregiving brings other adjustment challenges and demands. Today, the typical caregiver is middle aged and often caught in what has been called the "sandwich" or "squeeze" generation. That is, they have their aging parents on one end of the generational cycle, their children on the other, and themselves in the middle. As a result of this squeeze, middle-agers frequently face growing pressures as they simultaneously cope with the needs of their aging parents and their offspring (Bumagin 2006). This is a good example of two developmental crises colliding— one family at midlife and the other experiencing the later life transition.

Couples at midlife are also typically confronted with competing role responsibilities and time demands. The rigors of providing regular care while maintaining one's own household are physically and psychologically exhausting. The loss of personal freedom, the lack of time for social and recreational activities, and other restrictions are often part of the sacrifices to be made.

The pressures become more intense when the female caregiver, who traditionally shoulders most of the work, is employed outside of the home (Prieto 2008; Haber 2007; Bumagin, 2006).

The Dark Side of Caregiving: Elder Abuse

The often unrelenting rigors and demands of caregiving have been known to produce a dark side to intergenerational care: abuse of the elderly. Researchers (e.g., Schimer 2005; Matthews 2004; Carp 2000) report that the abuse of the elderly takes many forms, including neglect, verbal and emotional abuse, physical assault, and financial exploitation. As many as 1 million aged Americans are estimated to suffer maltreatment each year, and this figure is expected to rise in years to come.

The abuser of an elderly person is likely to be a parent's middle-aged caregiver, often the daughter. Robert Pierce and Rosilee Trotta (1986) write that the female caregiver often is experiencing some kind of personal crisis, such as alcohol or drug addiction, illness, or financial problems. The combination of personal crisis coupled with the new task of caring for an aged parent often creates a situation that increases the likelihood of abuse. As we have seen throughout this chapter, the pileup of demands or prior strains complicates the family crisis and creates considerable disequilibrium.

Other researchers (e.g., Nerenberg 2007) write that abusers are typically normal persons who are encountering escalating stress levels. For middle-aged female caregivers, such stress may accompany their traditional nurturing role. They most likely start caring for an elderly parent at the time when their own teenagers are beginning to leave home. Being placed back into a nurturing role, just when it is expected that this responsibility is finished, may prove overwhelming.

A persistent theme in the literature (e.g., Nerenberg 2007; Brandl 2006; Ambrogi and London 1985) is that pressured caregivers often face a workload without relief. They point out that a dependent, frail elder often requires constant, physically and emotionally demanding care. Caregivers may have to get up several times during the night to take the elder to the toilet to manage incontinence, thus interrupting their own needed sleep. And if the elder has had a stroke and is severely disabled, the caregiver may have to bathe, dress, and feed the elder. All of this drains precious coping resources and adds to the disequilibrium.

Despite caregivers' good intentions, many cannot easily meet the long-term demands of frail elders.

Gerontologists (e.g., Dell Orto 2007; Putnam 2006) tell us that for many caregivers, certain parts of assistance often prove more burdensome than others. For example, for some it is not the degree of physical impairment of the person being cared for, or even cognitive impairment, but rather changes in the elder's behavior. More specifically, personality changes that lead to unresponsiveness or unpredictability or to changes in past relationships often create caregivers' depression. Also, inconvenience in living arrangements—such as parents moving into children's homes or children moving into parents' homes—creates disequilibrium.

Caregiving Support and Assistance

In recent years, attention has been directed toward the needs of adult caregivers. A number of support groups have been established to help adult children better handle the pressures of caring for aging parents, including abusive tendencies. Such support groups have proven valuable in terms of providing resources and referrals, companionship, guidance, education, and reassurance (Gelfand 2006; AARP Public Policy Institute 2005; Gartska, Mc-Callion, and Toseland 2001). The reader is directed to Chapter 7, which provides a comprehensive listing of caregiving support groups.

Whether sharing a residence or tending to the needs of the elderly on a visitation basis, caregivers must reckon with the financial burden. The material support of an aging parent is an expensive venture, be it the amount of time given or actual dollars expended. The cash value of services performed by families far exceeds the combined cost of government and professional services to both elderly living in the community and those living in institutions. Experts (e.g., Feinberg and Newman 2004; Goodman et al. 2004; Skocpol 2000; Wisendale 2001) agree that policy makers need to pay more attention to the financial drain posed by caregiving.

Unfortunately, most people are not aware of how expensive caregiving is or how little coverage exists until the crisis hits. Medical costs at hospitals and nursing homes have increased dramatically, resulting in depletion of Medicare and Medicaid funds (Connell, Janevic, and Gallant 2001; Hudson and Gonyea 2000). If no one is at home to care for the elderly parent, services must be paid for from someone's pocket. Obviously, the continuing care for a loved one represents a very expensive venture (Roog et al. 2004; Simon-Rusinowitz et al. 2005).

The complexities attached to caregiving mean that adult children need to seriously address the issue of who is going to be the primary caregiver. Planning in advance is the key. When an aged parent is stricken with an illness or faces acute financial hardship, it is often too late to do the most effective planning. The time to work out financial and legal considerations possibly lurking ahead is *before* they occur, when parents are optimally healthy and content with their lives (Brodie and Gadling-Cole 2003).

Family discussions should take place repeatedly over the years. Nothing has to be decided definitively after the first conversation, since most strategies and decisions need to evolve. Family members usually need time to think about matters and refine their own particular ideas.

Family discussions and advance planning need not be restricted to finances, either. Honest, open discussions are needed about all aspects of family life. When this is done in productive and healthy ways, an assortment of parents' plans and wishes usually unfolds. Better yet, difficult situations in later years can be eased, since a well-informed adult child is in the best position to ensure that parents' best interests are protected and caregiving stress is kept at manageable levels (Hooyman and Kiyak 2008; Bumagin 2006; Brodie and Gadling-Cole 2003).

Summary

This chapter illustrates how family crises come in all shapes and sizes. Generally speaking, a crisis is a period of stress that has the potential for disrupting routines and sometimes causing overwhelming feelings of disequilibrium. Separate sections in the chapter explored *situational crises* (addiction, adolescent runaways, unemployment, infidelity, divorce, and chronic illness and disease) and *developmental crises* (caring for aging parents). Regardless of the crisis category, change in one part of the system creates a ripple effect and impacts other parts of the system.

A deliberate effort is made in this chapter to show how crises create many implications for family life, especially the lives of children. How the family perceives the stressor, its current state in terms of equilibrium or disequilibrium, and its previous experience in handling crises are critical factors in recovery. In the wake of stress and disequilibrium, many families benefit from outside intervention for support and assistance. Intervention efforts seek to employ the family's strengths and resources to help the unit regain stability. Therapy typically utilizes a systems approach, aimed at the individual within the context of the family, or within a support group setting.

References

AARP Public Policy Institute. 2005. *Family Caregiver Support Services: Sustaining Unpaid Family and Friends in a Time of Public Fiscal Restraint.* Washington, DC: AARP Public Policy Institute.

Ahrons, C. R. 1998. *The Good Divorce: Keeping Your Family Together when Your Marriage Comes Apart,* 2nd ed. New York: HarperCollins.

Ahrons, C. R. 2004a. *We're Still Family: What Grown Children Have to Say About Their Parents' Divorce.* New York: HarperCollins.

Ahrons, C. R. 2004b. "What Grown Children Have to Say about Their Parents' Divorce." *Children's Legal Rights Journal* 24:48–56.

Ahrons, C. R. 2004c. "Divorce: An Unscheduled Life Cycle Transition." In *The Family Life Cycle,* 3rd ed., edited by B. Carter and M. McGoldrick. New York: Allyn and Bacon.

Ahrons, C. R. 2007. "Family Ties after Divorce: Long-term Implications for Children." *Family Process* 46:53–65.

Ahrons, C. R., and J. Tanner. 2003. "Adult Children's Relationships with Their Fathers Twenty Years after Divorce." *Family Relations* 52:340–351.

Alleyne, S., L. Egodigwe, and T. E. Holmes. 2004. "How to Effectively Compete in a Tough Job Market: Getting in Gear for Career Success." *Black Enterprise* 34:73–81.

Ambrogi, D., and C. London. 1985. "Elder Abuse Laws: Their Implications for Caregivers." *Generations* 10 (1): 37–39.

American Medical Association. 2006. "Alcohol Abuse and Alcoholism." [Online information; retrieved 7/25/07.] http://jama.ama-assn.org/cgi/content/full/295/17/2100.

Andreas, J. B., T. J. O'Farrell, and W. Fals-Stewart. 2006. "Does Individual Treatment for Alcoholic Fathers Benefit Their Children? A Longitudinal Assessment." *Journal of Consulting and Clinical Psychology* 74 (1): 191–198.

Andrews, S. 2007. *Love, Marriage and Divorce.* Waco, TX: Library Binding.

Asenjo. B. 2007. "Addiction." [Online information; retrieved 7/21/07.] http://www.answers.com/topic/addiction.

Aviles, A., and C. Helfrich. 2004. "Life Skill Service Needs: Perspectives of Homeless Youth." *Journal of Youth and Adolescence* 33 (4): 331–342.

Baer, J. S., J. A. Ginzler, and P. L. Peterson. 2003. "DSM-IV Alcohol and Substance Abuse and Dependence in Homeless Youth." *Journal of Studies on Alcohol* 64 (1): 5–15.

Bailey, J. L. 2007. *The Parental Peace Accord.* Bloomington, IN: Author-House.

Baker, A. J. L., M. M. McKay, C. J. Hans., H. Schlange, and A. Auville. 2003. "Recidivism at a Shelter for Adolescents: First-Time versus Repeat Runaways." *Social Work Research* 27:84–94.

Baksh, N., and L. Murphy. 2007. *In the Best Interest of the Child.* Gardena, CA: Hohm Press.

Bell, N. S., T. C. Harford, C. H. Fuchs, J. E. McCarroll, and C. E. Schwartz. 2006. "Spouse Abuse and Alcohol Problems among White, African American, and Hispanic U.S. Army Soldiers." *Alcoholism: Clinical and Experimental Research* 30 (10): 1721–1733.

Beymer, J. K., and R. L. Hutchinson. 2002. "Profile of Problem Children from a Rural County in Indiana." *Adolescence* 37 (145): 183–191.

Black, C. 2007. "Survey Reports More Women Are Having Extramarital Affairs." [Online article; retrieved 8/23/07.] http://www.associatedcontent.com/article/231316/survey_reports_more_women_are_having.html.

Black, D. W., P. O. Monahan, M. Temkit, and M. Shaw. 2006. "A Family Study of Pathological Gambling." *Psychiatry Research* 141 (3): 295–303.

Borgman, Christine. 2003. *From Gutenberg to the Global Information Infrastructure: Access to Information in the Networked World.* Cambridge, MA: MIT Press.

Bouvard, M. G. 2007. *Healing: A Life with Chronic Illness.* Lebanon, NH: University Press of New England.

Bradley, A. 2006. "Online Infidelity—Is Your Partner Having a Cyber Affair?" [Online article; retrieved 8/23/07.] http://www.article99.com/news-and-society/relationships/article.php?art=9891.

Brandl, B. 2006. *Elder Abuse Detection and Intervention: A Collaborative Approach.* New York: Springer.

Brentano, C. 2007. *Divorce: Causes and Consequences.* New Haven, CT: Yale University Press.

Brodie, K., and C. Gadling-Cole. 2003. "The Use of Family Decision Meetings when Addressing Caregiver Stress." *Journal of Gerontological Social Work* 41:89–100.

Brody, E. 2006. *Women in the Middle: Their Parent Care Years*. New York: Springer.

Brown, J. M. 2004. "The Effectiveness of Treatment." In *The Essential Handbook of Treatment and Prevention of Alcohol Problems*, edited by N. Heather and T. Stockwell. New York: Wiley.

Browne, M. H., and M. M. Browne. 2007. *You Can't Have Him, He's Mine*. Avon, MA: Adams Media.

Bumagin, V. 2006. *Caregiving: A Guide for Those Who Give Care and Those Who Receive It*. New York: Springer.

Burbank, P. 2006. *Vulnerable Older Adults: Health Care Needs and Interventions*. New York: Springer.

Cargan, L. 2007a. *Doing Social Research*. Lanham, MD: Rowman and Littlefield.

Cargan, L. 2007b. *Being Single: Myths and Realties*. Lanham, MD: Rowman and Littlefield.

Cargan, L., and J. H. Ballantine. 2006. *Sociological Footprints: Introductory Readings in Sociology*, 10th ed. Belmont, CA: Thomson Higher Education.

Carp, F. M. 2000. *Elder Abuse in the Family: An Interdisciplinary Model for Research*. New York: Springer.

Cauce, A. M., M. Paradise, J. A. Ginzler, L. Embry, C. J. Morgan, and Y. Lohr. 2000. "The Characteristics and Mental Health of Homeless Adolescents: Age and Gender Differences." *Journal of Emotional and Behavioral Disorders* 8 (4): 230–242.

Center for Substance Abuse Treatment. 2004. *Substance Abuse Treatment and Family Therapy*. Treatment Improvement Protocol Series, No. 39. Rockville, MD: Substance Abuse and Mental Health Services Administration.

Center on an Aging Society. 2005. *Caregivers of Older Persons: Data Profile*. No. 2, May. Washington, DC: Georgetown University.

Centers for Disease Control and Prevention. 2007. *Chronic Disease Prevention*. Atlanta, GA: Centers for Disease Control and Prevention.

Centers for Disease Control and Prevention and the Merck Foundation. 2007. *The State of Aging and Health in America 2007*. Whitehouse Station, NJ: The Merck Company Foundation.

Chalder, M., F. J. Elgar, and P. Bennett. 2006. "Drinking and Motivations to Drink among Adolescent Children of Parents with Alcohol Problems." *Alcohol and Alcoholism* 41 (1): 107–113.

Cherlin, A. J. 2003. "Family Demography." In *Encyclopedia of Population*, edited by P. Demeny and G. McNicoll. New York: Macmillan.

Cherlin, A. J. 2004a. *Public and Private Families: An Introduction*. New York: McGraw-Hill.

Cherlin, A. J. 2004b. "The Deinstitutionalization of American Marriage." *Journal of Marriage and Family* 66:848–861.

Cherlin, A. J. 2005. "American Marriage in the Early Twenty-first Century." *The Future of Children* 15 (2): 33–55.

Chou, C., L. Condron, and J. C. Belland. 2005. "A Review of the Literature on Internet Addiction." *Educational Psychology Review* 17 (4): 363–388.

Clarke, R., and W. Dempsey. 2001. "The Feasibility of Regulating Gambling on the Internet." *Managerial and Decision Economics* 22:125–132.

Connell, C. M., M. R. Janevic, and M. P. Gallant. 2001. "The Costs of Caring: Impact of Dementia on Family Caregivers." *Journal of Geriatric Psychiatry and Neurology* 14:179–188.

Conway, K. 2007. *Illness and the Limits of Expression.* Ann Arbor, MI: University of Michigan Press.

Corley, M. D. 2007. "Online Infidelity." [Online article; retrieved 8/22/07.] http://www.instituteforcouplescounseling.com/onlineinfidelity.htm.

Dalton, M. M., and K. I. Pakenham. 2002. "Adjustment of Homeless Adolescents to a Crisis Shelter: Application of a Stress and Coping Model." *Journal of Youth and Adolescence* 31 (1): 79–84.

Davis, N. 2007. *Lean on Me: Ten Powerful Steps to Moving beyond Your Diagnosis and Taking Back Your Life.* New York: Simon and Schuster.

Dawson, D. A., B. F. Grant, F. S. Stinson, P. S. Chou, B. Huang, and W. J. Ruan. 2005. "Recovery from DSM-IV Alcohol Dependence: United States, 2001–2002." *Addiction* 100 (3): 281–292.

Deegan, G. 2003. "Discovering Recovery." *Psychiatric Rehabilitation Journal* 26 (4): 368–376.

Dekel, R., E. Peled, and S. E. Spiro. 2003. "Shelters for Houseless Youth: A Follow-up Evaluation." *Journal of Adolescence* 26:201–212.

Dell Orto, A. E. 2007. *The Psychological and Social Impact of Illness and Disability.* New York: Springer.

DiClemente, C. 2003. *Addiction and Change: How Addictions Develop and Addicted People Recover.* New York: Guilford Press.

Duran, M. G. 2003. "Internet Addiction Disorder." [Online article; retrieved 7/22/07.] http://allpsych.com/journal/internetaddiction.html.

ElderCare Advocates. 2007. "Coping with a Chronic Illness in Your Family." [Online article; retrieved 8/28/07.] http://www.eldercareadvocates.com/pages/art22.htm.

Feinberg, L. F., and S. L. Newman. 2004. "A Study of 10 States since Passage of the National Family Caregiver Support Program: Policies, Perceptions and Program Development." *The Gerontologist* 44 (6): 760–769.

Fest, J. 2003. "Understanding Street Culture: A Prevention Perspective." *School Nurse News* 20 (2): 16–18.

Fetsch, R. 2006. "Coping Well with Unemployment." [Online article; retrieved 8/15/07.] http://www.ext.colostate.edu/emptrans/feature0209.html.

Fitzgerald, H., B. Lester, and B. Zuckerman. 2000. *Children of Addiction: Research, Health, and Public Policy Issues.* New York: Garland Science.

Foston, N. A. 2003. "How to Find a Job in a Tight Market." *Ebony* 58 (January): 52–59.

Gartska, T., P. McCallion, and R. Toseland. 2001. "Using Support Groups to Improve Caregiver Health." In *Aging, Communication, and Health,* edited by M. L. Hummert and J. F. Nussbaum. Mahwah, NJ: Lawrence Erlbaum Associates.

Gelfand, D. 2006. *The Aging Network: Programs and Services,* 6th ed. New York: Springer.

Gibson, P. 2002. "Barriers, Lessons Learned and Helpful Hints: Grandmother Caregivers Talk about Service Utilization." *Journal of Gerontological Social Work* 39:55–74.

Glass, S. P., and J. C. Staeheli. 2004. *Not "Just Friends": Rebuilding Trust and Recovering Your Sanity after Infidelity.* New York: Simon and Schuster.

Gleick, James. 2003. *What Just Happened: A Chronicle from the Information Frontier.* New York: Vintage.

Gnuschke, J. E., and B. L. Alvarado. 2007. "Wary and Watchful: The National Outlook for 2007–2008." *Business Perspectives* 18 (Winter): 1–9.

Goodman, C. C., M. Potts, E. M. Pasztor, and D. Scorzo. 2004. "Grandmothers as Kinship Caregivers: Private Arrangements Compared to Public Child Welfare Oversight." *Children and Youth Services Review* 26:287–305.

Grabenstein, C. C. 2007. *Divorced Parents Challenge: Eight Lessons to Teach Children Love and Forgiveness.* Calverton, MD: Collier Productions.

Graham, A. W., T. K. Schulz, and B. B. Wilford, eds. 2003. *Principles of Addiction Medicine,* 3rd ed. Annapolis Junction, MD: American Society of Addiction Medicine.

Greene, R. R. 2000. *Social Work with the Aged and Their Families.* New York: Aldine de Gruyter.

Griffiths, M. 2003. "Internet Abuse in the Workplace: Issues and Concerns for Employers and Employment Counselors." *Journal of Employment* 40 (2): 87–96.

Haber, D. 2007. *Health Promotion and Aging.* New York: Springer.

Halcon, L. L., and A. R. Lifson. 2004. "Prevalence and Predictors of Sexual Risks among Homeless Youth." *Journal of Youth and Adolescence* 33 (1): 71–82.

Hammer, H. 2003. "Vanishing Youngsters: No Easy Answers." *USA Today* 132 (September): 14–25.

Hammer, H., D. Finkelhor, and A. Sedlak. 2002. "Runaway/Thrownaway Children: National Estimates and Characteristics." *National Incidence Studies of Missing, Abducted, Runaway, and Thrownaway Children.* Washington, DC: Office of Juvenile Justice and Delinquency Prevention.

Hansen, D. 2007. *Broken Strings: Wisdom for Divorced and Separated Families.* Bloomington, IN: AuthorHouse.

Harrar, S., and R. M. DeMaria. 2006. *The Seven Stages of Marriage.* New York: Penguin.

Harvey, J., A. Wenzel, and S. Sprecher. 2004. *Handbook of Sexuality in Close Relationships.* Mahwah, NJ: Lawrence Erlbaum Associates.

Hertlein, K. M., and F. P. Piercy. 2006. "Internet Infidelity: A Critical Review of the Literature." *The Family Journal* 14:366–376.

Heyman, G. M. 2001. "Is Addiction a Chronic, Relapsing Disease?" In *Drug Addiction and Drug Policy: The Struggle to Control Dependence,* edited by G. M. Heymann and W. N. Brownsberger. Cambridge, MA: Harvard University Press.

Hodgins, D. C., K. Makarchuk, and N. Peden. 2002. "Why Problem Gamblers Quit Gambling: A Comparison of Methods and Samples." *Addiction Research and Theory* 10 (2): 203–208.

Hooyman, N., and H. A. Kiyak. 2008. *Social Gerontology.* Boston: Allyn and Bacon.

Hudson, R., and J. Gonyea. 2000. "Time Not Yet Money: The Politics and Promise of the Family Medical Leave Act." *Journal of Aging and Social Policy* 11 (2/3): 189–200.

Jackson, W. 2001. "Coping with Chronic Illness." [Online article; retrieved 7/2/08.] http://www.geocities.com/cfsdays/chronic.htm.

Jones, K. D., and N. B. Minatrea. 2001. "The Consequences of Internet Addiction: Implications for Counseling Practice." *Journal of Technology in Counseling* 2 (1): 22–43.

Kart, C. S., and J. M. Kinney. 2001. *The Realities of Aging: An Introduction to Gerontology,* 6th ed. Boston: Allyn and Bacon.

Kaysen, D., T. M. Dillworth, T. Simpson, A. Waldrop, M. E. Larimer, and P. A. Resick. 2006. "Domestic Violence and Alcohol Use: Trauma-Related Symptoms and Motives for Drinking." *Addictive Behavior* 32 (6): 1272–1283.

Kessler, D. (2007). "After a Job Loss." [Online article; retrieved 8/15/07.] http://davidkessler.biz/articles/afterjobloss.htm.

Kesten, D. 2004. *Addiction, Progression and Recovery: Understanding the Stages of Change on the Addiction Recovery Learning Curve.* Eau Claire, WI: PESI Healthcare.

Khantzian, E. J. 2001. "Addiction: Disease, Symptom or Choice?" *Counselor* 2 (6): 46–50.

King, H. 2007. "Coping with Job Loss." [Online article; retrieved 8/15/07.] http://oser.state.wi.us/docview.asp?docid=1143.

Kroll, B. 2004. "Living with an Elephant: Growing Up with Parental Substance Misuse." *Child and Family Social Work* 9 (2): 129–140.

Labeau, J. 2003. "Chronic Career Stress: What It Looks Like and What to Do about It." *Public Management* 85 (November): 8–16.

Lemanski, M. 2001. *A History of Addiction and Recovery in the United States.* Tucson, AZ: Sharp Press.

Manette, D. 2005. *Ultimate Betrayal: Recognizing, Uncovering, and Dealing with Infidelity.* Garden Park, New York: Square One.

Martz, E., and H. Livneh. 2007. *Coping with Chronic Illness and Disability: Theoretical, Empirical, and Clinical Aspects.* New York: Springer-Verlag.

Mathews, S. H. 2003. *Sisters and Brothers/Daughters and Sons: Meeting the Needs of Old Parents.* Bloomington, IN: Unlimited.

Matthews, F. 2004. "Doctors, Elder Abuse, and Enduring Powers of Attorney." *New Zealand Medical Journal* 117 (120): 612–616.

McMorris, B. J., K. A. Tyler, L. B. Whitbeck, and D. R. Hoyt. 2002. "Familial and 'On-the-Street' Risk Factors Associated with Alcohol Use among Homeless and Runaway Adolescents." *Journal of Studies on Alcohol* 63 (1): 34–44.

Miller, J. S. 2007. "Keeping the Family Calm after a Job Loss." [Online article; retrieved 8/15/07.] http://www.careerjournal.com/jobhunting/jobloss/19980311-miller.html.

Missing Children's Recovery Foundation. 2007. "Missing Children Statistics." [Online information; retrieved 8/14/07.] http://www.mcrf.us/Statistics.asp.

Mitchell, W. 2004. *The More You Know: Getting the Evidence and Support for a Troubled Relationship.* Greenville, SC: Eagle's Nest.

Mitchell, W. F. 2001. *Adultery: Facing Its Reality.* Binghamton, NY: Global Academic.

Moody, H. 2006. *Aging: Concepts and Controversies,* 5th ed. Thousand Oaks, CA: Sage.

Murphy, P. J. 2007. *Divorce and Separation.* Portsmouth, NH: Heinemann.

Natelson, B. H. 2007. *Your Symptoms Are Real: What to Do When Your Doctor Says Nothing Is Wrong.* New York: Wiley.

National Council on Economic Education. 2008. *EconEd Link.* [Online article; retrieved 8/12/07.] http://www.econedlink.org/lessons/index.cfm?lesson=EM754&page=teacher.

National Institute on Alcoholism and Alcohol Abuse. 2007. *A Guide to Action for Families.* Washington, DC: U.S. Department of Health and Human Services.

National Institute of Drug Abuse and Addiction. 2007. *Understanding Drug Abuse and Addiction.* Washington, DC: U.S. Department of Health and Human Services.

National Institute of Mental Health. 2007. *Gambling Addiction.* Washington, DC: U.S. Department of Health and Human Services.

National Runaway Switchboard. 2006. "2006 Annual Report: The Journey Continues." [Online information; retrieved 8/12/07.] http://www.1800runaway.org/downloads/pdfs/NRSAnnualReport_06.pdf.

Nerenberg, L. 2007. *Elder Abuse Prevention.* New York: Springer.

Neuman, M. G. 2002. *Emotional Infidelity.* New York: Crown.

Neville, Kristine. 2002. *Communicate and Connect to the Internet.* New York: Gateway.

Novak, M. 2006. *Issues in Aging.* Boston: Allyn and Bacon.

Oravec, J. 2000. "Internet and Computer Technology Hazards: Perspectives for Family Counseling." *British Journal of Guidance and Counseling* 28 (3): 309–324.

Ory, M. G. 1985. "The Burden of Care." *Generations* 10 (1): 15–17.

Ory, M. G. 2006. "Gerontological Research: Changes and Stabilities over Time." Paper presented at the American Public Health Association Annual Meeting, Washington, D.C., November 4.

Peluso, P. R. (2007). *Infidelity: A Practitioner's Guide to Working with Couples in Crisis.* Philadelphia: Routledge.

Petry, N. M. 2000. "Psychiatric Symptoms in Problem Gambling and Nonproblem Gambling Substance Abusers." *American Journal on Addictions* 9:163–171.

Pierce, R. L., and R. Trotta. 1986. "Abused Parents: A Hidden Family Problem." *Journal of Family Violence* 1:99–110.

Pitman, F. S. 1987. *Turning Points: Treating Families in Transition and Crisis.* New York: Norton.

Pollick, M. 2002. "Are Internet Relationships Infidelity?" [Online article; retrieved 8/22/07.] http://www.essortment.com/lifestyle/internetrelatio_ttus.htm.

Prieto, E. 2008. *Home Health Care Provider: A Guide to Essential Skills.* New York: Springer.

Putnam, M. 2006. *Aging and Disability.* New York: Springer.

Quinn, F. L. 2001. "First Do No Harm: What Could Be Done by Casinos to Limit Pathological Gambling." *Managerial and Decision Economics* 22:133–142.

Redfield, S. 2005. "Understanding and Addressing the Challenges of Job Loss for Low-Wage Workers." *Economic Perspectives* 29 (2): 67–72.

Reece, H. 2003. *Divorcing Responsibly.* Oxford, UK: Hart.

Roog, S. A., T. A. Knight, J. Koob, and M. J. Krause. 2004. "The Utilization and Effectiveness of the Family and Medical Leave Act." *Journal of Health and Social Policy* 18 (4): 39–52.

Rubinstein, R. L., M. Moss, and M. H. Kleban, eds. 2000. *The Many Dimensions of Aging.* New York: Springer.

RunawayTeens.org. 2007. "About Runaway Teens." [Online information; retrieved 8/13/07.] http://www.runawayteens.org/statistics.html.

Russell, M. 2007. "Addictive Behaviors and Addictions." [Online information; retrieved 7/21/07.] http://ezinearticles.com/?Addictions—Addictive-Behavior-and-Addictions&id=216914.

Schaffner, L. 1998. "Searching for Connection: A New Look at Teenage Runaways." *Adolescence* 33 (131): 619–623.

Schaie, K. W. 2007. *Social Structures: Demographic Changes and the Well-being of Older Persons.* New York: Springer.

Schimer, M. 2005. "Elder Abuse: The Attorney's Perspective." *The Clinical Gerontologist* 28 (2): 55–82.

Schulz, R., ed. 2006. *The Encyclopedia of Aging.* New York: Springer.

Schwartz, D. 2007. *Disease Management Directory and Guidebook.* Northboro, MA: HCPro, Inc.

Seaburn, D. 2001. "AAMFT Consumer Update: Chronic Illness." [Online information; retrieved 8/28/07.] http://www.aamft.org/families/Consumer_Updates/ChronicIllness.asp.

Sellman, J. D., S. Adamson, P. Robertson, S. Sullivan, and J. Coverdale. 2002. "Gambling in Midmoderate Alcohol-Dependent Outpatients." *Substance Use and Misuse* 37 (2): 199–213.

Shaffer, H. J. 2002. "Is Computer Addiction a Unique Psychiatric Disorder?" [Online article; retrieved 7/28/07.] http://www.psychiatrictimes.com/p020435.html.

Simon-Rusinowitz, L., K. Mahoney, D. Loughlin, and M. D. Sadler. 2005. "Paying Family Caregivers: An Effective Policy Option in the Arkansas Cash and Counseling Demonstration and Evaluation." In *Challenges of Aging on U.S. Families: Policy and Practice Implications,* edited by R. K. Caputo. New York: Haworth Press.

Skocpol, T. 2000. "Reaching for the Middle: What It Will Take to Build a Family-Friendly America." In *The Missing Middle: Working Families and the Future of American Social Policy.* New York: W. W. Norton.

Smoke, J. 2007. *Growing through Divorce.* Eugene, OR: Harvest House.

Son, A. J. 2002. "Information Packet: Runaway and Homeless Youth." [Online report; retrieved 8/13/07.] http://www.hunter.cuny.edu/socwork/nrcfcpp/downloads/information_packets/homeless_and_runaway_youth-pkt.pdf.

Sponaugle, G. C. (1989). "Attitudes Toward Extramarital Relations." In *Human Sexuality: The Societal and Interpersonal Context,* edited by K. McKinney and S. Sprecher. Norwood, NJ: Ablex Publishing Corporation.

Spring, J. A., and M. Spring. 2005. *How Can I Forgive You?* New York: HarperCollins.

Steadman, L. 2007. *It's a Breakup, Not a Breakdown.* Prince Albert, Canada: Polka Dot Press.

Substance Abuse and Mental Health Services Administration. 2004. *Substance Abuse Treatment and Family Therapy.* Washington, DC: U.S. Department of Health and Human Services.

Szinovacz, M. E. 2007. *Caregiving Contexts.* New York: Springer.

Temple, D. S. 2004. *Picking Up the Pieces: A Guide to Recovery from Betrayal and a Broken Heart.* Bloomington, IN: AuthorHouse.

Thomas, C. 2007. *Sociologies of Disability and Illness.* New York: Palgrave Macmillan.

Thompson, S. J., and V. K. Pillai. 2006. "Determinants of Runaway Episodes among Adolescents Using Crisis Shelter Services." *International Journal of Social Welfare* 15:142–149.

Thompson, S. J., and D. E. Pollio. 2006. "Adolescent Runaway Episodes: Application of an Estrangement Model of Recidivism." *Social Work Research* 30 (4): 245–261.

Thompson, S. J., A. E. Safyer, and D. E. Pollio. 2001. "Examining Differences and Predictors of Family Reunification among Subgroups of Runaway Youth Using Shelter Services." *Social Work Research* 25:163–172.

Toneatto, T., and D. Ferguson. 2003. "Effect of a New Casino on Problem Gambling in Treatment-Seeking Substance Abusers." *Canadian Journal of Psychiatry* 48 (1): 40–44.

Turner, J. S. 2002. *Families in America.* Santa Barbara, CA: ABC-CLIO.

Turner, J. S. 2003. *Dating and Sexuality in America.* Santa Barbara, CA: ABC-CLIO.

Tyler, K. A., and K. A. Johnson. 2006. "Trading Sex: Voluntary or Co-erced? The Experiences of Homeless Youth." *Journal of Sex Research* 43 (3): 208–214.

Tyler, K. A., L. B. Whitbeck, D. R. Hoyt, and K. A. Yoder. 2000. "Predic-tors of Self-Reported Sexually Transmitted Diseases among Homeless and Runaway Adolescents." *Journal of Sex Research* 37 (4): 369–377.

Underwood, H., and B. Findlay. 2004. "Internet Relationships and Their Impact on Primary Relationships." *Behaviour Change* 21 (4): 127–140.

U.S. Bureau of Labor Statistics. 2007. *Handbook of Labor Statistics.* Wash-ington, DC: U.S. Government Printing Office.

U.S. Census Bureau. 2006. *Statistical Abstract of the United States,* 125th ed. Washington, DC: U.S. Government Printing Office.

U.S. Census Bureau. 2007. *Statistical Abstract of the United States,* 126th ed. Washington, DC: U.S. Government Printing Office.

U.S. Department of Health and Human Services. 2007. *Health, United States, 2006.* Hyattsville, MD: National Center for Health Statistics

U.S. Department of Labor. 2008. "Employment Situation Summary." [Online information; retrieved 8/14/07.] http://www.bls.gov/news.release/empsit.nr0.htm

Van Leeuwen, J. M., C. Hopfer, S. Hooks, R. White, J. Petersen, and J. Pirkopf. 2004. "A Snapshot of Substance Abuse among Homeless and Runaway Youth in Denver, Colorado." *Journal of Community Health* 29 (3): 217–229.

Wallerstein, J., J. Lewis, and S. Blakeslee. 2000. *The Unexpected Legacy of Divorce: A 25 Year Landmark Study.* New York: Hyperion.

Weil, B. 2003. *Adultery: The Forgivable Sin,* 2nd ed. Poughkeepsie, NY: Vivisphere.

Wekerle, C., and A. M. Wall, eds. 2001. *The Violence and Addiction Equa-tion: Theoretical and Clinical Issues in Substance Abuse and Relationship Vio-lence.* New York: Brunner-Routledge.

Whitbeck, L. B., and D. R. Hoyt. 1999. *Nowhere to Grow: Homeless and Runaway Adolescents and Their Families.* New York: Aldine De Gruyter.

White, W. L., M. Boyle, and D. Loveland. 2002. "Alcoholism/Addiction as a Chronic Disease: From Rhetoric to Clinical Reality." In *Alcohol Problems in the United States: Twenty Years of Treatment Perspective,* edited by T. F. McGovern and W. L. White. New York: Haworth.

Willis, L. 2007. *Divorce.* Farmington Hills, MI: Thomson Gale.

Wills, J. 2007. *Promoting Health.* Boston: Blackwell.

Wisensale, S. 2001. "Federal Initiatives in Family Leave Policy: Formulation of the FMLA." In *Family Leave Policy: The Political Economy of Work And Family in America,* by S. Wisensale. New York: M. E. Sharpe.

Young, K. 2007. "New Research on Internet Addiction Legitimizes the Controversial Clinical Disorder." [Online article; retrieved 7/25/07.] http://www.netaddiction.com/newspr/cpbpr.htm.

3

Special U.S. Issues

Introduction

There is no mistaking the fact that we live in uncertain times. The horrific tragedy of September 11, 2001, reminded us of our vulnerabilities and the impact that life-altering circumstances have on family life. Trauma and turmoil have moved closer to all of us, whether it be in the form of airline crashes, highway fatalities, acts of terrorism, or hurricanes. Crises such as these—and countless others—put the modern American family to task and test its inner resolve and resiliency.

In this chapter, we examine some representative traumatic crises plaguing American families: domestic violence, school violence, natural disasters, deployed military families, and adolescent suicide. Given their unpredictable nature and the escalating numbers of families involved with these problems, never has the need been greater to understand traumatic crises, particularly in terms of preparing families for impending trauma (if possible) and providing support and family relief. Researchers (e.g., Goldenberg and Goldenberg 2008; Greenberg 2008; James 2008) acknowledge that understanding and preparing for traumatic crises can reduce accompanying feelings of helplessness and pave the way for the restoration of balanced family functioning. Some even discover that facing extreme adversity brings out the best in people.

Other families, though, are not so fortunate. Coping mechanisms are stretched to the limit or meet with failure. Residual trauma lingers for years, perhaps forever. Such families are staggered by traumatic crises, discovering that pressures are unyielding and stress levels unmanageable. Many survivors experience what is called an **acute stress disorder**, a psychological disturbance marked by intrusive and disturbing memories of the crisis, an exaggerated startle response, and a tendency to avoid the situation by withdrawing from it physically and psychologically. Simply put, they are unable to return to a normal range of functioning. For these families, the task of rebuilding and restoring family equilibrium looms insurmountable.

Domestic Violence

Marilyn Lane is an abused wife. Her husband has battered her about twice a month for 11 years. The physical abuse started six months after the wedding, and her husband has become more violent over time. Over the years, Marilyn has had three broken bones, contusions all over her body, and on one occasion, a gash that required 16 sutures to close during an emergency room visit. She has always chosen to strategically cover her wounds with extra makeup or clothing, blaming those that could be seen on falling down, accidentally bumping into large objects, or outdoor injuries.

Although the expression "Home sweet home" conjures up images of peace and safety, for the battered spouse there is no place worse than home. **Domestic violence** is most commonly applied to an intimate relationship between two adults in which one partner uses a pattern of assault and intimidating acts to assert power and control over the other partner. It is also referred to as *intimate partner violence.* Domestic violence is considered a traumatic family crisis because of its unpredictability, life-threatening potential, and the fact that it creates a sense of destruction and loss for the victims.

The most conservative estimates place the number of battered women of all races and classes at 2 to 4 million each year (National Organization for Women 2007). Abused partners may be married or not married; heterosexual, gay, or lesbian; living together, separated, or dating. Domestic violence can happen to anyone regardless of race, age, sexual orientation, religion, or gender. Although partner violence is particularly widespread, abusive behavior also gets directed toward children and teenagers. We need to acknowledge, too, that other forms of domestic violence exist: elder abuse (see Chapter 2), sibling abuse, husband abuse, and parent abuse (see Kiselica and Morrill-Richards 2007; Barnett, Miller-Perrin, and Perrin 2005; Turell 2003; Bonnie and Wallace 2003; Carp 2000). Our focus in this section is first on partner abuse, followed by child abuse.

It will prove helpful at the outset to distinguish between the different kinds of violence abuse that exist. According to the U.S. Department of Justice (2007), domestic violence can be physical, sexual, emotional, economic, or psychological actions or threats of actions that influence another person. This definition includes any behaviors that intimidate, manipulate, humiliate, isolate, frighten, terrorize, coerce, threaten, blame, hurt, injure, or wound someone.

Partner Abuse

When a woman begins to lose her sense of identity or self-worth to the point that she no longer feels safe expressing opinions or feelings to her partner, or she starts going along with things because she is afraid that her partner will react violently, she may be at risk for intimate partner violence. Unfortunately, circumstances will likely only get worse over time (Rondini 2007).

Intimate partner abuse can exert effects on a woman's health, both physically and psychologically. Physical harm, including contusions, fractures, and lacerations, is one obvious effect. Intimate partner abuse has also been connected to chronic health problems and even death—from either suicide because of depression or murder by the partner. Battered women are more likely to have arthritis, neck pain, pelvic pain, and migraine headaches. They also have an increased risk of menstrual problems and difficulties during pregnancy, including bleeding, anemia, and low birth weight (Harvard Medical School Family Health Guide 2006; Zink et al. 2006). The reader is encouraged to visit Chapter 6 (Figures 6.12, 6.13, 6.14, and 6.15), where more specific details on the topic of intimate partner violence appear.

The abusive partner uses various strategies to achieve power and control. He may intimidate and demean his partner by constantly criticizing her, taking full command of household finances, or telling her what she can wear, where she can go, and whom she can see. (While the majority of abusers in domestic violence situations are the male partner, the reader should recognize that women can also be the abusing partner.) Many batterers may play "mind games" with their partners, such as suggesting that she is hypersensitive, hysterical, or even mentally unbalanced. Often he makes sure that she is isolated from family, friends, and colleagues. His mental manipulation may also surface as pathological jealousy, such as making false accusations about her having an affair. Shortly, the partner realizes that she is cut off from all outside support and connections, no longer in touch with the people and services that could help her. This sense of isolationism is exactly the environment the abuser wishes to create (Harvard Medical School Family Health Guide 2006; Lee, Sebold, and Uken 2003).

What prompts abusive behaviors such as these? The abuser is a complicated puzzle, but a number of psychological and sociological factors have been cited (Loseke, Gelles, and Cavanaugh 2005; Kurst-Swanger and Petcosky 2003). The abusive partner often faces a pileup of pressures from work and the home, financial difficulties, and low levels of self-esteem. Many abusers feel the need to control and are usually lonely, are typically depressed, and have never learned how to contain their aggression or hostility. Substance use is often involved in many incidents of partner violence. When substance use and partner violence co-occur, substance use may play a facilitative role by precipitating or exacerbating violence (Wekerle and Wall 2002; Fazzone, Holton, and Reed 2001).

Intimate partner violence also appears to be a product of past learning. Children who were victims of violence often grow up and resort to similar methods of discipline with their partners or children. They learn early in life that aggressive force is an effective way of controlling the perceived unpleasant behaviors of others. Violent juvenile offenders are four times more likely to have grown up in homes where they saw violence. Children who have witnessed violence at home are also five times more likely to commit or suffer violence when they become adults (National Organization for Women 2007).

Child Abuse

Child abuse is a traumatic family crisis and is defined as harm to, or neglect of, a child by another person, whether adult or child. Child abuse happens in all cultural, ethnic, and income groups. Much like partner abuse, different forms of child abuse are seen. Child abuse can be physical, emotional, verbal, sexual, or neglectful. Abuse may cause serious injury to the child and may even result in death. Child abuse is perhaps the most alarming type of domestic violence because of the acute vulnerability of children, their inability to escape the trauma of the situation, and the degrees of physical punishment that they suffer (Ianelli 2005).

Maltreatment during infancy or early childhood can cause important regions of the brain to form improperly, leading to physical, mental, and emotional problems, such as sleep disturbances, panic disorder, and attention-deficit/hyperactivity disorder (Righthand, Kerr, and Drach 2003; Bancroft and Silverman 2002). See Figure 6.16 as well as Table 6.5 for more information on child maltreatment.

Child abuse can also extend to child sexual abuse. **Child sexual abuse** occurs when a child is used for sexual purposes by an adult or adolescent. It involves exposing a child to any sexual activity or behavior. It usually includes fondling and may include inviting a child to touch or be touched sexually. Other forms of sexual abuse include sexual intercourse, juvenile prostitution, and sexual exploitation through child pornography. In addition to the physical violation, sexual abuse is inherently emotionally abusive and is often accompanied by other forms of mistreatment. It is a betrayal of trust and an abuse of power over the child (McDowell 2006; Jaffe, Baker, and Cunningham 2004).

The statistics on physical and sexual child abuse are alarming and a cause for concern. An estimated hundreds of thousands of children are physically abused each year by a parent, close relative, or other adult perpetrator. An estimated 3 million children are reported each year as suspected victims of child abuse and neglect. One in three girls and one in five boys are sexually abused by an adult at some time during childhood (Centers for Disease Control and Prevention 2007a).

The family disequilibrium and emotional trauma of abuse remain long after the external bruises have healed. For instance, an adult who was physically abused as a child often has trouble establishing intimate personal relationships. Both men and women encounter trouble with physical closeness, touching, intimacy, and trust as adults. They are also at higher risk for anxiety, depression, substance abuse, medical illness, and problems at school or work. Adult women sexually molested as children are more likely than nonvictims to suffer from both physical and psychological problems. Men who were sexually abused as children may also suffer from depression, anxiety, and suicidal thoughts and behavior, especially if they were repeatedly abused (McDowell 2006; American Academy of Child and Adolescent Psychiatry 2008).

What motivates child abusers? Much like partner abuse, all of the causes of child abuse are not known. However, a significant amount of research points to parental behaviors and conditions that put children at risk for abuse: lack of parenting knowledge, especially nurturing qualities; depression or other mental health problems; onset of a financial crisis; exposure to domestic violence at an early age or to current violence; difficulty controlling anger and poor conflict resolution abilities; and substance abuse. Child sexual abusers share many of the same motivations, as well as the possibility of having been sexually violated as a youngster themselves.

Implications for Family Life

It should be obvious by now that the traumatic crisis of domestic violence poses many serious implications for family life. One might think the battered woman should just pack up her belongings and leave the abuser, but it is not that simple. For battered partners, deciding to leave an abusive relationship is a process more than a single action. As we have learned, isolation and fear may prevent a battered woman from leaving, even when she knows it is probably for the best. Lack of financial resources due to the batterer's economic control of the household often prevents the woman from leaving. And while community support is usually available, a woman in an abusive relationship often has difficulty asking for help (Harvard Medical School Family Health Guide 2006).

Melinda Smith and colleagues (Smith et al. 2007) add that most women cannot simply leave their homes, their jobs, their children's schools, their friends, and their relatives to escape their abuser. They depend upon police to enforce the law against physical abuse. However, law enforcement cannot act until a restraining order is violated or until the victim is physically harmed. Because of these factors, many battered women rationalize that it is easier to stay with their abuser than to try to leave and face the consequences (Cooper and Vetere 2005; Roberts 2002; Loue 2001).

Women can take a number of steps to protect themselves while getting out of an abusive situation, and people are waiting to help (Schewe 2002; Zorza 2002). An abused woman is in particular danger if she is thinking of leaving or tries to leave an abusive relationship; abusers often react with anger and hostility since their desire to control is threatened. When women leave, they often experience fear for their lives as well as their children's safety, not fear of an unpredictable future (Flannery 2006; Fowler 2003; Feindler, Rathus, and Silver 2003; Gondolf 2002; Geffner, Dutton, and Sonkin 2002).

It is therefore of the utmost importance for battered women to have some kind of safety plan and knowledge of expanded family resources (the second component of the Double ABCX model). Calling a domestic violence hotline is recommended, such as the National Domestic Violence Hotline at 1-800-799-SAFE (7233) or TTY 1-800-787-3224. Help is available to callers 24 hours a day, 365 days a year. Hotline advocates are available for victims and anyone calling on their behalf to provide crisis intervention; safety planning; information; and referrals to agencies in all 50 states, Puerto Rico, and the U.S. Virgin Islands. Assistance is available in English and Spanish, with access to more than 140 languages through interpreter services. More specific information regarding safety plans is readily available (e.g., Roberts and Roberts 2005; Shipway 2004; Jordan 2004; Mills 2003; Sever 2002).

As far as child abuse intervention is concerned, it must be kept in mind that battered youngsters will not just come out and tell adults they are being abused. Most fear what might happen to them if they tell. Some feel they are betraying the abuser. Still others believe that the abuse is their fault and should therefore feel ashamed to tell others. Because of such confusion in the face of this traumatic family crisis, it is important for adults to keep a watchful eye on possible signs of child abuse (beyond those of a physical nature). For more information on possible signs of child abuse, the reader is directed to the American Academy of Child and Adolescent Psychiatry (2008).

School Violence

Real life episodes of school shootings are as horrifying as they are tragic, prompting all of us to ponder the circumstances creating such violent behavior. For example, consider the case of 15-year-old Kipland Kinkel, who hardly captured the image of a real-life school shooter and murderer. In fact, he appeared to be an ordinary adolescent, gangly and unimposing, with freckles and a slight case of acne dotting his face. Growing up in Springfield, Oregon, he tended to be on the shy side, a youngster who did not have many friends and usually kept to himself. The Kinkel family appeared to be a supportive and nurturing one: parents Bill and Faith were highly successful educators and older sister Kristen was outgoing and popular, a happy-go-lucky and well-adjusted sibling.

But outward family appearances are sometimes deceiving, and much swirled beneath the surface during Kip's childhood and adolescence. He repeated the first grade due to his slow emotional and physical development, and his relationship with his father became strained. He often saw himself in competition with his older sister and usually ended up on the losing end. Kip continued to have problems in school, including being bullied, and by third grade had qualified for special education services. He was eventually diagnosed with dyslexia, a learning disability that alters the way the brain processes written material.

Matters would only get worse. As he got older, Kip became easily frustrated in school and at home and developed an uncontrollable temper. He became drawn to guns, knives, and explosives. He suffered from a failed relationship with a high school sweetheart. He began to retreat into himself, spending countless hours on the Internet, visiting pornographic sites and sites featuring graphic violence. After a brush with the law for throwing a 12-inch rock onto a car from an overpass, Kip was placed in psychotherapy by the Kinkels, where he was diagnosed with a major depressive disorder. He was hungry for attention, but an undercurrent of pent-up anger and hostility drove him to seek it in all the wrong ways. He was a powder keg ready to explode, the stressors in his life creating intense emotional upheaval.

Kipland Kinkel would leave behind a legacy of horror on May 20, 1998. After being expelled for bringing a handgun to school, one of many firearms he owned, he murdered both his parents. The next morning he drove to Thurston High School wearing a trench coat to hide the weapons he was carrying: a 9 mm Glock pistol, a Ruger .22 semiautomatic rifle, a Ruger .22 pistol, and a hunting knife taped to his leg. A backpack slung over his shoulder was filled with extra ammunition. As he calmly walked down a corridor leading to the cafeteria, he shot two students. Once in the cafeteria, he opened fire with his rifle without saying a word before he was overtaken by students and wrestled to the floor. The casualties: 2 students dead, 25 wounded. When the police arrived, Kinkel was arrested, and he is currently serving a 111-year prison term. He will never be eligible for parole.

Years ago, the school setting was considered a protective shield and an extension of parental supervision, an environment that posed few if any dangers and kept younger generations out of harm's way. However, an alarming number of school violence episodes beginning in the early 1990s changed such thinking, and safety in the classroom became an issue generating considerable public concern and attention (see, for example, Schreck and Miller 2003; Miller 2003; Addington et al. 2002). Chapter 6 provides various details on school violence (Figures 6.17, 6.18, 6.19, and 6.20).

Marlene Wong (2007) writes that over the past 20 years, almost 600 school shootings have taken place, not including planned or attempted shootings that were prevented. The United States leads the world in the number of school shootings, including those at elementary schools, high schools, and colleges. Moreover, a number of national surveys completed by high school youth indicated that many students felt that a shooting could happen in their school, some respondents identifying peers that they believed were most likely to perpetrate such a crime.

In response to this traumatic family crisis, a barrage of interventions was launched from educational leaders and national and state political leaders to tighten school security (e.g., Guerino et al. 2007; Jimerson, Brock, and Pletcher 2005; Crepeau-Hobson, Franci, and Marylynne 2005), and specialized training programs were aimed at teachers to upgrade their knowledge of school violence (e.g., Newman 2007; Trump 2002; Druck and Kaplowitz 2005; Kohm 2004; Wilde 2002; Hester 2003).

According to the *Report on Youth Violence* (U.S. Department of Health and Human Services, Office of the Surgeon General 2001) the United States has made laudable progress in gaining an understanding of the magnitude of the problem. We have made great strides in identifying and quantifying factors that, in particular settings or combinations, increase the probability that violence will occur. Furthermore, we have developed an array of interventions of well-documented effectiveness in helping young people whose lives are already marked by a propensity for violence as well as in preventing others from viewing violence as a solution to needs, wants, or problems.

These positive outcomes do not mean, however, that school shootings no longer happen. A public uneasiness about the topic still exists, and many parents today worry about the safety of their children in the classroom. Among teachers, Lesli Maxwell (2007) observes that each school shooting revives vexing questions and raises familiar fears for educators across the country who grapple daily with ensuring the safety of their students and staff.

The American Psychological Association (2007a) adds that when children see episodes of school violence such as shootings on television or on Web-based news flashes, it is natural for them to worry about their own school and their own safety, particularly if the violence occurred nearby or in a neighboring city or state.

In its reporting, the media leave no stone unturned when covering school shootings. The live television broadcasts are hauntingly similar: SWAT teams in full combat gear surrounding school property, traumatized parents ashen-faced and terrorized, bloodied survivors receiving emergency medical treatment, the call for more ambulances and body bags. Few, if any, will ever forget the above-mentioned 1998 Kinkel shootings or the one that followed in 1999 at Columbine High School in Littleton, Colorado (in which 14 students and 1 teacher were killed and 23 others were wounded).

The images of these tragic shootings and all others leave behind unsettled and troubling memories, making an uneasy population wonder whether what ignited such violence and, worse, if the nation's schools would experience more of this new brand of terrorism. Regarding the latter, the trail of violence since the Columbine shooting has spoken for itself (see the chronology of school shootings presented in Chapter 4).

Incidents involving other forms of school violence, while diminishing in occurrence, remain cause for concern. According to Jill DeVoe and colleagues (2004), for youths to reach their potential in school, schools must be safe and secure places for students, teachers, and staff members. Without a safe learning environment, educators may have trouble teaching and students may have difficulty learning. As Ken Druck and Matthew Kaplowitz (2005) report, school violence such as rape, robbery, theft, and aggravated assault affects one in every five teenagers. It is no wonder that many youngsters feel threatened in the midst of such violence. Because of such sentiments, many parents and other adults feel that America's schools are under siege (Maxwell 2006; Lubell and Vette 2006; Lavarello and Trump 2002).

Bullying and School Violence

Many students miss school because they fear attack or intimidation through bullying. **Bullying** is a form of violence that exposes a person to abusive actions repeatedly over time. It entails unwanted and repeated written, verbal, or physical behavior, including any threatening, insulting, or dehumanizing gesture, by an adult or a student that is severe or pervasive enough to create an intimidating, hostile, or offensive educational environment. It creates discomfort or humiliation for the victim and unreasonably interferes with the target person's school performance or participation (Florida Department of Education 2007; Shields and Cicchetti 2001; Swearer and Doll 2001).

Students who are bullied experience a flood tide of negative emotions. Feelings of persecution undermine feelings of safety and confidence. Fear, frustration, anger, and anxiety may lead to ongoing mood swings, illness, withdrawal from friends and family, an inability to concentrate, and loss of interest in school. Bullying can cause the targeted student to develop attendance and/or discipline problems, or fail at school altogether. In the worst scenarios, the bullied become suicidal or become retaliatory and violent (California Department of Education 2006; Espelage and Holt 2001; Shields and Cicchetti 2001). The reader is directed to Chapter 6 (Figures 6.21 and 6.22) for more information on bullying.

Obviously, the reactions experienced by those who are bullied connect directly to our topic of school shootings. The humiliation or degradation of bullying might be swallowed at the time, but anger tends to steadily brew. According to the Menninger Clinic (2005), in more than two-thirds of school shootings, clear cases of bullying by social groups and individuals have been established. Being bullied often combines with a troubling mix of easy access to violent and hate-laden media, weaponry, and information on strategies for terrorist attacks. Such was the case with the Kipland Kinkel shootings introduced at the beginning of this section. A school's response to bullying also deserves attention. A school climate that tolerates physical and relational aggression, especially by popular groups such as athletes or wealthier students, is at higher risk for violence.

Implications for Family Life

Exploring the underlying dynamics of school shootings or school violence in general is beyond the scope of this chapter. Rather, our focus is on the implications of school violence for the family. For those readers wishing to learn more about the motivations of the perpetrators of school violence, as well as school programming designed to curb school violence, a number of excellent publications exist. We direct attention to Maxwell (2007); Gross (2007); Lieberman (2006); Denmark (2005); Walker, Ramsey, and Gresham (2004); Sexton-Radek (2004); and Wessler and Preble (2003). In addition, Chapter 6 provides other details related to school violence (Figures 6.23 and 6.24).

When school violence poses a threat of serious injury or death, it can become a source of psychological distress for the child and the family. Understanding how children are impacted by this kind of traumatic crisis, including levels of distress expressed, can help the family system discover needed resources and needed adaptation skills. The latter will hopefully restore the family's equilibrium and overall resiliency (National Child Traumatic Stress Network 2007a).

Marlene Wong's (2007) review of the literature indicates that witnessing school shootings and other kinds of school violence affect different people in different ways. The American Psychological Association (2007a) concurs with this assessment and reports that every child will respond to this traumatic crisis differently. Some will have no ill effects; others may suffer an immediate and acute effect. Still others may not show signs of stress until sometime after the crisis event (Centers for Disease Control and Prevention 2007b).

According to the Centers for Disease Control and Prevention (2007b), it is natural for youngsters—no matter where they go to school—to worry about whether this type of incident may someday affect them. Parents, teachers, and school administrators need to join forces and communicate with one another not only about how to keep children safe but also about which children might need more reassurance and the best way to give it to them (American Psychological Association 2007a; Centers for Disease Control and Prevention 2007b). Talking with children about these tragedies, and what they watch or hear about them, can help put frightening or disturbing information into a better perspective to achieve family equilibrium. Along these lines, experts (e.g., American Psychological Association 2007a; Dorn 2005; Jones and Compton 2003) recommend that parents monitor how much exposure a child has to news reports of traumatic events, including those centering on recent school shootings.

Natural Disasters

When Hurricane Katrina unleashed its fury on the Gulf Coast of the United States on August 29, 2005, it was the third-strongest hurricane on record. Building up its strength in the Atlantic on August 23, it traveled landward and left immense devastation in its path along the north-central Gulf Coast. However, it saved its worst loss and property damage for New Orleans, arriving with 145 mile-per-hour winds, flooding the levee system, and placing about 80 percent of New Orleans under water. At least 1,836 people lost their lives in Hurricane Katrina and in the subsequent floods, about 400,000 jobs were lost, and about 1 million people became homeless (Clarke 2005; Comfort 2005; Friedman 2005; Mlakar 2005).

Hurricane Katrina is an example of a **natural disaster**, an extreme, sudden traumatic crises caused by environmental factors. Natural disasters can strike at any time, often with little or no warning, and can threaten the lives of people and destroy property in their wake. Examples of natural disasters are hurricanes, tsunamis, earthquakes, volcanic eruptions, extreme heat waves, droughts, floods, landslides and mudslides, tornadoes, volcanoes, and wildfires. Natural disasters are also classified as endemic stressors (see Chapter 1) because they are beyond our control and thus cannot be prevented. Rather, we must learn to live with them. They are especially dangerous because the changes they bring are comparatively rapid and affect our immediate environment and safety (Pararas-Carayannis 2007; Halpern and Tramontin 2007). Tables 6.6 and 6.7 and Figure 6.25 provide information on natural disasters occurring in 2006.

Lynne Borden (2003) points out that a distinction needs to be made between a natural disaster and a human-made disaster. While natural disasters are caused by forces of nature, *human-made disasters,* such as vehicle accidents, mining cave-ins, war, and terrorist attacks, pose a different set of challenges for families and often create greater distress than natural disasters. Terrorist attacks in recent years have created a seemingly unending array of traumatic crises: hijackings, bombings, kidnappings, executions, and mass murder. Individuals and families perceive these and all human-made disasters as involving someone or something (e.g., government, terrorists, business) that is to blame (Borden 2003).

Understanding the experience of families living with disaster requires considering the family system and the community context, including circumstances prior to, during, and after the disaster. Also, it is important to consider the impact of the disaster on the community. Each disaster is different, depending on its scope and intensity, and on characteristics of the community, family, and individual. Disasters can take their toll in many ways, including destruction of infrastructure; absence of electricity, sanitation, and potable water; destruction of physical contact with the outside world (e.g., roadways, phones, and bridges); vulnerability and exploitation due to disaster and media sensationalism; and potential recurrence (Borden 2003).

On a personal level, people often try to make sense of what happened and deal with the stress of the situation. Disasters create a tremendous amount of stress and anxiety for those directly and indirectly affected. In the days and weeks following the disaster, survivors typically experience a variety of reactions: fear and anxiety about the future, shock and disbelief, disorientation, difficulty making decisions or concentrating, recurring thoughts about the event, anger, and sadness and depression (Halpern and Tramontin 2007; Mental Health America 2007a). As we have seen throughout this book, the primary stressor has the potential of unleashing a multitude of secondary stressors.

Implications for Family Life

When a disaster strikes a family member or the whole family, the entire system experiences the aftermath. Traumatic crises have the ability to disrupt functions and routines within the family, such as parents' emotional nurturing, attention, and protection. Children may be especially at risk as traumatized parents often reduce physical contact and try to shield their offspring from the realities of what happened. Communication, intimacy, and expressiveness may be affected, resulting in a reduced capacity to cope with internal and external demands. Single parents may be at special risk, given the multiple resources that are drained following a disaster (Dyregrov 2007). Notice the connection here to the first component of the Double ABCX model, the pileup of family demands.

The needs of children and youth come to the forefront when a family experiences a natural disaster. According to one source (Lazarus, Jimerson, and Brock 2002), experiencing a dangerous or violent flood, storm, or earthquake is frightening even for adults, and the devastation to one's surroundings can be long lasting and distressing. Often an entire community is impacted, further undermining a child's sense of security and normalcy (Howitt and Leonard 2006). These factors present a variety of unique issues and coping challenges, including issues associated with specific types of natural disasters, the need to relocate when home and/or community have been destroyed, the role of the family in lessening or exacerbating the trauma, emotional reactions, and coping techniques (Halpern and Tramontin 2007). Such challenges embrace both psychological and social stressors (see Chapter 1).

According to the Federal Emergency Management Agency (2006), children look to parents or other caregivers for guidance on how to manage their reactions after the immediate threat is over. Children's coping with disaster or emergencies is often tied to the way parents cope. Children have uncanny radar and can pick up on adults' fears and sadness. Parents and adults can make disasters less traumatic for children by taking steps to manage their own feelings and plans for coping. Parents are almost always the best source of support for children in disasters.

To summarize, multitudes of families across the United States find themselves in the difficult position of dealing with the ramifications of an ongoing natural disaster (drought) or an immediate natural disaster (tornado, wildfire, hurricane). Regardless of the type or duration of the disaster, such unforeseen events create a traumatic crisis for families. Families affected by disaster are forced to cope with the immediate disaster and its long-term effects, in addition to the typical daily stressors faced by all families. Most families can learn to live with what has happened in a way that ensures the continued health of all concerned. If the disaster is dealt with openly and directly within the family, and children's and adolescents' needs are acknowledged and met, they can achieve family equilibrium and go on with their lives in a constructive manner (Zenere 2004; Borden 2003).

Deployed Military Families

It was an especially difficult good-bye for Ned and Rita Hart. Ned is a sergeant in the U.S. Army and was being deployed to Iraq, his second tour of duty in the Middle East. He is a veteran of the first Persian Gulf War but knows his deployment to Operation Iraqi Freedom will be a longer and much more dangerous haul. He was recently informed by his company commander that military deployments had been extended from 12 to 15 months.

Both Ned and Rita grew up in military families. They got married shortly after high school and Ned enlisted the next year. Since then, the Harts have brought two children into the world, Leah and Andrea. Both girls attend public school, and Rita works as a receptionist at a local pharmaceutical company.

Ned enlisted in the army for a number of reasons: family tradition, a chance to travel, a sense of adventure, and a desire to serve his country. Over the past year, though, he has found his loyalty wavering. He has lost a number of combat friends in Iraq, and now he wonders if his country is fighting against an enemy that can never be beat. He views his upcoming tour with a mixture of hope and fear, and recognizes that the road ahead represents dangerous and unsettling times. Leaving behind a loving wife and two beautiful children does not make separation any easier.

Rita shares the same uncertainties and anxieties, and saying good-bye is even worse than ever before. She has spent her adult life balancing army needs with personal and family needs, but her husband's current deployment into hostile territory for such an extended period is by far the most formidable challenge. She knows that the thought of perhaps becoming a widow will weigh heavily on her each day, as will the struggle of raising two children alone and trying to maintain household equilibrium.

Ned's deployment is hardly earth-shattering news. Since the terrorist attacks of September 11, 2001, military operations in Afghanistan and Iraq have required substantial increases in the number of U.S. service members deployed and the frequency with which units are sent overseas. Through December 2007, more than 1.4 million active-duty personnel and 400,000 reserve personnel had been deployed to those theaters and served a tour of duty. But Afghanistan and Iraq do not paint a complete picture of U.S. military involvement. The forces of the U.S. military are located in nearly 130 countries around the world, performing a variety of duties from combat operations to peacekeeping to training with foreign militaries. Some of these deployments have existed for nearly 50 years, as in Japan, Germany, and South Korea (Global Security 2007; U.S. Congress 2007).

Ned and Rita Hart join legions of other deployed military families who are forced to deal with an unpredictable, traumatic family crisis. The life-threatening potential of military deployment has become a fact of life for military families. Currently, 700,000 children in the United States have at least one parent deployed overseas for military duty; more than half a million children under the age of five are waiting for their active-duty National Guard or Reserve mother or father to come home. This total is the highest since World War II. Since 2001, 160,000 female troops have also been deployed, and 10 percent of them are single mothers (U.S. Congress 2007; American Psychological Association 2007b; Bennis and Leaver 2005).

Implications for Family Life

When a family member goes to war, the separation is usually painful for all concerned and results in a flood of unsettled emotions. Feelings such as pride, anger, fear, and bitterness can add to the distress of uncertainty. Anxieties mount if the military assignment is in a hostile environment, and intensified even further when the media transmit news of war atrocities, suicide bombings, and environmental destruction (Whealin and Pivar 2007).

Due to the sheer number of deployed service men and women in the world today, many military families face repeated deployments. In many instances, it is unknown when a deployment will end, which serves to elevate the tension and uncertainty of this family crisis. According to Simon Pincus and colleagues (2007) and Jennifer Morse (2007), it is possible to establish seven rather predictable emotional stages of deployment. Each stage is characterized both by a time frame and by specific emotional challenges for the family, which must be dealt with and mastered by the system. Failure to adequately negotiate these challenges can lead to disequilibrium within the system as well as within the deployed soldier. Morse's (2007) seven stages are described below.

Anticipation of Departure

Before the departure occurs, partners may feel a mixture of denial and anticipation of loss. As the deployment date edges closer, tempers often erupt as partners attempt to take care of all necessary preparations, obligations, and duties while simultaneously trying to make time for themselves and their loved one. This stage reappears during all future deployments.

Detachment and Withdrawal

Here, the soon-to-be-deployed partner becomes focused on the pending mission and connectedness with his or her unit. Regarding the latter, such bonding with one's unit may create emotional detachment from the family system. Sadness and anger might occur as couples seek to protect themselves from the pain and hurt of separation. As this stage happens more frequently, marital friction may increase. The creation of emotional insulation is seen by many as a coping strategy, but in reality it only serves to create more distance. It may well be that such "numbing" behaviors are preferable to feeling sad or distraught.

Emotional Disorganization

With repeated deployments, one might surmise that emotional upheaval and domestic instability would lessen. However, this is not always the case. While a military spouse may be used to the routine(s), he or she may also be experiencing "burnout" and fatigue from the last deployment (no doubt a pileup of stressors as captured by the Double ABCX model). Many spouses report feeling overwhelmed starting this stage again.

Recovery and Stabilization

During this stage, most partners recognize that they are resilient and able to meet the challenges attached to deployment. Confidence is achieved and a positive outlook emerges. With repeated deployments, however, partners may face difficulty rallying the emotional strength required. The quest for family equilibrium is not an easy journey, and some families struggle with it more than others.

Anticipation of Return

For most, this becomes a happy and hectic time, a period of anticipation preparing for the return of the service member. Family members need to discuss realistic plans and expectations for the return and reunion, the end result being the restoration of equilibrium.

Return Adjustment and Renegotiation

Once the service member is home, the family system must reestablish its expectations and renegotiate its roles. If the returning veteran has experienced war-related injuries and/or stress-related symptoms, the complexities of family adjustment magnify. It goes without saying that combat fatalities pose additional stressors and create other waves of family upheaval and disequilibrium.

The key to establishing household stability is engaging in open and honest communication. The family must also reckon with the lingering effects of combat stress on the returning service member. The existing literature exposes how difficult this transition can be (see, for example, Mental Health America 2007b; Drummet, Coleman, and Cable 2003; Patterson 2002). Those service members suffering from combat stress are often guarded, are often irritable, and prefer solitude. Some may resort to substance abuse in an attempt to "numb" the emotional pain and dark memories. Efforts to renegotiate family stability and equilibrium may trigger marital friction.

Reintegration and Stabilization

This final stage can take up to six months as the family regains equilibrium, although lingering combat stress can lengthen the duration. For most, family dynamics capture renewed vitality and harmony. However, disequilibrium may return should additional stressors be encountered, such as the family being ordered to establish a new residence upon the return of the service member. Back-to-back deployments create stress and a return of the family to the first stage.

What can military families do to best weather this traumatic crisis? According to Lorraine Gallagher (2007), having a primary caretaker dispatched to a war zone can be one of the most stressful events a family can experience. She recognizes that military deployment is hard on everyone and offers some relatively simple guidelines that can make deployment easier and enable the time to pass more quickly for all concerned. These guidelines are discussed below.

The importance of sustaining effective family communication cannot be overstated. It is important for families to discuss how they are feeling about all of the changes that are taking place or pending. By sharing feelings and providing mutual support, the transition will be smoother and will enable the family to achieve resiliency. Gallagher (2007) suggests spending as much family time as possible before the departure. This need for connectedness is especially important if children are involved. Depending on their developmental level, youngsters might not understand what is happening and may not be able to express what they are feeling. Parents and caregivers need to help them understand and provide the special attention needed to get them through deployment with minimal adjustment problems.

Another guideline is for the family to seek help when it is needed. It is very important for family members to keep their spirits high and offer mutual support. This can be accomplished, at least in part, by family members and service members writing and calling each other. They can also send pictures to show how someone has changed or how the kids have grown. Some send tape recordings or videos to each other. Finally, deployed military families need to be encouraged to seek out more formal support and assistance if needed (the notion of expanded family resources in the Double ABCX model). People who have had previous mental health problems and who have survived past trauma may also want to check in with a mental health care professional. Nearly every military installation has a family service center, family support center, or community service center where persons can access information, referral, counseling, and crisis intervention services (Hoshmand and Hoshmand 2007; Mental Health America 2007b; Martin et al. 2004; Drummet, Coleman, and Cable 2003).

Before closing, we need to acknowledge that fairly recent research has uncovered a dark side to deployed military families: child maltreatment. More specifically, researchers (Gibbs et al. 2007) have suggested that children are more likely to experience maltreatment at home during large-scale military deployments, raising concerns about the impact of war on military personnel and their families across the United States.

Gibbs and colleagues (2007) conducted a large-scale investigation to measure the impact of the 9/11 terrorist attacks on military and nonmilitary families. The sample consisted of 1,771 Texas families of noncommissioned soldiers who had been combat-deployed at least once between 2001 and 2004. The researchers chose to study Texas families because of the large military population there and the availability of data.

The researchers discovered that prior to October 2002, rates of child maltreatment were a bit higher among nonmilitary families compared with military families. However, after the United States began deploying larger numbers of troops to Afghanistan and Iraq in 2003, rates of abuse and neglect in military families surpassed the rates among nonmilitary families. More specifically, rates of child maltreatment in military families rose twice as high in the period after October 2002 compared with the period prior to this time. During the same time frame, the rate of substantiated child abuse and neglect was relatively stable for nonmilitary families. The higher rates of child maltreatment were associated with increases both in deployments and in returns from deployment. For more on the topic of child maltreatment, the reader is directed back to the section on domestic violence earlier in this chapter.

Although family support services are available in each branch of military services to assist deployed troops and their families, this investigation reveals that either deployed families are not able to access the resources available to them or the existing support services do not effectively respond to the needs of the deployed families. In other words, the family is not able to achieve the balance outlined in the ABCX model. The investigators emphasized that some type of additional intervention should be explored, perhaps providing more support and educational programs for family members during the deployment period.

Teenage Suicide

News of the suicidal death of 15-year-old Sean Riggins reverberated through the community. Neighbors bunched together and talked in hushed tones about what he did and how he did it, a four-story leap from an abandoned warehouse that resulted in massive head trauma. No one could understand how something so tragic could have happened.

Sean had suffered from depression since middle school. He became moody and irritable in the eighth grade, sometimes even defiant and rebellious, which prompted his parents to seek psychiatric assistance. After an initial evaluation and diagnosis, he was prescribed Zoloft and saw his therapist once a month. Things calmed down, at least for a little while. On the outside, it looked like Sean Riggins had regained his footing.

Entry into high school, though, placed Sean on a collision course with new pressures and challenges. He became the target of bullies, something he had experienced off and on in middle school. He kept the bullying to himself, swallowing whatever insults or humiliation that came his way, wanting desperately to come across as one of the guys. He had a girlfriend for a little while, but that relationship failed and ushered in a new wave of dejection and despondency.

During the winter of his freshman year, Sean's behavior changed. Although his grades were at acceptable levels, he began cutting classes and hanging out with the wrong crowd. Contact with his family was minimal—he didn't get along with his stepfather and rarely spent time with his older brother—and he began pulling more and more into himself. He lost interest in any outside activities and his moods became dark again, prompting his parents to schedule several appointments with Sean's psychiatrist. The psychiatrist increased Sean's medication and began seeing Sean biweekly instead of monthly. Little did anyone know that Sean had taken himself off the Zoloft; each day he tossed the unused tablets down the bathroom sink.

Sean's friends would remark later that he seemed agitated and preoccupied—more so than usual—before he chose to end his life. Most attributed his darkness to the upcoming term exams staring every freshman in the face. Sean, though, was on a downward spiral. He spent most of his days wasting time and evenings behind his bedroom door, listening to the Grateful Dead or staring vacantly at the television. When his parents checked in on him, he made sure he had an open textbook or notebook next to him, wanting to create the image of the serious and determined student. What he was really doing was planning to end his life, the only missing piece being how he was going to do it. The abandoned warehouse four blocks away beckoned and eventually provided him with the answer.

At an age when they are supposed to have everything to live for, about 2 million adolescents each year attempt suicide, and almost 700,000 receive medical attention for their attempt. In 2001, 2.6 percent of students reported making a suicide attempt that had to be treated by a doctor or nurse. It is estimated that each year in the United States, approximately 2,000 youth age 10 to 19 complete suicide, making suicide the third-leading cause of death among young people age 15 to 24, following unintentional injuries and homicide. As many as 25 suicides are attempted for each one that is completed (National Institute of Mental Health 2006; National Alliance on Mental Illness 2003). Table 6.8, contained in Chapter 6, charts suicide death rates for teenagers as well as those for other age brackets.

Recent trends in adolescent suicide are cause for concern. In 2007, the Centers for Disease Control and Prevention reported that the suicide rate rose 8 percent for young people between the ages of 10 and 24 from 2003 to 2004 (based on the latest numbers available). Such findings suggest a troubling reversal of fairly recent trends, a 25 percent decline in teenage suicide rates since the early 1990s. The suicide rate among preteen and young teen girls rose 76 percent, the causes of which are puzzling to health officials. Suicide rates among older adolescent females, those age 15 to 19, spiked 32 percent; rates for males in that age group increased by 9 percent. Males committed suicide far more often than females, accounting for about three-quarters of adolescent suicide (Centers for Disease Control and Prevention 2007c, 2007d).

Regarding this upswing in suicides, the declining use of antidepressants among adolescents is thought to play a role. Several years ago, federal regulators warned that antidepressants seemed to raise the risk of suicidal behavior among teenagers, so black box warnings were put on the drugs' packaging. With the recent outbreak, experts also noted a drop in the sales of antidepressants.

According to the National Institute of Mental Health (2006), suicidal behavior is complex. Some risk factors vary with age, gender, or ethnic group and may occur in combination or change over time. Suicide rates are highest among non-Hispanic whites and second highest among American Indian and Native Alaskan males. The lowest rates are found among non-Hispanic blacks, Asians and Pacific Islanders, and Hispanics. Although non-Hispanic white adolescents commit suicide at a much higher rate than non-Hispanic blacks, the suicide rate for non-Hispanic blacks has almost doubled over the last 20 years (Centers for Disease Control and Prevention 2007c, 2007d; Lipton 2006; Rudd et al. 2006).

As far as gender differences are concerned, males outnumber females four to one in the number of suicidal deaths reported each year. But as far as attempted suicides are concerned, females clearly outnumber males. Females also are more apt to allow for intervention and are more likely to "call for help" through a suicide attempt. Gender differences also appear when one considers the means teenagers use to commit suicide. Females tend to overdose on drugs or cut themselves. Males use firearms, hanging, or jumping more frequently. Given the fact that males choose more sudden, lethal methods, it makes sense that they are more likely to succeed in their attempts. Firearms are used in about 60 percent of all adolescent suicides (Penn State Medical Center 2006; Soreff 2006).

Adolescents often experience stress and confusion from situations occurring in their families, schools, and communities. Such feelings can overwhelm young people and lead them to consider suicide as a "solution" (Centers for Disease Control and Prevention, 2007c, 2007d). Where do such feelings originate? What motivates teenagers to take their lives? One persistent theme is depression; many have a pervasive feeling of worthlessness, apprehension, and hopelessness (see Figures 6.26 and 6.27 and Table 6.9 in Chapter 6 for a graphic portrayal of the link between depression and suicidal behavior). Such feelings create a sense of helplessness, a general feeling that life is not worth living. Other factors linked to adolescent suicidal behavior include previous suicide attempts, a family history of mental disorders or suicidal behavior, family violence (physical or sexual abuse), exposure to other adolescents who have committed suicide, being bullied, easy access to firearms, and aggressive and disruptive behavior (National Institute of Mental Health 2006; Soreff 2006; Caruso 2007). Finally, a connection between substance abuse and suicidal behavior is well documented in the literature (Agosti and Levin 2006; Brady 2006; Conner et al. 2006; Esposito-Smythers et al. 2006; Goldstein and Levitt 2006). Referring back to material covered in Chapter 1, it becomes obvious that suicidal teenagers have experienced a pileup of personal and family demands.

For adolescents who are already receiving psychiatric treatment, family therapy may be an effective approach to help parents and family members to understand better the problems of their adolescent. The goals of such education are to increase compliance with treatment, promote a partnership with the parents so that they can monitor the patient with regard to recurrences, and help the family learn how to cope with a child with a psychiatric illness (Berman 2006a, 2006b; National Alliance on Mental Illness 2003). As we have witnessed in all of our family crisis situations, a systems approach to the problem is the preferred mode of treatment.

Implications for Family Life

The death of a family member is a serious crisis at any time, but especially so with the sudden loss of a child or teenager. For parents, a traumatic crisis such as this is likely the most painful loss imaginable. The fact that suicide was involved intensifies the heartache and suffering. According to Peter Durand (2006), when a teenager dies by suicide, a number of reactions are often experienced.

First, family members have a strong and perpetual need to know what happened, yet so many unanswered questions will likely remain. The frustrating aspect of this need is that the facts have died with the teenager. The reality of the situation is that the family may never know what truly happened. Further contributing to the frustration is that family members spend considerable energy trying to make sense of a senseless incident.

It also needs to be recognized that the suicide leaves behind a legacy of guilt. It is not uncommon for family members to blame themselves for what happened—the "if onlys" and "I wishes." Such feelings can create extreme levels of anxiety and stress. An important part of grief work for family members is coming to the conclusion that they could not have done anything to prevent the suicide. Such acceptance may take time to evolve as family members share their guilt with someone they trust (Parkes 2002; Jordan 2001; Carlson 2000).

The value of support groups cannot be overstressed. For many survivors, an important facet of the healing process is the support and sense of connection they feel through sharing their grief with other survivors. The most common way this sharing occurs is through survivor support groups. Such groups provide a safe haven where survivors can share their experiences and offer supportive assistance to one another. Support groups can be an important way to connect with other survivors and enable the bereaved to be able to talk openly about suicide with people who really understand (American Foundation for Suicide Prevention 2007).

Summary

A traumatic crisis is an extreme variation of a situational crisis and is unpredictable and often life threatening. This chapter explored five kinds of traumatic crises: domestic violence, school violence, natural disasters, deployed military families, and adolescent suicide. Never has the need been greater to understand traumatic crises, given the escalating numbers of American families forced to deal with them.

The path to recovery is a difficult one. It is not uncommon for families to relive the trauma, in the process experiencing feelings of loss, vulnerability, and insecurity. Relapses are not uncommon, nor are secondary stressors accompanying the upheaval—problem drinking, domestic violence, abandonment, and health issues often entering the mix. Many survivors suffer from an acute stress disorder, a psychological disturbance marked by intense levels of insecurity and fear. Basic assumptions of safety and security are shattered in the wake of traumatic crises, often leading to feelings of vulnerability and insecurity. We acknowledged in this chapter that children and adults respond in different ways to traumatic crises. Both young and old need to be reassured that they are safe and assured that ongoing guidance and contact are available.

Recovery from traumatic crises and the restoration of control and confidence knows wide variation. The depth of impact from the crisis on the family influences the timetable of recovery time, and we must take into consideration the family's state of affairs when the crisis strikes, especially the presence of concurrent multiple stressors. Intervention specialists need to help the troubled family identify and share thoughts and images of the crisis, including an acceptance of what happened and intentions to chart a new path in life.

References

Abbott, Patrick L. 2004. *Natural Disasters*, 4th ed. New York: McGraw-Hill Higher Education.

Addington, L. A., S. A. Ruddy, A. K. Miller, and J. F. DeVoe. 2002. *Are America's Schools Safe? Students Speak Out*. Washington, DC: National Center for Education Statistics.

Agosti, V., and F. R. Levin. 2006. "One-Year Follow-up Study of Suicide Attempters Treated for Drug Dependence." *American Journal on Addictions* 15 (4): 293–296.

American Academy of Child and Adolescent Psychiatry. 2008. "Child Abuse: The Hidden Bruises." [Online information; retrieved 8/29/07.] http://aacap.org/cs/root/facts_for_families/child_abuse_the_hidden_bruises.

American Foundation for Suicide Prevention. 2007. "Coping with Suicide Loss: Support Groups." [Online information; retrieved 8/20/07.] http://www.afsp.org/index.cfm?fuseaction=home.viewPage&page.

American Psychological Association. 2007a. "Talking to Your Children about the Recent Spate of School Shootings." [Online article; retrieved 7/13/07.] http://www.apa.org/topics/schoolshooting.html.

American Psychological Association. 2007b. "Psychological Needs of Military Personnel and Their Families Are Not Being Met, Reports APA Task Force." [Online article; retrieved 8/3/07.] http://www.medical newstoday.com/articles/63863.php.

Bancroft, L., and J. G. Silverman. 2002. *The Batterer as Parent: Addressing the Impact of Domestic Violence on Family Dynamics.* Thousand Oaks, CA: Sage.

Barnett, O. W., C. L. Miller-Perrin, and R. D. Perrin. 2005. *Family Violence across the Lifespan: An Introduction.* Thousand Oaks, CA: Sage.

Bennis, Phyllis, and Erik Leaver. "The Iraq Quagmire: The Mounting Costs of War and the Case for Bringing Home the Troops." *Foreign Policy in Focus* (August 31, 2005).

Berman, A. L. 2006a. "Suicide Data: What the Family Therapist Needs to Know." *American Association for Marriage and Family Therapy* 6 (July/August): 7–10.

Berman, A. L. 2006b. "Risk Assessment, Treatment Planning, and Management of the At-Risk for Suicide Client." *American Association for Marriage and Family Therapy* 6 (July/August): 13–15.

Bolton, D., D. O'Ryan, O. Udwin, S. Boyle, and W. Yule. 2000. "The Long-Term Psychological Effects of a Disaster Experienced in Adolescence: General Psychopathology." *Journal of Child Psychology and Psychiatry and Allied Disciplines* 41:513–523.

Bonnie, R. J., and R. B. Wallace. 2003. *Elder Mistreatment: Abuse, Neglect, and Exploitation in an Aging America.* Washington, DC: National Academies Press.

Borden, L. 2003. "Supporting Families Following a Disaster." [Online fact sheet; retrieved 7/19/07.] http://ag.arizona.edu/fcs/supporting_families/01overview.html.

Bowen, G. L., J. A. Mancini, J. A. Martin, W. B. Ware, and J. P. Nelson. 2003. "Promoting the Adaptation of Military Families: An Empirical Test of a Community Practice Model." *Family Relations: Interdisciplinary Journal of Applied Family Studies* 52:33–44.

Brady, J. 2006. "The Association between Alcohol Misuse and Suicidal Behavior." *Alcohol and Alcoholism* 41 (5): 473–478.

California Department of Education. 2006. "Bullying Frequently Asked Questions." [Online information; retrieved 8/8/07.] http://www.cde.ca.gov/ls/ss/se/bullyfaq.asp.

Carlson, T. 2000. *Suicide Survivors Handbook.* Duluth, MN: Benline Press.

Carp, F. M. 2000. *Elder Abuse in the Family: An Interdisciplinary Model for Research.* New York: Springer.

Caruso, K. 2007. "Bullied Children Suffer Behavioral Problems; Are at Risk for Suicide." [Online article; retrieved 8/20/07.] http://www.suicide.org/bullied-children-suffer-behavioral-problems.html.

Centers for Disease Control and Prevention. 2007a. "Child Maltreatment: Fact Sheet." [Online fact sheet; retrieved 8/29/07.] http://www.cdc.gov/ncipc/factsheets/cmfacts.htm.

Centers for Disease Control and Prevention. 2007b. "School Violence: Tips for Coping with Stress." [Online article; retrieved 7/13/07.] http://www.cdc.gov/Features/SchoolViolence/.

Centers for Disease Control and Prevention. 2007c. "Suicide Prevention." [Online fact sheet; retrieved 8/20/07.] http://www.cdc.gov/ncipc/factsheets/suifacts.htm.

Centers for Disease Control and Prevention. 2007d. "Suicide Trends among Youths and Young Adults Aged 10–24 Years; United States, 1990–2004." *Morbidity and Mortality Weekly Report* 56 (35): 905–908.

Clarke, L. 2005. "Worst Case Katrina." *Social Science Research Council* 12:6–12.

Conner, K. R., V. M. Hesselbrock, M. A. Schuckit, J. K. Hirsch, K. L. Knox, and S. Meldrum. 2006. "Precontemplated and Impulsive Suicide Attempts among Individuals with Alcohol Dependence." *Journal of Studies on Alcohol* 67 (1): 95–101.

Cooper, J., and A. Vetere. 2005. *Domestic Violence and Family Safety: A Systemic Approach to Working with Violence in Families.* London: Whurr/Wiley.

Crepeau-Hobson, M., F. Franci, and G. L. Marylynne. 2005. "Violence Prevention after Columbine: A Survey of High School Mental Health Professionals." *Children and Schools* 27 (3): 157–165.

Denmark, F. L., ed. 2005. *Violence in Schools: Cross-National and Cross-Cultural Perspectives.* New York: Springer.

DeVoe, J. F., P. Kaufman, A. Miller, M. Noonan, T.D. Snyder, and K. Baum. 2004. *Indicators of School Crime and Safety.* 2004. Washington, DC: U.S. Department of Education and U.S. Department of Justice.

Dorn, C. 2005. *Innocent Targets: When Terrorism Comes to School.* Atlanta: Georgia Institute of Technology.

Druck, K., and M. Kaplowitz. 2005. "Preventing Classroom Violence." *Education Digest* 71 (2): 40–43.

Drummet, A. R., M. Coleman, and S. Cable. 2003. "Military Families under Stress: Implications for Family Life Education." *Family Relations* 52 (3): 279–294.

Durand, P. 2006. "When Someone Dies by Suicide." [Online information; retrieved 8/20/07.] http://www.griefworksbc.com/Suicide.asp.

Dyregrov, A. 2007. "Family Recovery from Terror, Grief and Trauma." [Online article; retrieved 7/16/07.] http://www.icisf.org/articles/Acrobat%20Documents/TerrorismIncident/Terrorovertime.html.

Espelage, D. L., and M. Holt. 2001. "Bullying and Victimization during Early Adolescence: Peer Influences and Psychosocial Correlates." *Journal of Emotional Abuse* 2 (3): 123–142.

Esposito-Smythers, C., A. Spirito, R. Uth, and H. LaChance. 2006. "Cognitive Behavioral Treatment for Suicidal Alcohol Abusing Adolescents: Development and Pilot Testing." *American Journal on Addictions* 15 (Suppl. 1): 126–130.

Fazzone, P. A., J. K. Holton, and B. G. Reed. 2001. *Substance Abuse Treatment and Domestic Violence.* Rockville, MD: U.S. Department of Health and Human Services.

Federal Emergency Management Agency. 2006. *Helping Children Cope with Disaster.* [Online information, retrieved 8/6/08.] http://www.fema.gov/rebuild/recover/cope_child.shtm

Feindler, E. L., J. H. Rathus, and L. B. Silver. 2003. *Assessment of Family Violence: A Handbook for Researchers and Practitioners.* Washington, DC: American Psychological Association.

Flannery, D. J. 2006. *Violence and Mental Health in Everyday Life: Prevention and Intervention Strategies for Children and Adolescents.* Lanham, MD: AltaMira Press.

Florida Department of Education. 2007. "Florida's Bullying Prevention Project." [Online information; retrieved 8/8/07.] http://www.fldoe.org/besss/bullying.asp.

Fowler, J. 2003. *A Practitioner's Tool for Child Protection and the Assessment of Parents.* Philadelphia: Jessica Kingsley.

Friedman, J. 2005. "Reflections on Katrina." *Policy and Practice of Public Human Services* 63 (4): 12–16.

Gallagher, L. C. 2007. "U.S. Military Deployment: When a Family Member Leaves." [Online article; retrieved 8/2/07.] http://www.operationhomefront.org/Info/info_deploy_familymember.shtml.

Geffner, R., D. G. Dutton, and D. J. Sonkin. 2002. *Intimate Violence: Contemporary Treatment Innovations.* Binghamton, NY: Haworth.

Gibbs, D. A., S. L. Martin, L. L. Kupper, and R. E. Johnson. 2007. "Child Maltreatment in Enlisted Soldiers' Families during Combat-Related Deployment." *Journal of the American Medical Association* 298 (5): 528–535.

Global Security. 2007. "Where are the Legions? Global Deployments of U.S. Forces." [Online information; retrieved 8/2/07.] http://www.global security.org/military/ops/global-deployments.htm.

Goenjian, A. K., L. Molina, A. M. Steinberg, and L. A. Fairbanks. 2001. "Post Traumatic Stress and Depressive Reactions among Adolescents after Hurricane Mitch." *American Journal of Psychiatry* 158:788–794.

Goldenberg, H., and I. Goldenberg. 2008. *Family Therapy: An Overview,* 7th ed. Belmont, CA: Thomson Learning.

Goldstein, B. I., and A. J. Levitt. 2006. "Is Current Alcohol Consumption Associated with Increased Lifetime Prevalence of Major Depression and Suicidality? Results from a Pilot Community Survey." *Comprehensive Psychiatry* 47 (5): 330–333.

Gondolf, E. W. 2002. *Batterer Intervention Systems: Issues, Outcomes, and Recommendations.* Thousand Oaks, CA: Sage.

Goodman, L. A., and D. Epstein. 2007. *Listening to Battered Women: A Survivor-Centered Approach to Advocacy, Mental Health, and Justice.* Washington, DC: American Psychological Association.

Greenberg, J. S. 2008. *Comprehensive Stress Management,* 10th ed. New York: McGraw-Hill.

Gross, K. A. 2007. "Good Policy, Not Stories, Can Reduce Violence." *Chronicle of Higher Education* 53 (35): B10.

Guerino, P., M. Hurwitz, M. E. Noonan, and S. E. Kaffenberger. 2007. *Crime, Violence, Discipline, and Safety in U.S. Public Schools: Findings from the School Survey on Crime and Safety.* Washington, DC: National Center for Education Statistics.

Halpern, J., and M. Tramontin. 2007. *Disaster Mental Health.* Belmont, CA: Thomson Learning.

Harrison, C. 2007. "Protect Children from Post-Traumatic Stress Disorder (PTSD) in a Natural Disaster." [Online article; retrieved 7/16/07.] http://www.associatedcontent.com/article/236676/protect_children_ from_posttraumatic.html.

Harvard Medical School Family Health Guide. 2006. "Recognizing Domestic Partner Abuse." [Online article; retrieved 8/29/07.] http://www. health.harvard.edu/fhg/updates/update1006d.shtml.

Hester, J. P. 2003. *Public School Safety: A Handbook.* Jefferson, NC: McFarland.

Hoshmand, L. T., and A. L. Hoshmand. 2007. "Support for Military Families and Communities." *Journal of Community Psychology* 35 (2): 171–186.

Howitt, A. M., and H. B. Leonard 2006. "Katrina and the Core Challenges of Disaster Response." *Fletcher Forum of World Affairs* 30(1): 215–221.

Ianelli, V. 2005. "Child Abuse Facts for Parents." [Online information; retrieved 8/29/07.] http://pediatrics.about.com/cs/pediatricadvice/a/child_abuse.htm.

Jaffe, P. G., L. L. Baker, and A. J. Cunningham. 2004. *Protecting Children from Domestic Violence: Strategies for Community Intervention.* New York: Guilford Press.

James, R. K. 2008. *Crisis Intervention Strategies,* 6th ed. Belmont, CA: Thomson Learning.

Jimerson, S. R, S. E. Brock, and S. W. Pletcher. 2005. "An Integrated Model of School Crisis Preparedness and Intervention: A Shared Foundation to Facilitate International Crisis Intervention." *School Psychology International* 26 (3): 275–296.

Jones, R. T., R. Fray, J. D. Cunningham, and L. Kaiser. 2001. "The Psychological Effects of Hurricane Andrew on Ethnic Minority and Caucasian Children and Adolescents: A Case Study." *Cultural Diversity and Ethnic Minority Psychology* 7:103–108.

Jones, S. J., and R. Compton, eds. 2003. *Kids Working It Out: Strategies and Stories for Making Peace in Our Schools.* San Francisco: Jossey-Bass.

Jordan, C. E. 2004. *Intimate Partner Violence: A Clinical Training Guide for Mental Health Professionals.* New York: Springer.

Jordan, J. 2001. "Is Suicide Bereavement Different? A Reassessment of the Literature." *Suicide and Life Threatening Behavior* 31 (1): 91–102.

Kiselica, M. S., and M. Morrill-Richards. 2007. "Sibling Maltreatment: The Forgotten Abuse." *Journal of Counseling and Development* 85:148–160.

Kohm, K. 2004. "Rebuilding School Culture to Make Schools Safer." *Educational Digest* 70 (3): 23–30.

Kurst-Swanger, K., and J. L. Petcosky. 2003. *Violence in the Home: Multidisciplinary Perspectives.* New York: Oxford University Press.

Lavarello, C., and K. S. Trump. 2002. "Schools Are Vulnerable to Attack." *National Academy Associate* 4 (6): 30–36.

Lazarus, P. J., S. R. Jimerson, and S. E. Brock. 2002. "Natural Disasters." In *Best Practices in School Crisis Prevention and Intervention,* edited by S. E. Brock, P. J. Lazarus, and S. R. Jimerson. Bethesda, MD: National Association of School Psychologists.

Lee, M. Y., J. Sebold, and A. Uken. 2003. *Solution-Focused Treatment of Domestic Violence Offenders: Accountability for Change.* New York: Oxford University Press.

Lieberman, A. F., and P. Van Horn. 2004. "Assessment and Treatment of Young Children Exposed to Traumatic Events." In *Young Children and Trauma: Intervention and Treatment,* edited by J. Osofsky. New York: Guilford Press.

Lieberman, J. 2006. *The Shooting Game: The Making of School Shooters.* Santa Ana, CA: Seven Locks Press.

Lipton, L. 2006. "Emergency Responders Management of Patients Who May Have Attempted Suicide." *Internet Journal of Rescue and Disaster Medicine* 5 (2): 1–5.

Litz, B. T., and M. J. Gray. 2004. "Early Intervention for Trauma in Adults: A Framework for First Aid and Secondary Prevention." In *Early Intervention for Trauma and Traumatic Loss,* edited by B. T. Litz. New York: Guilford Press.

Loseke, D. R., R. J. Gelles, and M. M. Cavanaugh. 2005. *Current Controversies on Family Violence.* Thousand Oaks, CA: Sage.

Loue, S. 2001. *Intimate Partner Violence: Societal, Medical, Legal, and Individual Responses.* New York: Kluwer.

Lubell, K. M., and J. B. Vette. 2006. "Suicide and Youth Violence Prevention: The Promise of an Integrated Approach." *Aggression and Violent Behavior* 11 (4): 167–175.

Martin, J. A., D. L. Mancini, G. L. Bowen, J. A. Mancini, and D. K. Orthner. 2004. *Building Strong Communities for Military Families.* NCFR Policy Brief, April. Minneapolis, MN: National Council on Family Relations.

Maxwell, L. A. 2006. "School Shootings in Policy Spotlight." *Education Week* 26 (7): 16–17.

Maxwell, L. A. 2007. "College Rampage Renews School Safety Concerns." *Education Week* 27 (4): 16–17.

McCann, E., and K. Olson. 2007. "Parents Should Talk to Children of Every Age About School Shootings." [Online article; retrieved 7/13/07.] http://www.extension.umn.edu/extensionnews/2005/schoolshooting07.html.

McCue, M. L. 2007. *Domestic Violence.* Santa Barbara, CA: ABC-CLIO.

McDermott, B. M., and E. Lee. 2005. "Posttraumatic Stress Disorder and General Psychopathology in Children and Adolescents Following a Wildfire Disaster." *Canadian Journal of Psychiatry* 50 (3): 137–143.

McDowell, B. M. 2006. "Caring for Child Victims: Countering the Effects of Domestic Violence." *Journal for Specialists in Pediatric Nursing* 11 (2): 129–132.

Menninger Clinic. 2005. "School Violence: Take School Climate & Bullying Seriously." [Online article; retrieved 8/8/07.] http://www.newswise.com/articles/view/513397/.

Mental Health America. 2007a. "Dealing with Stress After a Natural Disaster." [Online information; retrieved 7/19/07.] http://www1.nmha.org/reassurance/naturalDisaster.cfm.

Mental Health America. 2007b. "Operation Healthy Reunions: Coping with War-Related Stress." [Online information; retrieved 8/2/07.] http://www.mentalhealthamerica.net/reunions/infoWarStress.cfm.

Miller, A. 2003. *Violence in U.S. Public Schools.* Washington, DC: National Center for Education Statistics.

Mills, L. G. 2003. *Insult to Injury: Rethinking Our Responses to Intimate Abuse.* Princeton, NJ: Princeton University Press.

Mlakar, P. 2005. "Hurricane Katrina and Levee Failure." U.S. Army: Federal Document Clearing House congressional testimony. Washington, DC: U.S. Government Printing Office.

Morse, J. 2007. "A Closer Look for Current Conditions: A Fresh Glance at the Emotional Cycle." [Online article; retrieved 8/4/07.] http://www.hooah4health.com/deployment/familymatters/emotionalcyclesupport.htm.

National Alliance on Mental Illness. 2003. "Suicide in Youth." [Online article; retrieved 8/20/07.] http://www.nami.org/Content/ContentGroups/Helpline1/Suicide_in_Youth.htm.

National Association of School Psychologists. 2006. "Talking to Children about Violence: Tips for Parents and Teachers." [Online information; retrieved 7/14/07.] http://www.nasponline.org/resources/crisis_safety/talkingviolence.pdf.

National Child Traumatic Stress Network. 2007a. "Parenting in a Challenging World." [Online information; retrieved 7/10/07.] http://www.nctsnet.org/nccts/nav.do?pid=ctr_aud_prnt_chlg.

National Child Traumatic Stress Network. 2007b. "Age-Related Reactions to a Traumatic Event." [Online article; retrieved 7/20/07.] http://www.nctsnet.org/nctsn_assets/pdfs/age_related_reactions.pdf.

National Institute of Mental Health. 2006. "Suicide in the U.S.: Statistics and Prevention." [Online information; retrieved 8/20/07.] http://www.nimh.nih.gov/publicat/harmsway.cfm#references.

National Organization for Victim Assistance. 2002. *The Community Crisis Response Training Manual.* Washington, DC: National Organization for Victim Assistance.

National Organization for Women. 2007. "Violence against Women in the United States." [Online information; retrieved 8/28/07.] http://www.now.org/issues/violence/stats.html.

Natraian, M., ed. 2007. *Domestic Violence.* Aldershot, UK: Ashgate.

Newman, K. S. 2007. "Before the Rampage: What Can Be Done?" *Chronicle of Higher Education* 53 (35): 20.

Pararas-Carayannis, G. 2007. "Natural Disasters: International Decade for Natural Disaster Reduction (IDNDR)." [Online article; retrieved 7/2/07.] http://www.drgeorgepc.com/NaturalDisasters.html#anchor292767.

Parkes, C. 2002. "Grief: Lessons from the Past." *Death Studies* (26): 367–385.

Patterson, J. M. 2002. "Integrating Family Resilience and Family Stress Theory." *Journal of Marriage and the Family* 64:349–360.

Penn State Medical Center. 2006. "Understanding and Preventing Teen Suicide." [Online information; retrieved 8/20/07.] http://www.hmc.psu.edu/childrens/healthinfo/s/suicide.htm.

Pincus, S. H., R. House, J. Christenson, and L. E. Adler. 2007. "The Emotional Cycle of Deployment: A Military Family Perspective." [Online article; retrieved 7/4/07.] http://www.hooah4health.com/deployment/familymatters/emotionalcycle.htm.

Righthand, S., B. Kerr, and K. Drach. 2003. *Child Maltreatment Risk Assessments: An Evaluation Guide.* New York: Haworth.

Roberts, A. R. 2002. *Handbook of Domestic Violence Intervention Strategies: Policies, Programs, and Legal Remedies.* New York: Oxford University Press.

Roberts, A. R., and B. S. Roberts. 2005. *Ending Intimate Abuse: Practical Guidance and Survival Strategies.* New York: Oxford University Press.

Rondini, A. 2007. "Relationship Abuse." [Online information; retrieved 8/29/07.] http://www.plannedparenthood.org/news-articles-press/politics-policy-issues/medical-sexual-health/relationship-abuse-14715.htm.

Rudd, M. D., A. L. Berman, T. E. Joiner, Jr., M. K. Nock, M. Silverman, M. Mandrusiak, K. Van Orden, and T. Witte. 2006. "Warning Signs for Suicide: Theory, Research, and Clinical Applications." *Suicide and Life Threatening Behavior* 36 (3): 255–262.

Sample, D. 2003. "War on TV Affects Students of Deployed Parents, Parents, Teachers." [Online article; retrieved 8/2/07.] http://www.cfs.purdue.edu/mfri/pages/news/parent_goes_to_war.htm.

Schewe, P. A. 2002. *Preventing Violence in Relationships: Interventions across the Life Span.* Washington, DC: American Psychological Association.

Schreck, C. J., and J. M. Miller. 2003. "Sources of Fear of Crime at School: What Is the Relative Contribution of Disorder, Individual Characteristics, and School Security?" *Journal of School Violence* 2 (4): 57–79.

Sever, A. 2002. *Fleeing the House of Horrors: Women Who Have Left Abusive Partners.* Toronto: University of Toronto Press.

Sexton-Radek, K., ed. 2004. *Violence in Schools: Issues, Consequences, and Expressions.* Westport, CT: Praeger.

Shafir, N. 2006. "Effective Crisis Communications and Emergency Notification." *School Business Affairs* 72 (6): 6–10.

Shen, Y. J., and C. A. Sink. 2002. "Helping Elementary-Age Children Cope with Disasters." *Professional School Counseling* 5 (5): 322–330.

Shields, A., and D. Cicchetti. 2001. "Parental Maltreatment and Emotion Dysregulation as Risk Factors for Bullying and Victimization in Middle Childhood." *Journal of Clinical Psychology* 30:349–363.

Shipway, L. 2004. *Domestic Violence: A Handbook for Health Professionals.* New York: Routledge.

Silva, A. 2004. "Culturally Competent Crisis Response: Information for School Psychologists and Crisis Teams." [Online article; retrieved 8/2/07.] http://www.nasponline.org/resources/culturalcompetence/cc_crisis.pdf.

Smith, K. 2002. *Environmental Hazards: Assessing Risk and Reducing Disaster,* 3rd ed. New York: Routledge.

Smith, M., T. de Benedictis, J. Jaffe, and J. Segal. 2007. "Domestic Violence and Abuse: Help, Treatment, Intervention, and Prevention." [Online information; retrieved 8/28/07.] http://www.helpguide.org/mental/domestic_violence_abuse_help_treatment_prevention.htm.

Soreff, S. 2006. "Suicide." [Online article; retrieved 8/20/07.] http://www.emedicine.com/med/topic3004.htm.

Swearer, S. M., and B. Doll. 2001. "Bullying in Schools: An Ecological Framework." *Journal of Emotional Abuse* 2 (2/3): 7–23.

Trump, K. S. 2002. "Be Prepared, Not Scared." *Principal Magazine* 81 (5): 10–14.

Turell, S. C. 2003. "The Abuse of Men: Trauma Begets Trauma." *Sex Roles: A Journal of Research* 54 (6): 27–34.

U.S. Congress. 2007. "The All-Volunteer Military: Issues and Performance." Congressional Budget Office study. [Online report; retrieved 8/2/07.] http://www.cbo.gov/ftpdocs/83xx/doc8313/07-19-MilitaryVol.pdf.

U.S. Department of Health and Human Services, Office of the Surgeon General. 2001. *Report on Youth Violence.* Washington, DC: U.S. Government Printing Office.

U.S. Department of Justice. 2007. "About Domestic Violence." [Online information; retrieved 8/28/07.] http://www.usdoj.gov/ovw/domviolence.htm.

Walker, H. M., E. Ramsey, and F. M. Gresham. 2004. *Antisocial Behavior in School: Evidence-based Practices,* 2nd ed. Belmont, CA: Thomson/Wadsworth.

Wallace, H. 2007. *Family Violence: Legal, Medical, and Social Perspectives,* 5th ed. Needham Heights, MA: Allyn and Bacon.

Wekerle, C., and A. Wall. 2002. *The Violence and Addiction Equation: Theoretical and Clinical Issues in Substance Abuse and Relationship Violence.* New York: Brunner-Routledge.

Wessler, S., and W. Preble. 2003. *The Respectful School: How Educators and Students Can Conquer Hate and Harassment.* Alexandria, VA: Association for Supervision and Curriculum Development.

Whealin, J., and I. Pivar. 2007. "Coping When a Family Member Has Been Called to War." [Online article; retrieved 8/2/07.] http://www.operationhomefront.org/Info/info_deploy_called2war.shtml.

Wilde, J. 2002. *Anger Management in School: Alternatives to Student Violence,* 2nd ed. Lanham, MD: Scarecrow Press.

Wong, M. 2007. "Managing Threats: Safety Lessons Learned from School Shootings." [Online article; retrieved 7/13/07.] http://www.nctsnet.org/nctsn_assets/pdfs/UrbanED_Managing_Threats_MWongPhD.pdf.

Zenere, F. J. 2004. "How Children Cope with Trauma and Ongoing Threat." [Online article; retrieved 8/20/07.] http://www.nasponline.org/resources/crisis_safety/ongoingthreat.aspx.

Zink, T., C. J. Jacobson, S. R. Pabst., and B. S. Fisher. 2006. "A Lifetime of Intimate Partner Violence: Coping Strategies of Older Women." *Journal of Interpersonal Violence* 21 (5): 634–651.

Zorza, J. 2002. *Violence against Women: Law, Prevention, Protection, Enforcement, Treatment, Health.* Kingston, NJ: Civic Research Institute.

4

Chronology

1900 A devastating hurricane strikes Galveston, Texas, on September 18, killing approximately 8,000 residents (Alexander 2000).

About 6 percent of married women work outside the home (U.S. Bureau of Labor Statistics 2007).

The rate of divorce per 1,000 of total population is 1.3 (U.S. Census Bureau 2007).

1901 Noted family therapist and author Milton H. Erickson is born in Aurum, Nevada. Erickson will become a psychiatrist and psychologist regarded by many as a foremost practitioner of medical hypnosis. He will write many books on the discoveries he made while treating the many patients and families he encountered.

1904 Clara Barton resigns as head of the American Red Cross and is replaced by Mabel T. Boardman. Over the years, the organization will become an influential source of rescue and assistance to individuals and families in emergencies. Today, the American Red Cross is at the scene of more than 40,000 disasters a year, from house fires to floods and tornadoes.

1906   The San Francisco earthquake claims up to 3,000 lives. Within a matter of seconds, the city is thrown into chaos as the earth splits open and buildings topple over. Massive fires develop throughout the city. In all, 28,000 buildings are destroyed, 225,000 residents are left homeless, and property damage amounts to more than $400,000,000 in 1906 dollars (Abbott 2007).

1912   The first family court is established in Trenton, New Jersey, giving it jurisdiction to hear and determine all domestic relations disputes. Ohio will follow in 1914 with legislation creating the Division of Domestic Relations in the Hamilton County (Cincinnati) Court of Common Pleas with jurisdiction over divorce, alimony matters, delinquency, dependency, neglected and crippled children, adults contributing to or tending to cause delinquency or dependency, and failure to provide support (Hurst 1999).

1916   Family therapist Virginia Satir is born.

1918   The unemployment rate stands at 1.4 percent, but will skyrocket to 24.9 percent by 1933 (U.S. Bureau of Labor Statistics 2007).

1920   Don Jackson, an early contributor to the field of family therapy, is born.

1925   The Great Tri-State Tornado rips through Missouri, Illinois, and Indiana on March 18, killing 695 people, injuring more than 2,000, and destroying about 15,000 homes (Abbott 2007).

1929   The stock market crash occurs and leads to the Great Depression, leaving millions of families in financial ruination.

1930   The rate of divorces per 1,000 of total population is 1.6 (U.S. Census Bureau 2007).

1931   Family therapist, teacher, and author Jay Haley is born.

1935   A hurricane slams into the Florida Keys on September 2, claiming more than 500 lives (Alexander 2000).

Alcoholics Anonymous (AA) is founded by Bill Wilson and Don Smith in Akron, Ohio. Alcoholics Anonymous is a voluntary, worldwide fellowship of men and women from all walks of life who meet together to attain and maintain sobriety. The only requirement for membership is a desire to stop drinking. Today, it is estimated that more than 114,000 AA groups and more than 2,000,000 members are active in 180 countries.

1936 A tornado on April 6 kills 203 and injures 1,800 in Gainesville, Georgia (Alexander 2000).

1938 The National Council on Family Relations is established; the organization is designed for family professionals to plan and act together on concerns relevant to families.

A hurricane pounds the Atlantic U.S. coastline. In a matter of hours, 688 people are killed, 4,500 people are injured, and more than 75,000 buildings are damaged (Abbott 2007).

1940 The divorce rate per 1,000 of total population is 2.1 (U.S. Census Bureau 2007).

1942 The American Association for Marriage and Family Therapy is established, which is geared to the professional development of marriage and family therapists throughout the United States, Canada, and abroad.

1948 Sex researcher Alfred Kinsey and colleagues report in the book *Sexual Behavior in the Human Male* that approximately one-third of American husbands engage in extramarital sexual intercourse. Five years later, in *Sexual Behavior in the Human Female,* they report that one-fifth of American wives do the same.

1949 Reuben Hill publishes the now classic *Families under Stress,* which features the ABCX model of family stress and crisis.

Nearly three-quarters of all 65-year-old men are in the labor force. By 1985, this percentage will shrink to one-third (U.S. Bureau of Labor Statistics 2007).

1950   The divorce rate per 1,000 of total population is 2.6 (U.S. Census Bureau 2007).

Two wives of Alcoholics Anonymous members in New York, Lois W. and Anne B., form a clearinghouse committee to coordinate the family groups related to AA that had informally sprung up around the country. Starting with 87 initial inquiries, they send out questionnaires and receive responses from 56 groups. As a result of the questionnaires, the name Al-Anon Family Groups is chosen and the groups adopt the "Twelve Steps" of AA. Al-Anon's first book, *The Al-Anon Family Group: A Guide for the Families of Problem Drinkers,* will be published in 1955 (Al-Anon 1997).

1952   The Women's Bureau of the U.S. Department of Labor publishes *Women Workers and Their Dependents* and *Maternity Protection of Employed Women* (Pruitt and Rapoport 2008).

1954   Family therapist Murray Bowen becomes the first director of the Family Division at the National Institute of Mental Health.

1957   Parents without Partners is founded in New York City by two single parents, Jim Egleson, a noncustodial parent, and Jacqueline Bernard, a custodial parent. It is a support organization devoted to the welfare and interests of single parents and their families. As concerned parents, Egleson and Bernard feel isolated from society because of their marital status and decide to form a mutual support organization.

The Mental Research Institute is founded in Palo Alto, California. The institute is a training facility for the interactional study of individuals, families, and their communities.

1958   Therapists Don Jackson and Jay Haley emerge as influential figures in shaping the family therapy movement. Working in Palo Alto, California, the two explore family stress and crises against the backdrop of communications analysis.

1960   The divorce rate doubles from that recorded in 1900 (U.S. Census Bureau 2007).

Women in the labor force comprise 31 percent of all women, 39 percent of women with children age 6 to 17, and 19 percent of women with children under age 6 (Pruitt and Rapoport 2008).

1961   The first family therapy research journal, *Family Process,* is founded by Don Johnson, Jay Haley, and Nathan Ackerman. Since its inception, the journal has become a major resource for mental health and social service professionals who are looking for cutting edge research and clinical ideas about family and systems theory and practice.

Family therapist Jay Haley publishes *Strategies of Psychotherapy.*

The first state system of family courts is established in Rhode Island. Rhode Island will be followed by New York in 1962 and Hawaii in 1965. By 1980, 13 states will be operating or seriously studying the feasibility of family court consolidation (Hurst 1999).

1962   The state of New York rules that cases of intimate partner violence will be handled in civil court rather than criminal court. As a consequence, convicted men face lesser penalties than would have been handed down in criminal court.

1964   Family therapist and noted researcher Virginia Satir publishes *Conjoint Family Therapy.*

1966   One of the first school shootings in U.S. history takes place on August 1 at the University of Texas. Charles Whitman kills 15 persons and wounds 31.

The state of New York establishes that cruel and inhumane treatment at the hands of a spouse is grounds for

1966   divorce. However, the abused party must prove that a
(*cont.*)   sufficient number of physical assaults have occurred.

1968   The American Association of Suicidology is founded by
Edwin Shneidman and is organized to promote research,
public awareness programs, public education, and training for professionals and volunteers.

Internationally recognized family therapist Don Jackson
dies.

1969   California enacts the Family Law Act, thus becoming the
first state to legislate a "no fault" divorce concept. The
no-fault concept recognizes the breakdown of a marriage
as a ground for divorce and helps reduce the adversarial
process often associated with traditional divorce proceedings. In the years that follow, nearly every state will
adopt some form or variation of the no-fault divorce
concept.

1970   The divorce rate per 1,000 of total population is 3.5 (U.S.
Census Bureau 2007).

Women in the labor force comprise 41 percent of all
women, 49 percent of women with children age 6 to 17,
and 30 percent of women with children under age 6. Between 1970 and 1996, the number of children living in
single-parent families will more than double (Pruitt and
Rapoport 2008).

1971   The National Runaway Switchboard is founded in
Chicago. It is a centralized organization with free 24-hour
services, expertise in all youth-related issues, and an information clearinghouse of youth services.

In Philadelphia, one of the first feminist self-help groups,
Women in Transition, is established. It provides social
services and support for divorced or separated women,
battered wives, and single mothers.

1972   The Center for Family Learning is founded by family
therapist Phil Guerin in New Rochelle, New York. The

center becomes a distinctive and critically acclaimed family therapy program.

Rainbow Retreat, one of the earliest battered women's shelters, opens in Phoenix, Arizona.

1974   The National Clearinghouse on Child Abuse and Neglect is established. The organization provides information and technical assistance on child abuse, neglect, and related child welfare issues.

Family therapist Salvador Minuchin publishes *Families and Family Therapy,* a classic text identifying family structural components, such as subsystems and boundaries.

The Child Abuse and Neglect Prevention and Treatment Act assists states and other bodies to develop programs to identify and prevent abuse and to provide ameliorative services.

The National Institute on Aging (NIA) is formed. Its establishment represents a broad scientific effort to understand the nature of aging and to extend the healthy, active years of life. The NIA provides leadership in aging research, training, health information dissemination, and other programs relevant to aging and older people.

The National Institute on Drug Abuse (NIDA) is established as the federal focal point for research, treatment, prevention, training, services, and data collection on the nature and extent of drug abuse. The mission of NIDA is to lead the nation in bringing the power of science to bear on drug abuse and addiction.

1976   Pennsylvania establishes the first state coalition against domestic violence.

The National Organization for Women establishes its Task Force on Battered Women.

1977   The Family Caregiver Alliance (FCA) is founded, the first community-based nonprofit organization in the

1977
(*cont.*) United States to address the needs of families and friends providing long-term care of elders at home. The FCA will eventually offer programs at national, state, and local levels to support and sustain caregivers.

Oregon becomes the first state to enact legislation mandating arrest for perpetrators of domestic violence.

1978 Lenore Walker pens the critically acclaimed book, *The Battered Woman*. This book discusses the "learned helplessness" theory of battered women and the "cycle of violence."

1979 President Jimmy Carter presides over the White House Conference on Families and subsequently establishes the Office for Families.

1980 The divorce rate per 1,000 of total population is 5.2 (U.S. Census Bureau 2007).

The National Coalition against Domestic Violence holds its first national conference in Washington, D.C.

Women in the labor force comprise 52 percent of all women, 68 percent of women with children age 6 to 17, and 50 percent of women with children under age 6 who are divorced (U.S. Census Bureau 2007).

1981 The first annual Domestic Violence Awareness Week is celebrated across the United States.

1983 Hamilton McCubbin and Joan Patterson publish their findings regarding the Double ABCX model of family crisis.

1984 The number of divorces declines for the first time in two decades (U.S. Census Bureau 2007).

The Family Violence Prevention and Services Act is passed, identifying federal funding for programs serving domestic violence victims.

U.S. Surgeon General C. Everett Koop declares domestic violence the number one health problem in the United States.

1988   Family therapist and author Virginia Satir dies.

The Administration on Aging funds the first national resource base aimed at increasing public understanding. The National Center for Elder Abuse will emerge from this effort as a national resource for elder rights advocates, adult protective service, law enforcement and legal professionals, medical and mental health providers, public policy leaders, educators, researchers, and concerned citizens.

1989   Charles Figley publishes *Treating Stress in Families.*

The divorce rate per 1,000 of total population is 4.7 (U.S. Census Bureau 2007).

1991   More than 2.6 million cases of suspected child maltreatment are reported in the United States. More than four children a day die from maltreatment (Healthy Families America 2008).

1992   The U.S. surgeon general ranks abuse by husbands as the leading cause of injuries to women age 15 to 44 (National Organization for Women 2007).

1993   After taking nearly 10 years to work its way through Congress, the U.S. Family and Medical Leave Act is enacted. It entitles employees of all public agencies and private-sector companies employing 50 or more people to 12 weeks of unpaid leave for birth and care of newborns, adoption, illness of immediate family member, and medical leave for a serious health condition (Pruitt and Rapoport 2008).

1994   The Violence against Women Act combines tough law enforcement strategies with safeguards for victims of domestic violence and sexual assault. The act increases penalties for sex offenders and domestic abusers, provides

1994
(*cont.*) additional funding to assist state and local law enforcement agencies, and enhances restitution for victims of domestic violence. It receives an unprecedented $1.6 billion budget for violence prevention and services.

1995 Federal, state, and local governments spend about $11.2 billion on child protection (Children's Defense Fund 1995).

1996 Congress passes the Domestic Violence Option, which grants abused women exemptions from punitive welfare reform provisions. The National Organization for Women is instrumental in getting this congressional legislation passed.

1998 The National Institute on Drug Abuse releases *Preventing Drug Use among Children and Adolescents: A Research-Based Guide,* which describes the most successful concepts for preventing drug abuse among young people.

Jay Haley publishes *Learning and Teaching Therapy.*

The U.S. Department of Health and Human Services reports an estimated 903,000 cases of child maltreatment. Of the reported cases, 53.5 percent suffer neglect, 22.7 percent are physically abused, 11.5 percent are sexually abused, and the remainder suffer psychological abuse and medical neglect. More than one-quarter of the reported cases suffer more than one type of maltreatment. More than 1,000 children die of abuse and neglect (U.S. Department of Health and Human Services 2007b).

The National Domestic Violence Hotline (1-800-799-SAFE), funded by the federal Violence against Women Act, begins operation.

More than 1,200 battered women's shelters exist in the United States, sponsored by approximately 1,800 domestic violence agencies (National Organization for Women 2007).

It is estimated that almost 450,000 adults over age 60 are abused or neglected in their home. When including self-neglect, this number increases to more than 550,000 (National Center on Elder Abuse 1998).

About 60 percent of all married women living with their husbands work outside the home (U.S. Bureau of Labor Statistics 2007).

Constance Ahrons writes the best-selling book *The Good Divorce.*

2000   The divorce rate per 1,000 of total population is 4.1 (U.S. Census Bureau 2007).

Fatherless homes account for 63 percent of youth suicides, 90 percent of homeless/runaway children, 85 percent of children with behavior problems, 71 percent of high school dropouts, 85 percent of youths in prison, and well over 50 percent of teen mothers (U.S. Census Bureau 2007).

Nate Brazille, a 13-year-old at Lake Worth (Florida) middle school, kills a teacher, Barry Grunow, on the last day of classes (Lieberman 2006).

It is estimated that before the age of 18, one in four children is exposed to family alcoholism or addiction, or alcohol abuse. Children of alcoholics are significantly more likely to initiate drinking during adolescence and to develop alcohol use disorders. Parents' drinking behaviors and favorable attitudes about drinking have been associated with adolescents' initiating and continuing drinking (Grant 2000).

2001   More than half the states enact legislation to combat school bullying. The passage of these acts of legislation is motivated, at least in part, by tragic shootings at several U.S. high schools in the late 1990s and later reports that many perpetrators of school shootings had felt bullied or threatened by peers. Most state laws require or encourage that school officials (typically school boards) develop a policy to prohibit bullying. Research indicates that bullying is prevalent among American school children, directly

2001 involving approximately 30 percent of school children
(cont.) within a school semester (Nansel et al. 2001).

Fifteen-year-old Charles Andrew Williams kills 2 students and wounds 13 others at Santana High School in Santee, California (Lieberman 2006).

More than 50 million people provide care for a chronically ill, disabled, or aged family member or friend during any given year. About 30 percent of family caregivers caring for seniors are themselves age 65 or over; another 15 percent are between the ages of 45 and 54. The typical family caregiver of an elderly family member is a 46-year-old woman caring for her widowed mother who does not live with her. She is married and employed. Approximately 60 percent of family caregivers are women. The need for family caregivers will increase in the years ahead. People over 65 are expected to increase at a 2.3 percent rate, but the number of family members available to care for them will only increase at a 0.8 percent rate (U.S. Department of Health and Human Services 2001).

The National Center on Caregiving is established to advance the development of high-quality, cost-effective programs and policies for caregivers in every state in the United States. The center is sponsored by the Family Caregiver Alliance.

It is estimated that in the United States, nearly 2 million U.S. adolescents attempt suicide, and almost 700,000 receive medical attention for their attempt (American Academy of Child and Adolescent Psychiatry 2008). This year, 2.6 percent of adolescents report making a suicide attempt that has to be treated by a doctor or nurse. Approximately 2,000 youth age 10 to 19 complete suicide. This year, suicide is the third-leading cause of death among young people age 15 to 24, following unintentional injuries and homicide (American Academy of Child and Adolescent Psychiatry 2008).

2002 The average life expectancy in the United States is 76 years. Those retiring at age 62, on average, can expect to spend 15 to 20 years in retirement (U.S. Census Bureau 2007).

2003 The Federal Emergency Management Agency becomes part of the U.S. Department of Homeland Security. Its mission is to reduce the loss of life and property and to protect individuals and families from all hazards, including natural and man-made disasters.

Fourteen-year-old James Sheets shoots and kills the principal of Red Lion Area (Pennsylvania) Middle School in a crowded cafeteria before killing himself (Lieberman 2006).

John Jason McLaughlin, age 15, kills two students at Rocori High School in Cold Spring, Minnesota (Lieberman 2006).

It is believed that between 1 million and 2 million elderly Americans are physically abused, neglected, or exploited by family and/or care providers. Furthermore, for every case of maltreatment or self-neglect reported, approximately five more go unreported (Bonnie and Wallace 2002).

The National Institute on Drug Abuse releases its newly updated publication, *Preventing Drug Use among Children and Adolescents: A Research-Based Guide for Parents, Educators, and Community Leaders, Second Edition,* which reflects NIDA's expanded research program and knowledge base in the area of drug abuse prevention.

The National Center on Elder Abuse (NCEA) is established to provide information, data, and expertise to federal, state, and local agencies, professionals, and the public. It is operated as a partnership among six organizations, with the National Association of State Units on Aging serving as the lead agency. Other partners in NCEA are the National Committee for the Prevention of Elder Abuse; the Clearinghouse on Abuse and Neglect of the Elderly, operated by the College of Human Resources of the University of Delaware; the San Francisco Consortium for

2003
(cont.) Elder Abuse Prevention at the Goldman Institute on Aging; the National Association of Adult Protective Service Administrators; and the Commission on Legal Problems of the Elderly of the American Bar Association (National Center on Elder Abuse 2008).

2004 A total of 2,279,000 Americans get married this year, a rate of 7.8 marriages per 1,000 people. About 43 percent of all first marriages in 2004 end within the first 15 years, 10 percent after 5 years. Seventy-five percent of divorcees remarry, almost half within three years. The median age of those who divorce is as follows: men 30.5, women 29 (U.S. Bureau of the Census 2007).

Desmond Keels, age 16, fatally shoots one student and wounds three others outside Strawberry Mansion High School in Philadelphia (Lieberman 2006).

Florida is hit with four major hurricanes—Charley, Frances, Ivan, and Jeanne—with estimated losses at $22 billion (Federal Emergency Management Agency 2008).

2005 The number of people between the ages of 55 and 64 is estimated to grow by about 11 million between 2005 and 2025, placing a strain on grown children serving as caregivers (U.S. Census Bureau 2007).

Hurricane Katrina unleashes its fury on New Orleans and the Gulf Coast on August 29. At least 1,836 people lose their lives in the subsequent floods, and about 400,000 jobs are lost. One million residents become homeless (Federal Emergency Management Agency 2008).

Sixteen-year-old Jeff Weise kills his grandfather and companion, then arrives at Red Lake (Minnesota) High School and murders a teacher, a security guard, five students, and then himself (Lieberman 2006).

The Centers for Disease Control and Prevention reports that each year 3 million children are reported as suspected victims of child abuse and neglect (Centers for Disease Control and Prevention 2007a).

2006   It is estimated that one out of every seven children will run away before the age of 18. Seventy-five percent of runaways who remain at large for two or more weeks will become involved in theft, drugs, or pornography. Each year, approximately 5,000 runaway and homeless youth die from assault, illness, and suicide (National Runaway Switchboard n.d.).

One in 10 Americans has some form of disability, a figure amounting to about 24 million persons (U.S. Department of Health and Human Services 2007a).

Thirty-two-year-old Carl Charles Roberts IV shoots 10 schoolgirls at West Nickel Mines Amish School (Pennsylvania), the victims ranging in age from 6 to 13, and then himself. Five of the girls and Roberts die (*U.S. News and World Report* 2008).

Teenage suicide rates remain alarmingly high. More than 2 million teenagers attempt to take their lives each year. Suicide remains the third-leading cause of death among young people age 15 to 24 (U.S. Department of Health and Human Services 2007a).

The United States has nearly 1.4 million active military personnel, approximately 369,000 deployed outside the United States and its territories (Global Security 2007).

More than 200 wildfires in a 24-hour period in Texas destroy 15 homes, kill 10,000 cattle and horses, and burn 191,000 acres (Federal Emergency Management Agency 2008).

About 52 percent of men age 62 to 64 are employed, compared with 43 percent in 1995 and 42 percent in 1990 (U.S. Bureau of Labor Statistics 2007). Of men age 65 to 69, 31 percent are employed, compared with 27 percent in 1995 and 26 percent in 1990. Among women 62 to 64 years old, 41 percent are working, compared with 32 percent in 1995

2006   and 28 percent in 1990. Among women 65 to 69 years old,
(*cont.*)   23 percent are working, compared with 17 percent in 1995 and 1990 (Purcell 2006).

2007   Approximately 14 million people in the United States are addicted to alcohol (National Institute of Drug Abuse and Addiction 2007).

The number of unemployed persons reaches 7.1 million; the unemployment rate registers at 4.6. Rates are highest among nonwhite segments of the population (U.S. Bureau of Labor Statistics 2007).

Direct costs (judicial, law enforcement, and health system responses) of child maltreatment are estimated at $24 billion each year. The indirect costs (long-term economic consequences) of child maltreatment exceed an estimated $69 billion annually (Centers for Disease Control and Prevention 2007a).

The U.S. Department of Health and Human Services reports that about one in two elderly 65 years and older has a physical disability (U.S. Department of Health and Human Services 2007a).

Among adults over age 50, more than 1 in 10 is providing care to aging parents (Brody 2006).

It is estimated that more than one-half million children have at least one parent deployed overseas for military duty (Global Security 2007).

Douglas Chanthabouly, age 18, shoots fellow student Samnang Kok, 17, at Henry Foss High School in Tacoma, Washington (*U.S. News and World Report* 2008).

Jay Haley dies in his sleep at his home in San Diego. He is 83. Haley devoted his life to the study of individuals within intimate relationships. A gifted and prolific author, he wrote many of the most significant books and training materials in the field of family therapy.

Following a 25 percent decline in adolescent suicides since the early 1990s, the Centers for Disease Control and Prevention reports that the overall rate of suicide for youth rises 8 percent; the rate stands at 76 percent for preteen and young teen females (Centers for Disease Control and Prevention 2007b).

The deadliest outbreak in school shootings occurs April 16 at Virginia Tech University. Twenty-three-year-old Cho Seung-Hui kills two students in a residence hall then kills 30 more about two hours later in a classroom building. His suicide brings the death toll to 33. Fifteen other students are wounded (*U.S. News and World Report* 2008).

Every day, four women die in the United States as a result of domestic violence, which amounts to approximately 1,400 female deaths a year. The number of women killed by their intimate partners overall amounts to more than the number of soldiers killed during the Vietnam War (National Organization for Women 2007).

2008   Scores of tornadoes tear through Arkansas, Mississippi, Kentucky, and Tennessee, killing 59 people, injuring hundreds, and causing millions of dollars worth of property damage (Federal Emergency Management Agency 2008).

Former student Stephen Kazmierczak opens fire with a shotgun and two handguns from the stage of a lecture hall at Northern Illinois University. He kills five students and injures 16 others before committing suicide (*U.S. News and World Report* 2008).

References

Abbott, P. 2007. *Natural Disasters*, 6th ed. New York: McGraw-Hill.

Al-Anon. 1997. *Paths to Recovery: Al-Anon's Steps, Traditions and Concepts.* New York: Al-Anon Family Group Headquarters.

Alexander, D. 2000. *Confronting Catastrophe: New Perspectives on Natural Disasters*. New York: Oxford University Press.

American Academy of Child and Adolescent Psychiatry. 2008. "Facts for Families #10: Teen Suicide." [Online fact sheet; retrieved 3/4/08.] http://www.aacap.org/publications/factsfam/suicide.htm.

Bonnie, R. J., and R. B. Wallace. 2002. *Elder Mistreatment: Abuse, Neglect and Exploitation in an Aging America*. Washington, DC: National Academies Press.

Brody, E. 2006. *Women in the Middle: Their Parent Care Years*. New York: Springer.

Centers for Disease Control and Prevention. 2007a. "Child Maltreatment: Fact Sheet." [Online fact sheet; retrieved 8/29/07.] http://www.cdc.gov/ncipc/factsheets/cmfacts.htm.

Centers for Disease Control and Prevention. 2007b. "Suicide Prevention." [Online information; retrieved 8/20/07.] http://www.cdc.gov/ncipc/factsheets/suifacts.htm.

Children's Defense Fund. 1995. *Annual Report*. Washington, DC: Children's Defense Fund.

Federal Emergency Management Agency. 2008. "Major Disaster Declarations." [Online information; retrieved 3/1/08.] http://www.fema.gov/news/disasters.fema?year=2008#sev1.

Global Security. 2007. "Where Are the Legions? Global Deployments of U.S. Forces." [Online information; retrieved 8/2/07.] http://www.globalsecurity.org/military/ops/global-deployments.htm.

Grant, B. F. 2000. "Estimates of U.S. Children Exposed to Alcohol Abuse and Dependence in the Family." *American Journal of Public Health* 90 (1): 112–115.

Healthy Families America. 2008. *Promoting Healthy Families in Your Community: 2008 Resource Packet*. Chicago: Healthy Families America.

Hurst, H. 1999. "Family Courts in the United States." *Family Court Bulletin* Volume 1, Issue 1, 1–5.

Lieberman, J. 2006. *The Shooting Game: The Making of School Shooters*. Santa Ana, CA: Seven Locks Press.

Minnesota Board on Aging. 2008. "Timeline to Retirement: Project 2030." [Online report; retrieved 3/3/08.] http://www.dhs.state.mn.us/main/groups/aging/documents/pub/dhs_id_050399.pdf.

Nansel, T. R., M. Overpeck, R. S. Pilla, J. Ruan, B. Simons-Morton, and P. Scheidt. 2001. "Bullying Behaviors among US Youth: Prevalence and Association with Psychosocial Adjustment." *Journal of the American Medical Association* 285:2094–2100.

National Center on Elder Abuse. 1998. "National Elder Abuse Incidence Study." Center for Community and Development. Newark, DE: University of Delaware.

National Center on Elder Abuse. 2008. "NCEA Partners." [Online information; retrieved 8/11/08] http://www.ncea.aoa.gov/NCEAroot/Main_Site/About/Partners.aspx.

National Institute of Drug Abuse and Addiction. 2007. "Understanding Drug Abuse and Addiction." Washington, DC: U.S. Department of Health and Human Services.

National Organization for Women. 2007. "Violence against Women in the United States." [Online information; retrieved 8/28/07.] http://www.now.org/issues/violence/stats.html.

National Runaway Switchboard. n.d. "What to Do when Your Child Returns Home." [Online information; retrieved 8/13/07.] http://www.1800runaway.org/pub_mat/what_to_do.html.

Pruitt, B., and R. Rapoport. 2008. "Looking Backwards to Go Forward: A Timeline of the Work-Family Field in the United States since World War II." [Online report; retrieved 3/2/08.] http://wfnetwork.bc.edu/timelines/other/PRtimeline.pdf.

Purcell, P. 2006. "Older Workers: Employment and Retirement Trends." [Online report; retrieved 9/2/07.] http://www.wmitchell.edu/elderlaw/documents/CRSWorkers0906.pdf.

Robinson, A. G. 2002. *Earthshock: Hurricanes, Volcanoes, Earthquakes, Tornadoes, and Other Forces of Nature.* New York: Thames and Hudson.

U.S. Bureau of Labor Statistics. 2007. *Handbook of Labor Statistics.* Washington, DC: U.S. Government Printing Office.

U.S. Census Bureau. 2007. *Statistical Abstract of the United States,* 126th ed. Washington, DC: U.S. Government Printing Office.

U.S. Department of Health and Human Services. 2001. *Characteristics of Long-Term Care Users.* Rockville, MD: Agency for Healthcare Research and Quality.

U.S. Department of Health and Human Services. 2007a. *Health, United States, 2006.* Hyattsville, MD: National Center for Health Statistics.

U.S. Department of Health and Human Services. 2007b. *America's Children: Key National Indicators of Well-Being, 2007.* Hyattsville, MD: National Center for Health Statistics.

U.S. News and World Report. 2008. "Timeline of School Shootings." March 2, 12–14.

5

Biographical Sketches

Constance R. Ahrons

Constance R. Ahrons is a well-known educator, therapist, and author. She received her PhD in counseling psychology and her master's degree in social work from the University of Wisconsin, Madison. She is professor emerita from the Department of Sociology and former director of the Marriage and Family Therapy Doctoral Training Program at the University of Southern California (USC) in Los Angeles. Ahrons is currently the director of the Divorce and Marriage Consulting Association in San Diego.

Prior to joining the USC faculty, she taught at the University of Wisconsin, Madison. In 2000–2001, she was awarded a fellowship from the Radcliffe Institute for Advanced Study at Harvard University to launch longitudinal research on the effects of a parental divorce on grown children 20 years later. She was also named a senior scholar and founding cochair of the Council on Contemporary Families.

Ahrons is the author of the critically acclaimed books *The Good Divorce: Keeping Your Family Together when Your Marriage Comes Apart* and *We're Still Family: What Grown Children Have to Say about Their Parents' Divorce* (see Chapter 2 of this book). Ahrons is especially well known for her conceptualization of the divorce process and how it impacts the family system. She detailed the family transitions that accompany divorce, including the stages of individual cognition, family metacognition, separation, family reorganization, and family redefinition. For more information on these five stages, the reader is directed to the

137

section titled "Divorce" in Chapter 2 of the current book. Ahrons has received several prestigious awards and has published more than 40 articles in family studies research journals.

Joan Aldous

Joan Aldous is the William R. Kenan, Jr. Professor of Sociology at the University of Notre Dame. She received her PhD from the University of Minnesota in 1963 and is considered an expert in family systems and dynamics, family policy, and intergenerational relationships.

Aldous has received numerous honors and awards for her professional contributions to her discipline. She is past president of the National Council on Family Relations, received the prestigious Ernest W. Burgess Award for her research in the field, and was elected a member of the Council of the American Sociological Association.

Beyond receiving research grants from the National Institute of Mental Health and the National Science Foundation, Aldous has received recognition from the University of Notre Dame for her teaching and writing accomplishments. She is the author of more than 50 published articles as well as two books, including the critically acclaimed *Family Careers: Rethinking the Developmental Perspective*. Aldous has also served with the National Science Foundation and on National Institutes of Health review panels as well as on the Sociology Panel of the Graduate Record Examination for Educational Testing Services.

Paul J. Bohannan (1920–2007)

Paul J. Bohannan is a widely recognized authority on divorce and the many challenges it poses to family systems. Born in 1920 in Lincoln, Nebraska, Bohannan was raised in Indiana, Montana, and Colorado and received his bachelor's degree, then became a Rhodes Scholar at Oxford University. He eventually earned a doctorate in philosophy from Oxford and taught at Princeton University and Northwestern University. He then taught at the University of California at Santa Barbara before finishing a distinguished teaching career at the University of Southern California. Bohannon was recognized as an expert in anthropology, stepfamilies, aging, law, divorce, and American history, among other topics. Bohannon died in 2007 from complications stemming from Alzheimer's disease. He was 87.

His contributions to the study of divorce are particularly relevant to this reference manual. In an effort to better understand the complex dynamics of divorce, Bohannan identified six components or processes of divorce in a landmark book, *Divorce and After* (1970). These components are not sequential and can overlap. Bohannan felt that it is important to understand these processes in order to find order and direction in the emotional chaos that frequently accompanies divorce.

The **emotional divorce** typically begins long before the actual break. It is centered around the deteriorating marriage and the initial motivations for considering a divorce. A wide range of negative feelings and behaviors characterize this component, including betrayals, accusations, and lack of affection and support. Partners usually feel misunderstood, rejected, and disillusioned. In many instances, one or both partners have psychologically departed long before the actual physical separation.

During the **legal divorce**, couples go to court to sever the legal ties of marriage. The legal grounds for obtaining a divorce vary from state to state, so many couples find themselves lost in the shuffle of courtroom proceedings. Many partners never envisioned the many complexities of divorce proceedings or the amount of psychological energy needed to pursue divorce. Although couples typically experience relief once the legal separation is final, many exhibit varying levels of emotional sensitivity throughout the entire period.

The **economic divorce** occurs when couples have to decide how they will divide their money and property. This is no simple task, since complications arise due to tax laws. Legal assistance is usually needed, and couples often experience resentment, anger, and hostility concerning the redistribution of money and property. Bohannan also acknowledges that the economic divorce can prove difficult for two reasons: First, there is never enough money or property to go around, and second, people get attached to certain objects and may need them to support their image of themselves. As a result of these interacting forces, psychological turbulence is to be expected during this divorce component.

The **coparental divorce** focuses on the issue of child custody. The parental responsibility for child rearing and custody is determined by the court on the basis of the children's well-being.

Visitation rights for the parent not awarded custody must be determined. Worry and concern about the effects of divorce on children are frequently expressed during this stage. Bohannan points out that the issues of custody and economic settlement represent the two greatest difficulties couples face. Also, more divorces fail in the coparental aspect than in any other way.

The **community divorce** implies that a divorced person's status in the surrounding neighborhood changes in certain ways. Divorce is viewed differently by people, and separated individuals must learn to adapt to these varying perceptions. Sometimes relationships with friends are altered. Many divorced persons report feelings of isolation and loneliness, while some also feel degrees of social disapproval. To ease such feelings, the social support of friends and family members is often stressed. Some divorced persons regret that divorcing one's spouse involves "divorce" from one's in-laws. Conversely, in-laws may become "out-laws." However, many divorced persons keep in touch with those they now call "the children's relatives."

Finally, the **divorce from dependency** focuses on the importance of divorced parties regaining psychological autonomy. The shift from being in a couple-oriented situation to being a single person requires role realignment and considerable psychological adjustment. Expectedly, those couples who maintained high levels of independence in their marriages are likely to regain autonomy more rapidly than are those marriage partners who were dependent on one another.

Elaine M. Brody

Elaine M. Brody is former associate director of Research at the Philadelphia Geriatric Center and past president of the Gerontological Society of America. She has been a force in gerontological social work research for decades, including landmark research exploring the dynamics and struggles of adult female children caring for their aging parents.

In her critically acclaimed book, *Women in the Middle: Their Parent Care Years*, Brody examines the effects of caregiving on the mental health, careers, and family life of women. Her research disclosed that caregiving has a profound impact on women, who provide the bulk of parent care. Although many female caregivers derive satisfaction from helping a parent, the added responsibilities often create stress, depression, and curtailed employment, as well as conflict within their own families. Brody is credited with raising the consciousness level of executives from large companies all across the nation, who began to realize how caring for aging parents impacts the employee ranks.

Among her many other accomplishments, Brody was a professor of clinical psychiatry at the Medical College of Pennsylvania and adjunct associate professor of social work in psychiatry at the School of Medicine at the University of Pennsylvania. She received an honorary doctorate from the Medical College of Pennsylvania and was elected a Distinguished Scholar of the National Academies of Social Work Practice. In 1985, she received the Brookdale Award of the Gerontological Society of America and, in 1982, received the Distinguished Alumni Award of the University of Pittsburgh School of Social Work.

Brody has also served on editorial boards of many professional journals and on peer review committees at the National Institute of Mental Health, the Administration on Aging, and a number of foundations. She was a member of the Congressional Advisory Panel on Alzheimer's Disease and of the Brookings Institution Advisory Panel on Long Term Care. She has directed nearly two dozen federally financed research studies on subjects such as individualized treatment of mentally impaired aged; mental and physical health practice of older people; women, work, and care of the aged; and marital status, parent care, and mental health. She is in demand as a guest speaker and workshop consultant at universities, foundations, hospitals, and governmental and voluntary agencies. She has also testified many times before committees of the U.S. House of Representatives and the U.S. Senate.

Sarah M. Buel

Sarah M. Buel has devoted her entire professional life to working with battered women, abused children, and juveniles within the legal system. She is a clinical professor at the University of Texas School of Law and codirector of the campus Domestic Violence Clinic. Buel is cofounder of the University of Texas Voices Against Violence program, a service that offers comprehensive, coordinated services for victims of sexual assault, intimate partner violence, and stalking.

Buel has served as special counsel for the Texas District and County Attorneys Association, providing training, technical, and case assistance to prosecutors throughout Texas. For six years she was a prosecutor, most of that time with the Norfolk County District Attorney's Office in Quincy, Massachusetts, helping to establish its award-winning domestic violence and juvenile programs. Previously, Buel served as a victim advocate, state policy coordinator, and legal aid paralegal.

Buel's background is testimony to her drive and determination. As a domestic violence survivor, she committed herself to improving the court and community response to abuse victims. She was a welfare mother for a short time before spending seven years working full time in the day while attending college at night to obtain her undergraduate degree in 1987. She graduated cum laude from Harvard Law School in 1990, where she founded the Harvard Battered Women's Advocacy Project, the Harvard Women in Prison Project, and the Harvard Children and Family Rights Project.

Robert N. Butler

Robert N. Butler is an internationally known gerontologist, author, and consultant. He was born in New York and received a medical degree from Columbia University's College of Physicians and Surgeons in 1953. He has been Brookdale Professor and chairman of the Gerald and May Ellen Ritter Department of Geriatrics and Adult Development of Mount Sinai Medical Center in New York City since 1982. As chairman of the first department of geriatrics in an American medical school, Butler is a leader in improving the quality of life for older people, including caregiving in multigenerational households.

Before he came to Mount Sinai, Butler worked at the National Institutes of Health, where he created the National Institute on Aging in 1976 and served as its first director. Under his leadership, the need for federal funding for research in gerontology gained recognition. He was particularly outspoken about the few service-related research activities available to enhance the health and social service delivery to the elderly in terms of efficiency, cost, and quality. Butler felt that future research on aging has to be unusually inventive and take advantage of a broad range of collaboration in seeking to telescope its natural development.

A prolific writer, Butler won the Pulitzer Prize in 1976 for his book *Why Survive? Being Old in America,* a penetrating social analysis of the elderly in the United States. He is a member of the Institute of Medicine of the National Academy of Sciences and is a founding Fellow of the American Geriatrics Society. Butler has also served as a consultant to the U.S. Senate Special Committee on Aging, the National Institute of Mental Health, the Commonwealth Fund, and numerous other organizations.

Nancy Chandler

Nancy Chandler received her master's degree in social work from the University of Georgia and currently serves as executive director of the National Children's Alliance (NCA), a nonprofit membership organization that represents more than 500 children's advocacy centers throughout the United States. NCA provides training, technical assistance, and networking opportunities to communities seeking to plan, establish, and improve children's advocacy centers. As executive director, Chandler oversees management of NCA's finances, resource development, training, program development, communications, membership services, and staff supervision.

Chandler is a strong advocate of children's rights and the prevention of child maltreatment. She has spoken at more than 300 conferences and workshops throughout the United States. She serves on the National Advisory Committee for Darkness to Light, a primary prevention program aimed at reducing the incidence and consequence of child sexual abuse.

Before moving to Washington, D.C., Chandler served as the executive director of the Memphis Child Advocacy Center, where she was instrumental in formulating plans for the operations of the center, coordinating the work of the multidisciplinary team, fund-raising, and collaborating on the renovation of the center. She is a member of the Academy of Certified Social Workers and the National Association of Social Workers, which named her Tennessee Social Worker of the Year in 1994. Chandler was also a member of Leadership Memphis and a founding board member of the National Network of Children's Advocacy Centers.

Andrew J. Cherlin

Andrew J. Cherlin is a professor in the Sociology Department at Johns Hopkins University. He earned his undergraduate degree from Yale University in 1970 and completed his doctoral studies in sociology at the University of California at Los Angeles in 1976. He is considered an expert in the fields of public policy, family studies, divorce, and remarriage and has published extensively in these areas.

In his 1992 book, *Marriage, Divorce, and Remarriage,* Cherlin provides readers with a comprehensive examination of marriage dissolution, including demographic trends, explanations for divorce rates, consequences of separation, and racial as well as class implications. In *Public and Private Families,* published in 2004, he explores the larger social structures in which family relations are embedded and the activities of private life such as dating, courtship, and cohabitation.

In 1989–1990, Cherlin was chair of the Family Section of the American Sociological Association, and in 1999, he was president of the Population Association of America. Cherlin is a recipient of a MERIT (Method to Extend Research in Time) Award from the National Institutes of Health for his research on the effects of family structure on children.

Milton H. Erickson (1901–1980)

Milton H. Erickson was born in 1901 in Aurum, Nevada. He is considered one of the founders of strategic family therapy, a short-term approach to counseling that emphasizes problem-focused intervention. Erickson was known for his development of pragmatic and flexible therapeutic approaches, as well as helping his clients devise alternative problem-solving strategies. Erickson was also considered one of the leading practitioners of medical hypnosis in the United States.

Erickson completed his undergraduate degree in psychology at the University of Wisconsin and received his medical degree at Colorado General Hospital. Among his appointments, Erickson served as chief psychiatrist at Worcester (Massachusetts) State Hospital, director of psychiatric research at Wayne County General Hospital and Infirmary in Michigan, and professor of psychiatry at Wayne State University and Michigan State University.

Throughout his professional life, Erickson maintained a private practice and spent time researching, consulting, and conducting seminars on strategic family therapy. He was the founding president of the American Society for Clinical Hypnosis as well as the founder and editor of that organization's professional journal. Erickson was also a fellow of both the American Psychiatric Association and the American Psychological Association.

Patricia Fennell

Patricia Fennell is a nationally recognized expert on chronic illnesses, trauma, forensics, and hospice care. Fennell received an undergraduate sociology degree from the College of St. Rose in New York and a graduate degree in social work from the State University of New York at Albany. Her organization, Albany Health Management Associates, treats and examines health care concerns through clinical care, consulting, and professional education utilizing the Fennell Four Phase Treatment (FFPT) approach.

The FFPT model is a multiphased approach that provides a narrative framework and cognitive map for patients and families, helping them describe, understand, and adapt to life with a chronic condition. The model can be summarized as follows:

In Phase One, **Crisis**, the person moves from onset of illness, which may be specifically detectable or may happen gradually, to an emergency period when the patient knows that something is seriously wrong. The task of the individual, caregivers, and clinicians during this phase is to cope with urgency and trauma.

In Phase Two, **Stabilization**, the individual discovers that he or she fails, sometimes repeatedly, to return to normal regardless of interventions or behavior. The task in this phase is to initiate stabilization and life restructuring.

In Phase Three, **Resolution**, the individual recognizes deeply that his or her old life will never return. Early in this phase, most experience profound existential despair. The task of this phase is to begin establishing an authentic new self and start developing a supportive, meaningful philosophy.

In Phase Four, **Integration**, the individual defines a new self in which illness may be an important factor, but it is not the only or even the primary one in his or her life. Integration of the illness into a meaningful life is the goal the individual seeks.

The FFPT model is regarded as a highly practical, internationally utilized, and empirically validated treatment model that recognizes the influences of cultural, psychosocial, and physical factors in both assessment and treatment. It addresses the complexity of chronic conditions by matching best medical practices to the model's four phases. By intervening with therapies suited to the patient's or family's current phase, health care providers can help families break out of patterns of repeated crises that usually require more extensive resources in response.

Fennell frequently lectures and consults on chronic illness issues with health care organizations, including the Centers for Disease Control and Prevention, U.S. Department of Health and Human Services, Fortune 150 organizations, and patient advocacy groups. Her research affiliations include Cornell University, Ithaca, New York; Vrije Universiteit, Brussels, Belgium; New Castle, Australia Research Consortium; DePaul University, Chicago; and Capital Region Sleep Center, Albany, New York. She is the author of numerous research and lay press articles, as well as the recent books *The Chronic Illness Workbook: Strategies and Solutions for Taking Back Your Life* and *Managing.*

Charles Figley

Charles Figley is one of the world's foremost authorities on the topics of stress and crises. He is director of the Florida State University Traumatology Institute. He is also a Fulbright Fellow and professor in the College of Social Work at Florida State University. Figley is formerly professor of Family Therapy and Psychology at Purdue University. He received his doctoral degree from Pennsylvania State University and his undergraduate degree from the University of Hawaii.

Figley has written more than 200 scholarly works, including 19 books and scores of articles for research journals. Among his book titles are *Mapping the Wake of Trauma, Burnout in Families,* and *Helping Traumatized Families.* He has also served as editor of a number of research publications, including the *Journal of Traumatic Stress, Innovations in Psychology, Traumatology: The International Journal,* and the Psychosocial Stress Book Series. Most of Figley's research has been guided by and contributes to theories and interventions that are evidence based and that prevent, limit, or eliminate unwanted stress and crises.

For years, Figley has been committed to applying his research and expertise toward solving human problems. Many of his efforts have been through the collective efforts of the international humanitarian organization the Green Cross, which he helped establish following the Oklahoma City bombing in 1995. Also, in response to the growing tensions in the Middle East and the deployment of thousands of troops to that region, he organized an emergency meeting of military mental health professionals shortly after the start of the Middle East crisis in 1990. He organized similar workshops and training conferences in 1991. Additionally, in response to the Columbine High School shooting in 1999, Figley provided extensive consultation to the state of Colorado, including a series of articles in helping mental health providers cope.

Figley has been elected to the highest level, fellow, in six professional organizations: the American Psychological Association, the American Psychological Society, the American Association for the Advancement of Psychology, the American Association for Marriage and Family Therapy, the American Orthopsychiatric Association, and the Society for the Psychological Study of Social Issues. He has presented keynote addresses nationally and internationally.

Figley has received dozens of awards throughout his long career, perhaps the most gratifying of which was his selection by the leading traumatology organization in the world, the International Society for Traumatic Stress Studies, as its final winner of its coveted Pioneer Award. The award recognizes traumatologists whose lifetime achievement substantially advanced the field. The American Psychological Association named Professor Figley Family Psychologist of the Year in 1997. A year prior, the Florida State University School of Social Work's student body named him Professor of the Year. In 2005, Figley received the Lifetime Achievement Award by the International Critical Incident Stress Foundation.

James L. Framo (1922–2001)

James L. Framo was a notable contributor to the fields of psychology and family therapy. He received his bachelor's and master's degrees from Pennsylvania State University and his doctoral degree from the University of Texas. He was a professor of psychology at

Alliant International University in San Diego and also taught at Temple University in Philadelphia. Framo had a long and distinguished career and was highly respected for his many contributions to the field, including a number of critically acclaimed books and research articles. He died from a stroke in 2001 at the age of 79.

Framo was a founding member and former president of the American Family Therapy Association and was recognized as an early proponent of family-of-origin therapy. Much of his writing focused on that approach, explaining the rationale for involving the patient's family of origin in helping to resolve psychological issues. Among his more prominent book titles are *Family Interaction: A Dialogue between Family Researchers and Family Therapists; Family Therapy: Major Contributions; Explorations in Marital and Family Therapy: Selected Papers of James L. Framo; Family-of-Origin Therapy: An Intergenerational Approach;* and *Coming Home Again: A Family of Origin Consultation.*

Among Framo's other achievements, he was a founder of the American Family Therapy Academy (AFTA), served as its second president, and received the AFTA Distinguished Achievement Award in 1984. He also served as president of the Family Institute of Philadelphia and was a fellow in both the American Association for Marriage and Family Therapy and the American Psychological Association. He served in an editorial capacity for several important research journals, including *Family Process,* the *Journal of Sex and Marital Therapy,* and the *Journal of Divorce and Remarriage.* Framo conducted hundreds of professional workshops around the United States, as well as in Canada, Mexico, Italy, Switzerland, Germany, Denmark, Ireland, Israel, Australia, the former Soviet Union, and Central Asia.

Frank F. Furstenberg Jr.

Frank F. Furstenberg Jr. is a widely recognized authority in the field of family studies research. He is the Zellerbach Family Professor of Sociology and a research associate in the Population Studies Center at the University of Pennsylvania. Furstenberg completed his undergraduate degree at Haverford College in Pennsylvania in 1961 and earned his doctoral degree in 1967 from Columbia University.

Furstenberg has published numerous books and research articles on divorce, remarriage, and stepparenting. Among his more notable books are *Divided Families: What Happens to Children When Parents Part, Adolescent Mothers in Later Life,* and *Teenage Sexuality, Pregnancy and Childbearing.*

His current research projects focus on the family in the context of disadvantaged urban neighborhoods, adolescent sexual behavior, cross-national research on children's well-being, urban education, and the transition from adolescence to adulthood. He is the chair of the MacArthur Foundation Research Network on the Transition to Adulthood. In October 1966, he was made a member of the Institute of Medicine of the National Academy of Science.

Richard J. Gelles

Richard J. Gelles is an internationally known expert on domestic violence. He is currently chair of the Child Welfare and Family Violence Program in the School of Social Work at the University of Pennsylvania. Gelles received his undergraduate degree from Bates College (1968), a master's degree in sociology from the University of Rochester (1971), and a PhD in sociology from the University of New Hampshire (1973).

Gelles is the author or coauthor of 21 books and more than 100 articles and chapters on family violence. His 1997 book *Intimate Violence in Families* paints a sobering portrait of hidden victims of familial violence—siblings, parents, and the elderly—as well as an examination of violence within gay and lesbian couples. He also explores emotional and psychological abuse, sexual abuse, neglect, and abandonment. Gelles informs readers what is known about intervention and treatment program effectiveness, with special attention to intensive family preservation programs and men's treatment programs. In an earlier book, *International Perspectives on Family Violence,* Gelles offers a worldview of domestic abuse, in the process offering convincing evidence that battering is a universal social problem.

Gelles is a member of the National Academy of Science's Panel on Assessing Family Violence Interventions. He also served as vice president for publications for the National Council on Family Relations. From 1973 to 1981, Gelles edited the journal *Teaching Sociology* and earned the Outstanding Contributions to Teaching Award in 1979 from the American Sociological Association. Gelles has presented innumerable lectures to family studies organizations and policy-making and media groups.

Ann M. Goetting

Ann M. Goetting is a professor of sociology at Western Kentucky University. She received her doctoral degree from Western Michigan University, and her teaching specialties are family systems, divorce and remarriage, family violence, and gender issues. She has coedited one book, *Individual Voices, Collective Visions: Fifty Years of Women in Sociology*, with Sarah Fenstermaker, and authored two more, *Homicide in Families and Other Special Populations* and *Getting Out: Life Stories of Women Who Left Abusive Men*. Currently, Goetting is executive editor of *Humanity & Society*, the journal of the Association for Humanist Sociology. Beyond her research pursuits, Goetting serves as an expert witness for battered women who kill abusers in self-defense and for those who have lost child custody to their batterers.

One of Goetting's more interesting contributions to the literature has been her reformulation of Paul Bohannan's components and processes of the divorce experience (readers are directed back to the biography of Bohannan and his analysis of the different sides to marital dissolution). Goetting reformulated Bohannan's divorce components and fashioned six processes of remarriage. She feels that each of these components requires adaptation and adjustment. As with Bohannan's conceptualization, these components may not occur to all remarried people with the same intensity or in the same order.

The **emotional remarriage** involves the reinvestment of emotions in a relationship so that comfort and love can be secured. This may be fear provoking for some, since loss and rejection loom as distinct possibilities. Obviously, failure can lead to disappointment as well as damage to one's identity and self-concept.

The **legal remarriage** involves the legal complexities associated with the new lifestyle. Beyond the child support, alimony, and property division that were associated with one's first marriage, other legal ramifications await remarrieds. For example, it must be determined which spouse—past or present—legally deserves the life and accident insurance inheritance, medical coverage, or pension rights. For that matter, one's financial obligations to children from a previous marriage, such as support for a college education, also need to be determined. As one can see, the new marriage can often create legal complications, particularly when the former marriage is considered.

The **economic remarriage** is the reestablishment of a marital household as a unit of economic productivity and consumption. The existence of children from a former marriage often complicates matters and creates financial instability. The remarriage also creates the problem of resource distribution, in other words, how the household's money is to be spent and who gets how much of what is available.

The **coparental remarriage** occurs if children are involved, either from one side of the marriage or both. The process of combining children to form a new, blended family is a formidable task in scope. To be sure, a number of adjustments and adaptations loom important: Brothers and sisters may have been separated, relationships with grandparents may have been severed, or alienation from friends and a familiar community may have occurred. Families differ in the time it takes them to adjust, as adults form new and meaningful relationships while children are faced with adjusting to a new home, a new school, new friends, or separation from a parent.

The **community remarriage** involves reentry into the world of couples. In the process, unmarried friends, especially those of the opposite sex, may be lost for lack of a common lifestyle. Married life is often intolerant of relationships with former friends and is thus an obstacle that has to be faced.

The **remarriage from independency** entails changing one's conjugal identity from individual to couple. This means giving up the personal freedom and independence established for the previous divorce and adjusting to a lifestyle in which a partner is expected to be an involved, intimate partner.

Bernard Guerney Jr. and Louise Guerney

Bernard Guerney Jr., PhD, and Louise Guerney, PhD, are internationally recognized as two of the most prominent and innovative practitioners of marital and family therapy in the United States. Experts in a systems approach to family disequilibrium, the husband and wife have made numerous contributions in writing, teaching, and practicing individual, marital, and group counseling. Both received their master's and doctoral degrees at Pennsylvania State University.

Bernard Guerney Jr. is professor emeritus of counseling psychology and of human development and family studies at

Pennsylvania State University, where he founded and directed the Individual and Family Consultation Center. He is also adjunct professor of psychology and family studies at the University of Maryland. He founded and directs the National Institute of Relationship Enhancement in Bethesda, Maryland. Bernard Guerney is approved as a therapist-supervisor by the American Association for Marriage and Family Therapy and has produced scores of articles and book chapters; four books; and numerous training manuals, audiotapes, and videotapes.

Louise Guerney is a licensed psychologist with a concentration in clinical child psychology. She is also a registered play therapist supervisor and past chairman of the Board of Directors of the International Association for Play Therapy. Together with her husband, Louise Guerney is recognized as the creator of filial family therapy, a unique family intervention model that teaches parents how to become the primary therapeutic agents for their children through the medium of play therapy. Louise Guerney is also a fellow of the American Psychological Association (APA) and of the Maryland Psychological Association. She is a faculty member of the National Institute of Relationship Enhancement in Bethesda, Maryland, where she conducts training programs for professionals in play and filial therapies and parent education leadership. She is an editor of the *International Journal of Play Therapy* and *The Family Journal.* Dr. Guerney is professor emeritus at Pennsylvania State University and for 23 years was head of the parent-child programs at Penn State's Individual and Family Consultation Center. She has published manuals for parents and parent educators for these programs and has coauthored the book *Helping Your Child.*

For their work in family therapy, the Guerneys have received a number of national awards and recognitions. Bernard Guerney is a fellow in four APA divisions: clinical psychology, counseling and psychotherapy, behavioral medicine, and marital/family therapy; and a certified group therapist. Louise Guerney received the 1988 Marriage and Family Therapy Award for Contributions to the Field of Marriage and Family Therapy, awarded by the Family Therapy Section of the National Conference of Family Relations, and together with her husband was awarded the 1983 Mace Medal for Contributions to Marital Enrichment, awarded by the Association for Couple and Marital Enrichment.

Jay Haley (1923–2007)

Jay Haley was a well-known family therapist, teacher, and author. Haley held degrees from the University of California at Los Angeles, the University of California at Berkeley, and Stanford University. He was one of the founders of family therapy, having earned that distinction with Don Jackson and other notable therapists at the Mental Research Institute in Palo Alto, California, in 1958. Haley promoted strategic therapy, which places an emphasis on short-term, focused efforts to solve specific problems.

In addition to his work at the Mental Research Institute, Haley served as director of family therapy research at the Philadelphia Child Guidance Clinic and was a consultant to the Family Committee Group for the Advancement of Psychiatry. He also served as editor of the research journal *Family Process*. Haley taught at the University of Maryland, Howard University, and the University of Pennsylvania.

Haley regularly conducted workshops and seminars on family therapy. He also authored numerous books, including *Strategies of Psychotherapy, Problem-solving Therapy, Ordeal Therapy,* and *Learning and Teaching Therapy.*

E. Mavis Hetherington

E. Mavis Hetherington was a professor of psychology for many years at the University of Virginia and retired in 1999. She obtained her PhD in psychology at the University of California at Berkeley. Hetherington is a past president of the Developmental Psychology Division of the American Psychological Association and of the Society for Research in Child Development in Adolescence. She has authored and edited many books in the areas of child and adolescent development and has contributed dozens of articles to professional research journals.

Hetherington is well known for her work on the effects of divorce, one-parent families, and remarriage on children's development. Her book *For Better or for Worse: Divorce Reconsidered* provides readers with an in-depth investigation of marital dissolution and its effects on children. The book summarizes findings from the Virginia Longitudinal Study of Divorce, which analyzed how children and their families adapted to divorce over the course of time. Hetherington's longitudinal study followed an initial group of 72 children of divorce and their families as they began remarrying; becoming stepparents; and, in some cases, getting divorced once again. In all, Hetherington tracked more than 1,400 individuals over the course of 30 years.

From her long-term perspective, Hetherington identifies distinct pathways into and out of divorce. She identifies the kinds of marriages that predispose a couple to divorce and others that do not. She also pinpoints "windows of change" that allow some people to transform the challenges of divorce into an opportunity. As Hetherington follows families through the life process of divorce, she shows how women and girls experience divorce differently from men and boys; why single mother–son relationships and stepfather-daughter relationships are often difficult; why divorce presents a greater risk to adolescent children; and how mentoring and authoritative parenting can provide the needed buffering against the negative effects of divorce.

This captivating look at the underlying dynamics of America's divorce-prone society is a valuable reference. Hetherington shows that while some barely survive divorce's effects, others actually thrive. She offers readers an important first step in recognizing the obstacles likely to be encountered and the choices to be made, so that the pathway out of divorce need not be a prescribed path of dissolution but one of healing and ultimate fulfillment.

Reuben Hill (1912–1985)

Reuben Hill is recognized as one of the pioneers of family studies and the creator of the widely referenced ABCX family stress model. Hill received his bachelor's degree from Utah State University and his doctorate from the University of Wisconsin. He joined the faculty at the University of Minnesota in 1957, at which time he launched the Minnesota Family Studies Center. In 1976, he was named Regents Professor and retired from the university in 1983 as an emeritus professor. He was also a visiting Fulbright scholar at the Institute of Sociology and Psychology at the University of Oslo in 1985.

Over the span of his career, Hill penned 20 books and more than 150 articles on various aspects of family dynamics. He placed a particular emphasis on a family development perspective, constantly exploring ways to make it more systematic, cumulative, and applied. The interplay between a developmental perspective and family therapy was of particular interest to Hill. He was also influential in the development of the research journal *Family Process*. He was a member of its board of directors between 1977 and 1983, was an advisory editor since 1964, and remained a valuable consultant throughout his professional career.

His book *Families under Stress* (1949) is considered a classic in the field and groundbreaking in its detailed explanation of family stress and disequilibrium. In it, he expounds upon a new theory of family crisis, which he dubs the ABCX model. The model grew out of Hill's observations of deployed military families, most notably the reactions of wives and children when their loved ones left to fight in World War II. He was intrigued by how some families adjusted well while others experienced intense disequilibrium. The ABCX model was Hill's effort to explain such reactions: the stressor (A), resources (B), family definition of the stressor (C), and the actual crisis (X). Hill argued that examining each component enables clinicians to analyze the stressful event, the family supports available, and the outcome (Chapter 1 of this book contains a detailed explanation of the ABCX model).

Hill received many awards in recognition of his contributions to the field, including the Regents Professorship; the first Burgess Award given by the National Council on Family Relations (NCFR); and the Reuben Hill Research Award, which is given annually in his name by NCFR for the best research or theory paper in the family field.

Don Jackson (1920–1968)

Don Jackson was one of the early contributors to the field of family therapy. He graduated from Stanford University's School of Medicine in 1943 and launched a career that spanned teaching, therapy, and research. Many leaders in the field of family therapy acknowledge Jackson as a major contributor to the understanding of family dynamics and therapeutic intervention. More specifically, Jackson was instrumental in developing interactional family therapy, which emphasizes that the key to understanding family members is to focus on their present-day behaviors, not past influences.

Before his untimely death in 1968 at the age of 48, Jackson published more than 125 articles and book chapters and seven books. Two of the titles he coauthored, *Mirages of Marriage* and *Human Communication,* are regarded as classic family therapy textbooks. Additionally, he cofounded the journal *Family Process* with colleagues Jay Haley and Nathan Ackerman. He also helped to launch the national publishing firm Science and Behavior Books.

In 1958, Jackson helped to establish the Mental Research Institute in Palo Alto, California, and worked with such notable therapists as Jay Haley and Virginia Satir. Among his many honors and awards, Jackson won the Frieda Fromm-Reichmann Award for contributions to understanding schizophrenia, the Edward R. Strecker Award for contributions to in-patient treatment of hospitalized patients, and a special citation from the American Psychiatric Association.

Hamilton McCubbin

Hamilton McCubbin is chief executive officer of the Kamehameha Schools system in Hawaii. Prior to this position, McCubbin was dean of the School of Human Ecology at the University of Wisconsin at Madison (UWM). McCubbin received undergraduate and graduate degrees from (UWM). He received his doctoral degree in 1970 and then pursued postdoctoral studies at Yale University, the University of Minnesota, and Stanford University, where he was an Andrew Mellon Fellow.

Included among his professional and academic administrative appointments are professor of Child and Family Studies and director of the Family Stress, Coping and Health Project, both with the School of Human Ecology at UWM; assistant director of the Agricultural Experiment Station, College of Agriculture and Life Science, UWM; director for the Center for Excellence in Family Studies, UWM; and director of the Institute for the Study of Resiliency in Families at UWM.

An internationally recognized authority in child and family studies with more than 100 published professional articles and 25 books, he is particularly well known as one of the creators of the Double ABCX model of family crisis. Building from the earlier work of Hill's ABCX model, McCubbin and fellow researcher Joan Patterson proposed four components: the pileup of family demands (aA), family adaptive resources (bB), family definition and meaning (cC), and family adaptation balancing (xX). The Double ABCX model contains what can be called a feedback loop; the outcome of one component feeds into the next component. For instance, if a family is faced with repeated stressors but has good supports and a positive interpretation, a sense of confidence is nurtured. The family uses this confidence to handle new stressors, which is termed *bonadaptation*. Should this not be the case and the family suffers from inadequate support and negative interpretation, maladaptation occurs.

McCubbin has served as an administrator or advisory board director to institutions such as the State of Wisconsin Council on Human Concerns and Services; the National Parenting Association; the Kuwait International Advisory Committee for the Government of Kuwait; the University of the United Arab Emirates; and the Drug and Alcohol Rehabilitation Program at the Presidio in San Francisco.

Virginia Satir (1916–1988)

Virginia Satir is recognized as one of the pioneers of family therapy. She believed that the family unit was an integral force in the growth and development of its members. Because individuals are constantly changing and evolving, the family must create optimal levels of functioning. She was particularly interested in improving patterns of family communication and problem-solving strategies.

Satir attended graduate school at the University of Chicago. Early in her career she worked with families at the Dallas Child Guidance Center and later at the Illinois State Psychiatric Institute. In 1959, Satir was invited to join Don Jackson and a team of therapists to launch the Mental Research Institute in Palo Alto, California. The Mental Research Institute would become the first formal program in family therapy in the United States.

Satir's first book, *Conjoint Family Therapy,* was published in 1964 and is considered a classic in the field. She has written many other books, including *Peoplemaking* in 1972 and *The New Peoplemaking* in 1988. Satir is also the author of many articles and conducted workshops and training seminars on the topic of family therapy. She remained involved in the family therapy movement for almost 50 years. She died in 1988 from pancreatic cancer.

Gregory A. Thomas

Gregory A. Thomas is deputy director of Planning and Response in the National Center for Disaster Preparedness at the Columbia University Mailman School of Public Health. Thomas assists communities and schools around the United States in the assessment and improvement of their current levels of emergency preparedness. Prior to his position with Columbia University, he served as the executive director of the Office of School Safety and Planning with the New York City Department of Education. As the senior law enforcement/security official there, he worked closely with federal, state, and local officials to address security- and disaster-related issues that arose for the many schools in the Lower Manhattan area affected by the terrorist attacks of September 11, 2001. Thomas attended college at the University of Maryland, Eastern Shore, where he received his bachelor of arts degree in sociology, and the Brooklyn campus of Long Island University, where he received his master of science degree in criminal justice.

Thomas is the author of the 2005 book *Freedom from Fear: A Guide to Safety, Preparedness, and the Threat of Terrorism.* The book provides an overview of the history of terrorism, puts the current global situation into perspective, and offers a wealth of advice on how to cope during all kinds of disasters and emergencies. The book addresses common fears about terrorism and offers suggestions on how to reduce anxiety about potential attacks, such as airplane hijacking and dirty bombs. It also outlines how to set up emergency plans for the office and at home and explains how to speak to children about terrorism and violence. Thomas advocates that readers prepare for natural disasters that may occur in their communities, including natural disasters such as hurricanes and tornadoes.

Thomas's professional affiliations include membership in the National Organization of Black Law Enforcement Executives, the largest organization of minority criminal justice officials in the United States; the Commission on Accreditation for Law Enforcement Agencies, where he served as an assessor of police departments and law enforcement agencies across the United States; and the professional advisory board of the National Center for School Crisis and Bereavement, based at Cincinnati Children's Hospital. Thomas also serves on the board of directors of the Hope Program, an award-winning New York City–based program that helps impoverished New Yorkers find and keep jobs.

In recognition of his professional and civic accomplishments, Thomas received the Thurgood Marshall Scholarship Fund Awards for Outstanding Community Service and Outstanding Board Leadership and a distinguished alumni citation from the National Association for Equal Opportunity in Higher Education. He is the first recipient of the Outstanding Young Alumnus Award from the University of Maryland, Eastern Shore.

Judith S. Wallerstein

Judith S. Wallerstein is considered one of the world's foremost authorities on the effects of divorce on children. Wallerstein attended Columbia University, attended the Topeka Institute for Psychoanalysis, and received her PhD in psychology from Lund University in Sweden. She is the founder and executive director of the Judith Wallerstein Center for the Family in Transition in Marin County, California. The Wallerstein Center conducts research and provides education and counseling for separated, divorced, and remarried families. Wallerstein has also taught at the School of Social Welfare and the School of Law at the University of California at Berkeley as well as at the University of Kansas and the Menninger School of Psychiatry.

Wallerstein is best known for her longitudinal research focusing on the long-term effects of divorce on children, which she translated into several successful books. Her 1996 book *Surviving the Breakup: How Children and Parents Cope with Divorce* grew out of her California Children of Divorce Study, launched in 1971. At that time, Wallerstein began studying a group of 131 children whose parents were all going through a divorce. She tracked the youngsters from childhood through their adolescent struggles and into adulthood. Her book *Second Chances: Men, Women and Children a Decade after Divorce* comprised the 10- and 15-year follow-up reports on her research.

Her book *The Unexpected Legacy of Divorce: A 25-Year Landmark Study* describes the feelings, expectations, and memories of divorce that these youngsters carried into adulthood and brought into their own intimate relationships. Using a comparison group of adults who grew up in the same communities, Wallerstein shares how adult children of divorce essentially view life differently from those who did not experience divorce as children. Wallerstein contends that for children of divorce, every life stage presents unique reminders and manifestations of earlier marital dissolution. Even in adulthood, the divorce experienced in childhood affects personality, the ability to trust, and the ability to cope with change.

Wallerstein also coauthored *The Good Marriage: How and Why Love Lasts*, based on her research examining 50 stable and fulfilling marriages between 1990 and 1991. Wallerstein describes what she considers the four basic types of marriage: romantic, rescue, companionate, and traditional. She identifies the stages through which a marriage evolves and explains the nine psychological tasks—including separating from the family of origin and making a safe place for conflict—that must be undertaken by anyone committed to building a good marriage.

Glen W. White

Glen W. White is the director of the Research and Training Center on Independent Living at the University of Kansas and the Research and Training Center on Measurement and Interdependence in Community Living. White earned his master's degree from Winona State University and his doctorate from the University of Kansas.

Past president of the National Association of Rehabilitation Research and Training Centers and past president of the American Public Health Association's Disability Forum, White is currently a professor in the Department of Applied Behavioral Science at the University of Kansas and conducts teaching and research in the areas of behavioral and community psychology and disability studies. He also has a joint academic appointment with the University of Kansas Medical School Department of Preventive Medicine.

White has a strong interest in conducting research and training activities in the areas of full community participation, disaster preparation and emergency response for people with disabilities and advocacy, and has been working with disability organizations in Peru and Vietnam. For the past several years, he also has been developing a systematic line of research in the areas of health promotion and prevention of secondary conditions.

A Phi Beta Delta inductee for international scholarly achievement, White has had several national appointments, including serving on the Centers for Disease Control and Prevention's National Center on Environment and Health National Advisory Committee and as a board member of the 21-member Commission on National and Community Service (since renamed the Corporation for National and Community Service), serving under U.S. presidents George H. W. Bush and Bill Clinton.

William Wilson (1895–1971) and Robert Smith (1879–1950)

William Wilson and Robert Smith are recognized as cofounders of Alcoholics Anonymous (AA), a worldwide organization that provides assistance to individuals struggling with alcohol addiction. Alcoholics Anonymous offers the problem drinker a way to live a full and satisfying life without the use of alcohol. The purpose of AA is for alcoholics to stay sober and help other alcoholics achieve sobriety.

Alcoholics Anonymous was founded in 1935. Wilson and Smith, both problem drinkers, saw alcoholism as a physical and spiritual disease and vowed to provide supportive guidance to alcoholics. Their belief and experience provided the basis for AA and, most important, the concept of the "Twelve Step" program, guidelines used to overcome addictive or dysfunctional behaviors. This program grew with the formation of autonomous groups, first in the United States and then around the world. Today, more than 1,000 AA groups are active worldwide. The Twelve-Step program has also generated successful programs for eating disorders, gambling, narcotics, and sex addiction as well as for people affected by others' addictions.

Devising a plan to help millions of people, Bill Wilson, a stockbroker, and Bob Smith, a surgeon, experienced little success at first. However, the Twelve-Step concept eventually caught on, culminating in a book that captured the mission of the program, causing AA's membership to mushroom. This publication, called *Alcoholics Anonymous*, was released April 10, 1939. Still in circulation, the book contains inspiration and insight into the steps needed to overcome alcoholism. Among the steps is the member's admittance of the problem, regular attendance at meetings, the member's right to anonymity, and a commitment to abstinence. A pivotal feature of AA's philosophy is the support members give each other. Members establish regular contact with a sponsor for support purposes.

Of particular relevance to this book was the founding of Al-Anon in the 1950s by Lois Wilson, wife of Bill Wilson. Al-Anon was adapted from Alcoholics Anonymous and is a Twelve-Step program for relatives and friends of problem drinkers. Members share their experience, strength, and hope in order to solve their common problems. They believe that alcoholism is a family illness and that changed attitudes can aid recovery. Al-Anon is not allied with any sect, denomination, political entity, organization, or institution; does not engage in any controversy; and neither endorses nor opposes any cause. There are no dues for membership.

In 1957, Alateen was formed in California by a teenage son of AA/Al-Anon parents. As the name implies, Alateen is a youth/young adult program of Al-Anon. The program follows many of the same steps as its parental organization, yet is more geared to teenagers and children. These traditions include the Twelve Steps and the concept of supportive assistance from the membership. There are no dues or fees required for attendance, and the only requirement for membership is that a problem of alcoholism exists in a relative or friend. Today, Al-Anon serves more than 33,000 groups in 112 countries, including 4,000 Alateen groups. Al-Anon membership worldwide is estimated at 600,000.

6

Data and Documents

Introduction

This chapter provides readers with a statistical portrait of family stress and crises. Americans are a very curious people, as the statistical graphics, surveys, studies, and opinion polls that the media continually bombard us with suggest. The fact that so much of this research is concerned with marriage and family life—including its ups and downs—is understandable if we look closely at our culture. As we have seen in previous chapters, family life has always been an integral and important part of our lives, and whatever turbulence comes our way invariably piques our attention. Exploring the many sides to family life is part of our nature, embracing us in some fashion from birth until death and, as this volume has shown, presenting us with a wide assortment of problems and challenges to explore.

Regardless of the discipline, to learn about something, we must have valid and reliable information. That is the goal of the statistical portraits contained in this chapter: to provide accurate, meaningful, and reliable information to the general public, as well as to others who are engaged in such fields as research, education, and therapy. Statistical portraits can help us see data related to family stress and crises clearly and systematically, which in turn promotes careful, critical, and systematic thinking. On a practical level, research in family stress and crises can help us make informed decisions about our behavior, allow us to compare our behaviors and attitudes with those of other people, and enable us to better understand the complexities of family stress and crisis.

Researchers gather data and graphically convey their findings in many different ways. In the pages that follow, a wide assortment of graphics is presented that consists of tables, which usually show quantitative data, as well as figures, which often consist of charts or graphs. All of the graphics included in this chapter have been carefully selected to accompany important sections of the book, such as material related to addiction, domestic violence, school shootings, and chronic illness.

In addition to complementing important textual material, the statistical portraits in this chapter are used to summarize key points or provide a visual display when words alone cannot adequately describe a concept. The graphics thus serve to offer a variation of text material, in the process providing readers with ways to better understand important concepts and visual aids to better remember them.

Many of the tables and figures in this chapter represent displays of demographics, or population trends, as they relate to family crisis issues. The statistical portraits are drawn from government sources, such as the U.S. Department of Health and Human Services, the Centers for Disease Control and Prevention, the Population Reference Bureau, and the Bureau of Justice Statistics. All sources provide timely and insightful information regarding the focus of this volume.

The data in this chapter follow the progression of topics covered in Chapters 2 and 3 of this book. The most available data are aligned with most of the topics presented in these two chapters: addiction, unemployment, divorce, chronic illness and disease, caring for aging family members, domestic violence, school violence, natural disasters, deployed military families, and adolescent suicide.

Addiction

The National Survey on Drug Use and Health (NSDUH) is the primary source of statistical information on the use of illegal drugs by the American population. NSDUH is a division of the Department of Health and Human Services. Conducted by the federal government since 1971, the survey collects data annually by administering questionnaires to a representative sample of the population through face-to-face interviews at the respondent's place of residence. The survey is an excellent source of information on the use of illicit drugs and the nonmedical use of lawful drugs, as well as alcohol and tobacco products. The sample consists of civilian, noninstitutionalized persons in the United States age 12 years or older (U.S. Department of Health and Human Services 2006a).

Overall, the survey revealed that approximately 22.6 million persons (9.2 percent of the population age 12 and older) may have had either substance abuse or dependency problems in the past year. Of this total, 3.2 million were dependent on or abused both alcohol and illicit drugs; 3.8 million were dependent on or abused illicit drugs but not alcohol; and 15.6 million were dependent on or abused alcohol but not illicit drugs. Marijuana was the most commonly used illicit drug (14.8 million), followed by illicit drugs other than marijuana (9.6 million). Particularly disturbing was the increased misuse of prescription drugs. For example, nonmedical use of prescription drugs among young adults increased from 5.4 percent in 2002 to 6.4 percent in 2006, due largely to an increase in the nonmedical use of pain relievers.

Figure 6.1 shows how many people (in millions) used illicit drugs in the past month, as well as the specific illicit drugs (marijuana, illicit drugs other than marijuana, psychotherapeutics, pain relievers, cocaine, tranquilizers, stimulants, hallucinogens, inhalants, methamphetamine, crack, Ecstasy, sedatives, heroin, OxyContin, LSD, and PCP). Note that some illicit drugs carry a footnote marker (indicated with a 1 following the category). This is because estimates for methamphetamine use incorporate data from new survey questions added in 2005 and 2006 that are not included in estimates for use of illicit drugs other than marijuana, use of psychotherapeutics, or stimulant use.

Among the more positive findings, current illicit drug use has declined among America's adolescents. The reader is directed to Figure 6.2, where a bar graph displays the respondents' age in years and the percentage using illicit drugs in the past month. Note that for each age group, there are bars representing 2002, 2003, 2004, 2005, and 2006. Among adolescents between the ages of 12 and 17, the percentage using illicit drugs in the past month was 11.6 percent in 2002, 11.2 percent in 2003, 10.6 percent in 2004, 9.9 percent in 2005, and 9.8 percent in 2006. Among young adults age 18 to 25, the percentage using illicit drugs in the past month was 20.2 percent in 2002, 20.3 percent in 2003, 19.4 percent in 2004, 20.1 percent in 2005, and 19.8 percent in 2006. Among adults age 26 or older, the percentage using illicit drugs in the past month

FIGURE 6.1
Use of Specific Illicit Drugs during Past Month among Persons Age 12 or Older, 2006

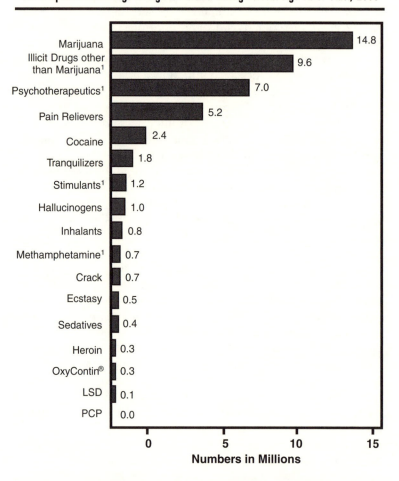

Source: U.S. Department of Health and Human Services. 2006a. *Results from the 2006 National Survey on Drug Use and Health: National Findings.* Office of Applied Studies. Washington, DC: U.S. Government Printing Office.

was 5.8 percent in 2002, 5.6 percent in 2003, 5.5 percent in 2004, 5.8 percent in 2005, and 6.1 percent in 2006.

The use of selected drugs among persons age 12 or older reflected gender differences. By this measure, males were more likely than females to be illicit drug users. Figure 6.3 shows that the rate of past-month marijuana use for males was about double the rate for females (8.1 vs. 4.1 percent). However, males and fe-

FIGURE 6.2
Drug Use among Persons Age 12 or Older
during the Past Month, by Age, 2002–2006

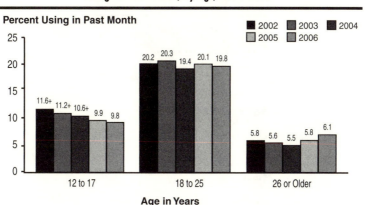

Source: U.S. Department of Health and Human Services. 2006a. *Results from the 2006 National Survey on Drug Use and Health: National Findings.* Office of Applied Studies. Washington, DC: U.S. Government Printing Office.

males had similar rates of past-month use of stimulants (0.5 percent for both males and females), tranquilizers (0.8 percent for males and 0.6 percent for females), hallucinogens (0.5 percent for males and 0.3 percent for females), and inhalants and methamphetamine (0.4 percent for males and 0.2 percent for females in both categories of illicit drugs).

The survey also queried respondents about alcohol consumption, including current, binge, and heavy usage. Figure 6.4 displays age in years, and the percentage using alcohol in the past month is displayed. Fourteen age categories are identified, and for each age category, the bar is divided into three sections corresponding to three types of alcohol use: (1) current alcohol use, which does not include binge use or heavy use; (2) binge alcohol use, which does not include heavy use; and (3) heavy alcohol use. Individual estimates may not sum to the total due to rounding. One can see that alcohol consumption is particularly prevalent during the young adult years. Among 21- to 25-year-olds, 68.6 percent were past-month alcohol users; this statistic can be broken down further as follows: 22.5 percent were current alcohol users (nonbinge or heavy use), 29.3 percent were binge alcohol users (nonheavy use), and 16.7 percent were heavy alcohol users. Among 26- to 29-year-olds, 63.5 percent were past-month alcohol users; this statistic can be broken down further as follows: 25.2 percent were current alcohol

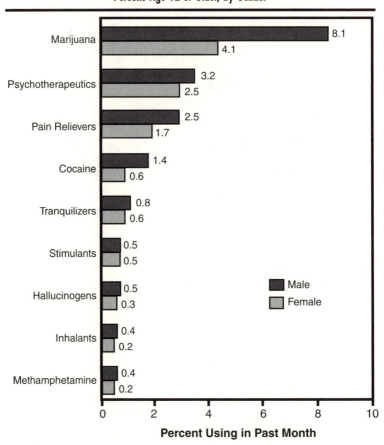

FIGURE 6.3
Use of Selected Drugs during the Past Month among
Persons Age 12 or Older, by Gender

Percent Using in Past Month

Source: U.S. Department of Health and Human Services. 2006a. *Results from the 2006 National Survey on Drug Use and Health: National Findings.* Office of Applied Studies. Washington, DC: U.S. Government Printing Office.

users (nonbinge or heavy use), 26.4 percent were binge alcohol users (nonheavy use), and 11.9 percent were heavy alcohol users.

Much like the trend uncovered in the use of other drugs, the consumption of alcohol reflected gender differences, as Figure 6.5 reveals. In this bar graph, which separates each gender and the total of all persons within various age groupings, there are bars representing 2002, 2003, 2004, 2005, and 2006. Among all persons age 12 to 20, the percentage using alcohol in the past

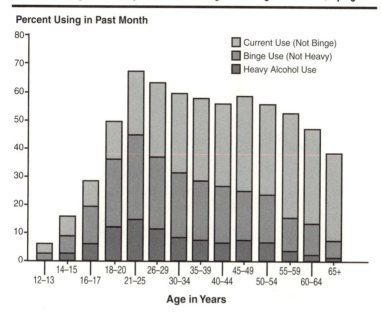

Source: U.S. Department of Health and Human Services. 2006a. *Results from the 2006 National Survey on Drug Use and Health: National Findings.* Office of Applied Studies. Washington, DC: U.S. Government Printing Office.

FIGURE 6.5
Current Alcohol Use among Persons Age 12 to 20, by Gender, 2002–2006

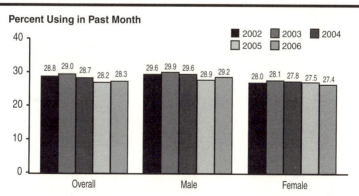

Source: U.S. Department of Health and Human Services. 2006a. *Results from the 2006 National Survey on Drug Use and Health: National Findings.* Office of Applied Studies. Washington, DC: U.S. Government Printing Office.

TABLE 6.1

Admissions, Age 65 or Older, by Primary Substance at Admission: 1995–2005

	1995	1996	1997	1998	1999	2000	2001	2002	2003	2004	2005
Admissions Age 65 or Older (thousands)	12.1	11.7	11.4	11.6	11.7	12.2	11.5	11.6	11.5	11.7	11.3
Primary Substance					*Percent*						
Alcohol	84.7	84.8	83.6	83.1	80.5	80.4	78.7	77.8	78.5	74.4	75.9
Opiates	6.6	6.5	7.3	7.5	7.9	8.2	9.2	9.2	9.3	8.8	10.5
Cocaine	2.1	2.0	1.9	2.3	2.6	2.9	2.6	2.9	3.2	3.9	4.4
Sedatives	0.5	0.5	0.7	0.3	0.2	0.3	0.4	0.4	0.4	0.8	1.3
Marijuana	0.9	0.9	1.0	0.9	1.2	1.2	1.0	1.2	1.4	1.3	1.0
Stimulants	0.3	0.3	0.3	0.2	0.5	0.5	0.4	0.8	0.6	0.6	0.8
Tranquilizers	0.7	0.8	0.7	0.7	0.7	0.8	1.2	0.9	0.8	0.6	0.6
Other	4.2	4.2	4.5	5.0	6.4	5.7	6.5	6.8	5.8	9.6	5.5

Source: Substance Abuse and Mental Health Services Administration, Office of Applied Studies. 2007. *The DASIS Report: Adults Aged 65 or Older in Substance Abuse Treatment: 2005.* Rockville, MD: Substance Abuse and Mental Health Services Administration.

month was 28.8 percent in 2002, 29.0 percent in 2003, 28.7 percent in 2004, 28.2 percent in 2005, and 28.3 percent in 2006. Among males age 12 to 20, the percentage using alcohol in the past month was 29.6 percent in 2002, 29.9 percent in 2003, 29.6 percent in 2004, 28.9 percent in 2005, and 29.2 percent in 2006. Among females age 12 to 20, the percentage using alcohol in the past month was 28.0 percent in 2002, 28.1 percent in 2003, 27.8 percent in 2004, 27.5 percent in 2005, and 27.4 percent in 2006.

Before closing this chapter section, a word or two needs to be said about substance abuse among the elderly. As we learned in Chapter 2, the U.S. population is aging, a demographic trend bringing important consequences for substance abuse treatment. In 2005, Americans age 65 or older comprised approximately 37 million people in the United States—13 percent of the total population— and 11,300 people from this age bracket were admitted to substance abuse treatment facilities. In each year from 1995 to 2005, alcohol was the most frequently reported primary substance of abuse for admissions age 65 or older. Between 1995 and 2005, primary opiate admissions increased from 6.6 to 10.5 percent of admissions age 65 or older. Table 6.1 displays more detail on this

TABLE 6.2
Projections of Occupations with the Largest Job Decline, 2004–2014
(numbers in thousands of jobs)

Occupation	Employment		Change	
	2000	2014	Number	Percent
Farmers and Ranchers	1,065	910	−155	−14.5
Stock Clerks and Order Fillers	1,566	1,451	−115	−7.3
Sewing Machine Operators	256	163	−93	−36.5
File Clerks	255	163	−93	−36.3
Order Clerks	293	230	−63	−21.4
Mail Clerks and Mail Machine Operators,				
Except Postal Service	160	101	−59	−37.1
Computer Operators	149	101	−49	−32.6
Secretaries, Except Legal, Medical, and Executive	1,934	1,887	−48	−2.5
Cutting, Punching, and Press Machine Setters,				
Operators, and Tenders, Metal and Plastic	251	208	−43	−17.2
Telemarketers	415	373	−42	−10.0

Source: U.S. Bureau of Labor. 2005. *Monthly Labor Review,* November, Washington, DC: U.S. Government Printing Office.

problem, including the kinds of substance abuse leading to admission to treatment centers.

Unemployment

As pointed out in Chapter 2, unemployment is a fact of life for many workers today. Unemployment rates are influenced by a number of factors, such as the instability of the economy, automation, or the overabundance of workers in a selected career. A glance at Table 6.2 examines those occupations with the largest *numerical* job declines. Changes in technology or business practices will reduce the demand for most of the listed occupations. More specifically, advances in manufacturing technology, such as faster machines and more automated processes, and a shift of assembly and other production activities to countries with lower labor costs are expected to decrease employment for a number of production and related occupations. Farmers and ranchers will see a job decline as market pressures and improved farm technology result in the consolidation of farms into fewer and larger units. Advances in computer, optical scanning, and voice recognition technologies and growth in electronic business will reduce demand for many office and administrative support occupations (such as file clerks and order clerks). Other declining occupations in this group include mail clerks and mail machine operators, except postal service; computer operators and secretaries, except legal, medical, and executive; word processors and typists; meter readers for utilities; telemarketers; and office machine operators, except computer operators.

Divorce

Divorce rates hit an all-time peak in 1946 and then steadily declined until the late 1950s. At that time, and until recently, the proportion of first marriages ending in divorce sharply increased. The approximately one million divorces granted in 1974 marked the first time in American history that more marriages ended in divorce than through death. Between 1970 and 1980, the number of divorces in the United States increased almost 70 percent. In 2000, approximately one million divorces were granted (U.S. Census Bureau 2008).

One method of computing the frequency of divorce is to examine the crude divorce rate. The crude divorce rate indicates the number of divorces per 1,000 members of the population in a given year. In the United States in 1999, there were about 4.2 divorces per 1,000 population. This is considered a high rate of divorce. The 4.2 crude divorce rate at that time was almost double the rate recorded in 1965. The rate then hovered at this level for a few years, and since has steadily declined. The divorce rate in 2006 was 3.6—the lowest rate since 1970 (U.S. Census Bureau 2008). Crude divorce rates, along with live birth-, death, and marriage rates, between 1960 and 2006 are shown in Table 6.3.

The media often report that almost 50 percent of all marriages end in divorce. This statement is very misleading; such a statistical analysis must be placed into a proper perspective. This percentage was arrived at by comparing all divorces granted in one year with the marriages performed in that same year. This method of calculation is quite different from the crude divorce rate and tends to be less than straightforward. Divorces granted in any year are the result of marriages performed in ear-

TABLE 6.3
Live Births, Deaths, Marriages, and Divorces: 1960 to 2006

| | | Number | | | | | Rate per 1,000 population | | | |
| | | Deaths | | | | | Deaths | | | |
Year	Births (1,000)	Total (1,000)	Infant[1] (1,000)	Marriages[2] (1,000)	Divorces[3] (1,000)	Births	Total	Infant[1]	Marriages[2]	Divorces[3]
1960	4,258	1,712	111	1,523	393	23.7	9.5	26.0	8.5	2.2
1965	3,760	1,828	93	1,800	479	19.4	9.4	24.7	9.3	2.5
1970	3,731	1,921	75	2,159	708	18.4	9.5	20.0	10.6	3.5
1971	3,556	1,928	68	2,190	773	17.2	9.3	19.1	10.6	3.7
1972	3,258	1,964	60	2,282	845	15.6	9.4	18.5	10.9	4.0
1973	3,137	1,973	56	2,284	915	14.8	9.3	17.7	10.8	4.3
1974	3,160	1,934	53	2,230	977	14.8	9.1	16.7	10.5	4.6
1975	3,144	1,893	51	2,153	1,036	14.6	8.8	16.1	10.0	4.8
1976	3,168	1,909	48	2,155	1,083	14.6	8.8	15.2	9.9	5.0
1977	3,327	1,900	47	2,178	1,091	15.1	8.6	14.1	9.9	5.0
1978	3,333	1,928	46	2,282	1,130	15.0	8.7	13.8	10.3	5.1
1979	3,494	1,914	46	2,331	1,181	15.6	8.5	13.1	10.4	5.3
1980	3,612	1,990	46	2,390	1,189	15.9	8.8	12.6	10.6	5.2
1981	3,629	1,978	43	2,422	1,213	15.8	8.6	11.9	10.6	5.3
1982	3,681	1,975	42	2,456	1,170	15.9	8.5	11.5	10.6	5.1
1983	3,639	2,019	41	2,446	1,158	15.6	8.6	11.2	10.5	5.0
1984	3,669	2,039	40	2,477	1,169	15.6	8.6	10.8	10.5	5.0
1985	3,761	2,086	40	2,413	1,190	15.8	8.8	10.6	10.1	5.0
1986	3,757	2,105	39	2,407	1,178	15.6	8.8	10.4	10.0	4.9
1987	3,809	2,123	38	2,403	1,166	15.7	8.8	10.1	9.9	4.8
1988	3,910	2,168	39	2,396	1,167	16.0	8.9	10.0	9.8	4.8
1989	4,041	2,150	40	2,403	1,157	16.4	8.7	9.8	9.7	4.7
1990	4,158	2,148	38	2,443	1,182	16.7	8.6	9.2	9.8	4.7
1991	4,111	2,170	37	2,371	1,187	16.2	8.6	8.9	9.4	4.7
1992	4,065	2,176	35	2,362	1,215	15.8	8.5	8.5	9.3	4.8
1993	4,000	2,269	33	2,334	1,187	15.4	8.8	8.4	9.0	4.6
1994	3,953	2,279	31	2,362	1,191	15.0	8.8	8.0	9.1	4.6

continues

lier years. The divorce rate has never reached one in every two marriages.

It needs to be pointed out, too, that divorce does not affect all social groups equally. The poor and the poorly educated, members of the working class, and those who marry young have higher divorce rates than better-educated and middle-class professionals. To illustrate, black women are more likely to experience first marital dissolution and Asian women are less likely to

TABLE 6.3   continued

		Number					Rate per 1,000 population			
		Deaths					Deaths			
Year	Births (1,000)	Total (1,000)	Infant[1] (1,000)	Marriages[2] (1,000)	Divorces[3] (1,000)	Births	Total	Infant[1]	Marriages[2]	Divorces[3]
1995	3,900	2,312	30	2,336	1,169	14.6	8.7	7.6	8.9	4.4
1996	3,891	2,315	28	2,344	1,150	14.4	8.6	7.3	8.8	4.3
1997	3,881	2,314	28	2,384	1,163	14.2	8.5	7.2	8.9	4.3
1998[4]	3,942	2,337	28	2,244	1,135	14.3	8.5	7.2	8.4	4.2
1999[4]	3,959	2,391	28	2,358	(NA)	14.2	8.6	7.1	8.6	4.1
2000[4]	4,059	2,403	28	2,329	(NA)	14.4	8.5	6.9	8.3	4.1
2001[4]	4,026	2,416	28	2,345	(NA)	14.1	8.5	6.8	8.2	4.0
2002[5]	4,022	2,443	28	2,254	(NA)	13.9	8.5	7.0	7.8	3.9
2003[5]	4,090	2,448	28	2,245	(NA)	14.1	8.4	6.9	7.7	3.8
2004[5]	4,112	2,398	28	2,279	(NA)	14.0	8.2	6.8	7.8	3.7
2005[5,6]	4,143	2,432	28	2,249	(NA)	14.0	8.2	6.8	7.6	3.6
2006[5,6]	4,269	2,416	28	2,160[7]	(NA)	14.3	8.1	6.6	7.3[7]	3.6

Notes: NA Not available. [1]Infants under 1 year, excluding fetal deaths; rates per 1,000 registered live births. [2]Includes estimates for some states through 1965 and also for 1976 and 1977, and marriage licenses for some states for all years except 1973 and 1975. Beginning 1978, includes nonlicensed marriages in California. [3]Includes reported annulments and some estimated state figures for all years. [4]Divorce rate excludes data for California, Colorado, Indiana, and Louisiana; population for this rate also excludes these states. [5]Divorce rates exclude data for California, Georgia, Hawaii, Indiana, Louisiana, and Minnesota in 2005 and 2006; California, Georgia, Hawaii, Indiana, and Louisiana in 2004; California, Hawaii, Indiana, Louisiana, and Oklahoma in 2003; and California, Indiana, and Oklahoma in 2002. Populations for these rates also exclude these states. [6]Provisional data. Includes nonresidents of the United States. [7]Excludes Louisiana.

Source: U.S. Census Bureau. 2008. *Statistical Abstract of the United States,* 127th ed. Washington, DC: U.S. Government Printing Office.

experience first marital dissolution compared with white or Hispanic women.

Before closing, a few comments are warranted regarding remarriages. The United States has one of the highest remarriage rates in the world. Statistics indicate that for those age 25 and older, 52 percent of men and 44 percent of women are remarried. This statistic means that in the United States today, divorce tends to be a transitional rather than a terminal event for those committed to marriage. However, it is important to point out that the pathways to remarriage are varied. For example, partners can be single, divorced or widowed with no children, divorced or widowed with custody of children, divorced or widowed without custody of children, or divorced or widowed with custody of some children but not others (U.S. Census Bureau 2008; Cooper 2007).

Those who choose to remarry tend to do so within a relatively brief time frame. The average interval between divorce and remarriage is approximately three and one-half years. Widowed men and women who do remarry tend to take longer to remarry than do divorced individuals, even when age is considered. A divorced person at any given age has a greater chance of marrying a second time than a never-married person has of marrying a first time. Finally, women and men in remarriages tend to differ in age by a greater margin than do women and men in first marriages. In both first marriages and remarriages, the man is the same age or older than the woman in most marriages (Cooper 2007).

The probability of remarriage is highest among white divorced women and lowest among black divorced women, and white divorced women tend to remarry more quickly. Also, remarriage is more likely among women who were under age 25 at divorce than among women age 25 and over at divorce. Rapid remarriage is also more likely among females who were married when they were young and who had less than a college education. Women with no children at the start of the second marriage are the least likely to experience a second marital disruption. Among those with children at remarriage, those with any unwanted children are more likely to experience a second marital disruption than those with no unwanted children. Additionally, women who live in communities with higher male unemployment, lower median family income, higher poverty, and higher receipt of welfare are more likely to experience the second marital breakup (U.S. Census Bureau 2008; Cooper 2007).

Rates of remarriage among blacks are lower than those of white non-Hispanics, and remarriage rates have been declining among blacks over the last two decades. Because of lower marriage rates and higher rates for divorce and the presence of illegitimate children, it appears that the low rate for black remarriage reinforces a pattern in which a much smaller proportion of the life course is spent in conventional two-parent families among blacks than among whites, with many more years spent in female-headed households both in childhood and for women as adults (Cooper 2007).

Divorce rates among the remarried are high. It is estimated that 60 percent of all remarriages eventually end in divorce. However, the divorce rate varies by the type of remarriage. Research indicates that when only one of the partners is remarried and the other is single, chances for divorce are no greater than they are for marriages in which both partners are in a first marriage. However, the chances for divorce escalate if both partners were previously married and have no children. The chances for divorce also tend to rise if both partners were previously married and one or both of them brought children into the remarriage (Stewart 2007).

About 65 percent of remarriages involve children from the prior marriage and form blended families. The number of step-families has been steadily increasing over the past few decades. To illustrate, 1,300 stepfamilies are formed daily, and each year 500,000 adults become new stepparents. About 6.4 million chil-dren, representing approximately one-tenth of U.S. children, live with one stepparent and one birth parent. Today, one of three Americans is now a stepparent, a stepchild, a stepsibling, or some other member of a blended family (Popkin and Einstein 2007; Stewart 2007).

The most common stepfamilies where children reside are stepfather families or combined stepfather-stepmother families. Regarding the latter category, the man's children from the prior marriage typically do not reside in the blended family. Further-more, some children who are not now stepchildren will become stepchildren before age 18, and some children who were for-merly stepchildren will see their parent and stepparent divorce. It is estimated in the next several years that the blended family will be the predominant family form in the United States (Cooper 2007; Lebey 2005; Marsolini 2006).

Chronic Illness and Disease

According to the U.S. Department of Health and Human Services (2007a), chronic disease and illness can affect both the young and the old. The Department of Health and Human Services ana-lyzed trends in chronic disease and illness, including childhood impairments. In the survey used, younger generations with ac-tivity limitation were identified through questions about specific limitations in such activities as walking, self-care, and play, as well as the current use of special education or early intervention services. Estimates of the number of children with an activity limitation varied depending on the type of limitations included and the methods used to identify them. In the Department of

Health and Human Services study, youngsters who were reported having more than one chronic health condition as the cause of their activity limitation were counted in each reported category (U.S. Department of Health and Human Services 2007a).

A closer look at the survey data reveals that chronic health conditions causing activity limitation in children varied by age. Speech problems, mental retardation, and asthma were the primary causes of activity limitation among children under five years of age. Learning disabilities and attention deficit/hyperactivity disorder (ADHD or ADD) tended to be the leading causes of activity limitation among all school-age children. Among younger school-age children (5 to 11 years of age), speech problems were another important cause of activity limitation. Among older school-age children (12 to 17 years of age), other mental, emotional, and behavioral problems were identified as important causes. Figure 6.6 displays selected chronic health conditions causing limitations of activity among children by age.

Among working-age adults (18 through 44 years of age), the U.S. Department of Health and Human Services (2007a) reported that arthritis and other musculoskeletal conditions were the most frequently mentioned conditions causing limitation. Mental illness was the second-leading cause of activity limitation, followed by fractures or joint injury. Among adults between the ages of 45 and 64 years, heart and circulatory conditions were the second-leading cause of limitation. Mental illness and diabetes were other widely reported conditions. For adults between the ages of 55 and 64, arthritis or other musculoskeletal conditions, heart and circulatory conditions, and diabetes headed the list of chronic health conditions. See Figure 6.7 for more detail on the age groupings and the accompanying chronic conditions.

It is important to point out the linkage between chronic health conditions and income, especially with advancing age. According to the U.S. Department of Health and Human Services (2007a), the percentage of persons reporting three or more chronic conditions tends to increase as income declines. Adults with three or more chronic conditions included persons ever diagnosed with three or more of the following conditions: hypertension, heart disease, stroke, emphysema, diabetes, cancer, arthritis, or asthma.

Among adults 75 years of age and over, the percentage of persons with three or more chronic conditions did not vary significantly by income. Adults 55 to 64 years of age in the lowest income

FIGURE 6.6
Selected Chronic Health Conditions Causing Limitation of
Activity among Children, by Age

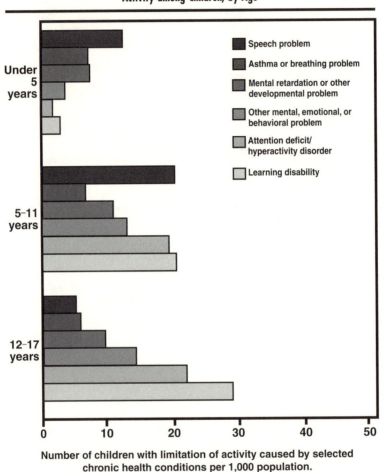

Number of children with limitation of activity caused by selected
chronic health conditions per 1,000 population.

Source: U.S. Department of Health and Human Services. 2007a. *Health, United States, 2006.* Washington, DC: U.S. Government Printing Office.

group (below 100 percent of the poverty level) were as likely to have three or more chronic conditions as older adults 75 years of age and over in the highest income group. Figure 6.8 provides more detail on the relationship between chronic health conditions and income.

FIGURE 6.7
Selected Chronic Health Conditions Causing Limitation of Activity among Working-age Adults, by Age

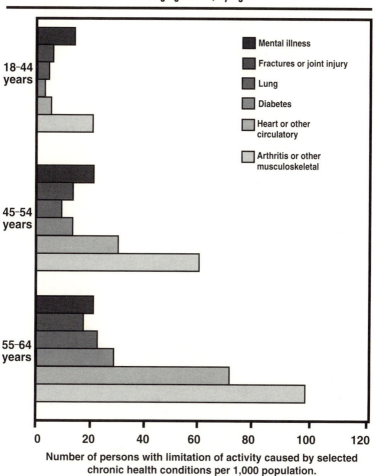

Number of persons with limitation of activity caused by selected chronic health conditions per 1,000 population.

Source: U.S. Department of Health and Human Services. 2007a. *Health, United States, 2006.* Washington, DC: U.S. Government Printing Office.

Finally, the U.S. Department of Health and Human Services (2007a) explored chronic health conditions among the population over the age of 65. Not surprisingly, advancing age often brings chronic health conditions, some more serious than others. Figure 6.9 shows that arthritis and other musculoskeletal conditions

FIGURE 6.8
Three or More Chronic Conditions among Adults 45 Years of Age and Over,
by Age and Percent of Poverty Level

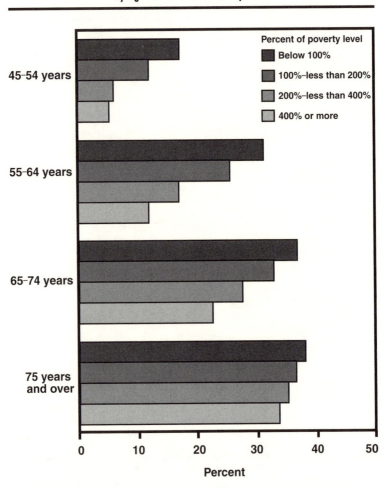

Source: U.S. Department of Health and Human Services. 2007a. *Health, United States, 2006.* Washington, DC: U.S. Government Printing Office.

were the most frequently mentioned chronic conditions causing limitation of activity during later life. Heart and circulatory conditions were the second-leading cause of limitations. Among adults 85 years and over, senility, vision conditions, and hearing problems were frequently mentioned causes of activity limitation.

FIGURE 6.9
Selected Chronic Health Conditions Causing Limitation of Activity among Older Adults, by Age

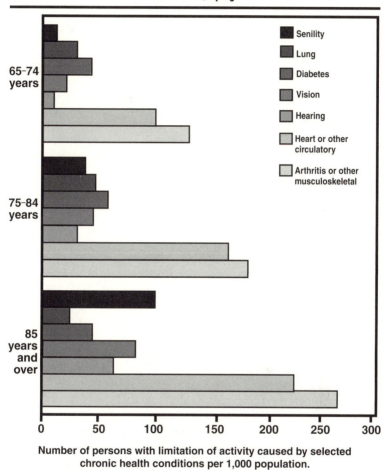

Number of persons with limitation of activity caused by selected chronic health conditions per 1,000 population.

Source: U.S. Department of Health and Human Services. 2007a. *Health, United States, 2006.* Washington, DC: U.S. Government Printing Office.

Caring for Aging Family Members

It is no longer a secret that people today are living longer than ever before. According to the U.S. Department of Health and Human Services (2007a), population projections indicate that the rate of growth for the total population from now until 2050 will

FIGURE 6.10
Elderly Population Growth Compared to the General Population, 1950–2050

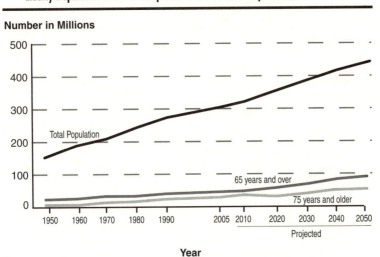

Source: U.S. Department of Health and Human Services. 2007a. *Health, United States, 2006.* Washington, DC: U.S. Government Printing Office.

be slower, but older age groups will continue to grow more rapidly than the total population. By 2029, all of the baby boomers (those born in the post–World War II period 1946–1964) will be age 65 years and over. As a result, the population age 65 to 74 years will increase from 6 percent to 10 percent of the total population between 2005 and 2030. As the baby boomers age, the population 75 years and over will also rise from 6 percent to 9 percent of the population by 2030 and continue to grow to 12 percent in 2050. By 2040, the population age 75 years and over will exceed the population 65 to 74 years of age (see Figure 6.10).

Most of today's elderly reside in family settings, although living arrangements differ considerably between men and women as they age. To illustrate, more than half of older, non-institutionalized persons lived with their spouse in 2006. About 10.9 million, or 71.9 percent, of older men, and 8.5 million, or 41.9 percent, of older women lived with their spouse. However, the proportion of elderly living with their spouses decreased with age, particularly among women. Only 29.8 percent of women over age 75 lived with their spouses (U.S. Department of Health and Human Services 2007b).

Approximately 30 percent (almost 11 million) aged, non-institutionalized persons in the United States live alone. Broken down by gender, this total includes about 8 million women and 3 million men. These totals account for about 38 percent of aged women and almost 20 percent of aged men. It should be noted that the proportion of elderly persons alone increases with advanced age. To illustrate, almost half of women age 75 and over live alone (U.S. Department of Health and Human Services 2007b).

In 2006, more than 670,000 grandparents age 65 or over maintained households in which grandchildren were present. Additionally, more than 800,000 grandparents over 65 years lived in parent-maintained households in which their grandchildren were present. Almost 2 million elderly citizens lived in households with grandchildren present in the house. Approximately 450,000 grandparents over age 65 had primary responsibility for the grandchildren living with them. For a statistical analysis of this information, the reader is directed to Table 6.4.

It is not uncommon for older grandchildren to lend a hand and assist their grandparents with day-to-day chores and routines. When the elderly need more intensive care, that care is more likely to originate from adult offspring. More than 20 million persons in the United States are informal caregivers, providing unpaid help to older persons who live in the community and have at least one limitation in their activities of daily living. These caregivers include spouses, adult children, and other relatives and friends (U.S. Department of Health and Human Services 2007b). However, it needs to be recognized that while most people age 65 and older live in households and receive care from adult offspring or other family members, the probability of living in a nursing home increases with age (see Figure 6.11).

Domestic Violence

One of the more extensive investigations of domestic violence was undertaken by the Bureau of Justice Statistics (2006a). Utilizing the National Crime Victimization Survey, it analyzed data related to domestic violence using an ongoing, nationally representative sample of households in the United States. The survey data included information about survivors of domestic abuse (age, gender, race, ethnicity, marital status, income, and educational level),

TABLE 6.4
Grandparents Living with Grandchildren by Race and Sex: 2005

Race, Hispanic origin, and sex	Grandparents living with grandchildren, total[1]	Grandparents responsible for grandchildren		
		Total	30 to 59 years old	60 years old and over
Grandparents living with own Grandchildren under 18 years old (1,000)	5,743	2,459	1,677	782
PERCENT DISTRIBUTION				
Total	100.0	100.0	100.0	100.0
White alone	59.3	60.4	60.1	60.9
Black or African American alone	21.0	25.5	25.3	26.0
American Indian and Alaska Native alone	1.6	2.2	2.2	2.0
Asian alone	6.8	2.8	2.1	4.3
Native Hawaiian and Other Pacific Islander alone	0.3	0.2	0.3	0.2
Some other race alone	9.7	7.5	8.4	5.4
Two or more races	1.4	1.5	1.6	1.2
Hispanic or Latino[2]	22.2	18.1	19.9	14.4
White alone, not Hispanic or Latino	47.5	50.4	49.4	52.6
Male	36.0	37.2	35.5	40.9
Female	64.0	62.8	64.5	59.1

Notes: [1]Covers both grandchildren living in grandparent's home and grandparents living in grandchildren's home. [2]Persons of Hispanic origin may be of any race.

Source: U.S. Census Bureau. 2008. *Statistical Abstract of the United States,* 127th ed. Washington, DC: U.S. Government Printing Office.

criminal offenders (gender, race, approximate age, and victim-offender relationships), and the nature of the crime (e.g., time and place of occurrence, use of weapons, nature of injury). The incidents of domestic violence were reported by those persons residing in households, not the homeless or those living in institutional settings such as shelters for the homeless. About 77,200 households and 134,000 individuals age 12 and older were interviewed.

FIGURE 6.11
Nursing Home Population by Age: 2000 (Percent Distribution)

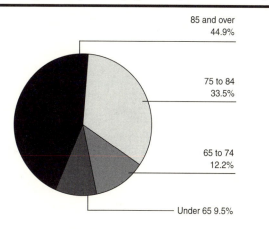

85 and over
44.9%

75 to 84
33.5%

65 to 74
12.2%

Under 65 9.5%

Source: U.S. Census Bureau. 2005. *65+ in the United States: 2005.* Current Population Reports, P23–209. Washington, DC: U.S. Government Printing Office.

Figure 6.12 shows that for white females, the rate of nonfatal intimate partner violence began at 9.8 per 1,000 persons age 12 or over in 1993 and decreased to 3.1 in 2005. For black females, the rate of nonfatal intimate partner violence began at 11.9 in 1993, then climbed to 13.3 in 1995. After 1995, the rate decreased to 3.8 in 2003. It fluctuated as it increased to 4.6 in 2005, during which time it spiked to 6.6. For white males, the rate of nonfatal intimate partner violence began at 1.6 in 1993 and increased to 1.7 in 1994. The rate then decreased to a low of 0.5 in 2003. After 2003, it fluctuated as it increased to 0.7 in 2005, during which time it reached a high of 1.1.

Physical assault against one's intimate partner can lead to the assailant killing the abused partner. The number of white female homicide victims began at 840 in 1976 and fluctuated, with a low of 821, as it increased to 1,002 in 1985. After 1985, the number decreased, reaching 749 in 1997. After 1997, it fluctuated, with a high of 862, as it increased to 789 in 2005. The number of black female homicide victims began at 709 in 1976 and decreased, reaching a low of 316 in 2004. The number of white male homicide victims began at 467 in 1976 and fluctuated, with a low of 452, as it increased to 528 in 1981. Then the number dropped to a low of 174

FIGURE 6.12
Nonfatal Intimate Partner Victimization Rate by Gender and Race, 1993–2004

Rates per 1,000 persons age 12 or older

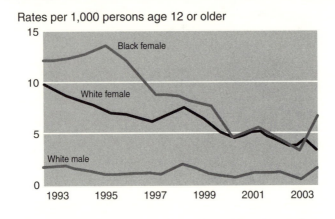

Source: Bureau of Justice Statistics. 2006a. *Intimate Partner Violence in the United States.* Washington, DC: Bureau of Justice Statistics.

in 2001. It next fluctuated, with a high of 195, as it increased to 183 in 2004. The number of black male homicide victims began at 820 in 1976 and dropped to a low of 138 in 2004, where it remained constant until 2004. See Figure 6.13 for more details.

The Bureau of Justice Statistics (2006a) also found that for females in all age categories, nonfatal intimate partner victimization declined over time. Females in the age ranges of 16 to 19, 20 to 24, and 25 to 34 were at a greater risk of nonfatal intimate partner violence. Females in the age ranges of 12 to 15, 50 to 64, and 65+ were at the lowest risk of nonfatal intimate partner violence (see Figure 6.14).

One's marital status posed certain risks for partner violence. On average, from 2001 to 2004, both females and males who were separated or divorced had the greatest risk of nonfatal intimate partner violence, while persons who were married or widowed reported the lowest risk of violence. For separated females, the rate of nonfatal intimate partner violence began at 92.3 per 1,000 persons age 12 or over in 1993 and decreased to a low of 26.6 in 2002. Then the rate increased to 49.0 in 2004. For divorced females, the rate of nonfatal intimate partner violence began at 26.2 in 1993 and decreased to 8.5 in 2004. For married females, the rate of nonfatal intimate partner violence began at 3.1 in 1993 and

FIGURE 6.13

Homicides of Intimates by Gender and Race of Victim, 1976–2004

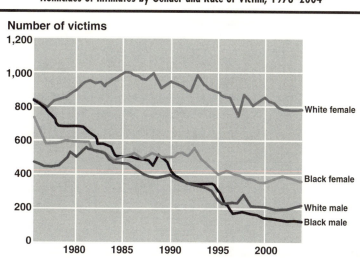

Number of victims

Source: Bureau of Justice Statistics. 2006a. *Intimate Partner Violence in the United States.* Washington, DC: Bureau of Justice Statistics.

FIGURE 6.14

Nonfatal Intimate Partner Victimization Rate for Females by Age, 1993–2004

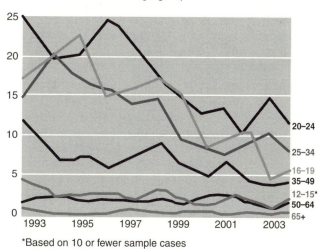

Rates per 1,000 females in age group

*Based on 10 or fewer sample cases

Source: Bureau of Justice Statistics. 2006a. *Intimate Partner Violence in the United States.* Washington, DC: Bureau of Justice Statistics.

FIGURE 6.15
Nonfatal Intimate Partner Victimization Rate for Females by
Marital Status, 1993–2004

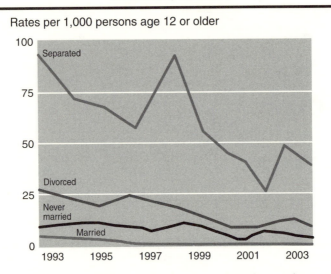

Rates per 1,000 persons age 12 or older

Source: Bureau of Justice Statistics. 2006a. *Intimate Partner Violence in the United States.* Washington, DC: Bureau of Justice Statistics.

climbed to 3.2 in 1994. Then the rate fell, reaching 0.9 in 2004. For females never married, the rate of nonfatal intimate partner violence began at 11.5 in 1993 and increased to 12.3 in 1995. Then the rate decreased to 4.4 in 2004 (see Figure 6.15).

As we learned in Chapter 3, child abuse is a widespread type of domestic abuse. According to the U.S. Department of Health and Human Services (2007c), child maltreatment takes many different forms, including physical, sexual, and psychological abuse, as well as neglect. Maltreatment is often associated with a number of negative consequences for youngsters, including substance abuse, lower school achievement, juvenile delinquency, and mental health problems. Some forms of maltreatment are connected to long-term physical, emotional, and social problems, and even death. For example, "shaken baby syndrome" can result in paralysis, mental retardation, or cerebral palsy. As Figure 6.16 reveals, the highest rates of substantiated maltreatment for children are between the ages of 0 and 3, followed by the age range of 4 to 7. The lowest rates of substantiated maltreatment for children are between the ages of 16 and 17.

FIGURE 6.16
Rate of Substantiated Maltreatment Reports of Children Ages 0–17
per 1,000 Children, 1998–2005

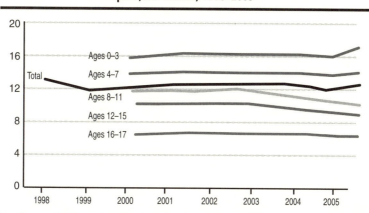

Note: The count of child victims is based on the number of investigations by Child Protective Services that found the child to be a victim of one or more types of maltreatment. The count of victims is, therefore, a report-based count and is a "duplicated count," since an individual child may have been maltreated more than once. The number of states reporting varies from year to year. States vary in their definition of abuse and neglect.

Source: U.S. Department of Health and Human Services. 2007c. *America's Children: Key National Indicators of Well-Being, 2007.* Washington, DC: U.S. Government Printing Office.

Although the U.S. Department of Health and Human Services (2007c) reports that neglect is the most common type of maltreatment across all age groups, types of maltreatment vary by age. In 2005, 73 percent of substantiated child maltreatment reports for children age 0 to 3 involved neglect, compared with 53 percent for adolescents age 16 and older. On the other hand, 23 percent of substantiated reports for teens age 16 and older involved physical abuse, and 17 percent involved sexual abuse. Among substantiated reports for children age 0 to 3, 12 percent involved physical abuse and 2 percent involved sexual abuse. Table 6.5 provides more detail.

School Violence

School violence committed by children and adolescents in the recent past has generated considerable concern among the general public, and social scientists have launched a wave of research

TABLE 6.5
Child Maltreatment: Percentage of Substantiated Maltreatment Reports,
Maltreatment Type and Age, 2005

Characteristic	Physical Abuse	Neglect	Medical Neglect	Sexual Abuse	Psychological Abuse	Other Abuse	Unknown
Overall	16.6	63.4	2.0	9.4	6.9	13.9	1.1
Age							
Age 0–3	12.2	73.1	2.7	2.1	5.5	14.9	1.2
Age 4–7	15.6	64.6	1.7	8.9	7.1	13.4	1.1
Age 8–11	17.6	60.3	1.7	11.2	8.1	13.7	1.1
Age 12–15	21.3	53.8	1.7	17.3	7.4	13.1	1.1
Age 16–17	23.2	52.7	1.8	16.7	6.6	13.9	0.9
Unknown or Missing	23.0	55.9	0.5	16.2	8.7	3.9	0.1

Note: Based on data from 49 states. The count of child victims is based on the number of investigations by Child Protective Services that found the child to be a victim of one or more types of maltreatment. The count of victims is, therefore, a report-based count and is a "duplicated count," since an individual child may have been maltreated more than once. Substantiated maltreatment includes the dispositions of substantiated, indicated, or alternative response-victim. States vary in their definition of abuse and neglect. Rows total more than 100 percent since a single child may be the victim of multiple kinds of maltreatment.

Source: Department of Health and Human Services. 2007c. *America's Children: Key National Indicators of Well-Being, 2007.* Washington, DC: U.S. Government Printing Office.

aimed at finding causes, consequences, and ways to curb it. One of the more comprehensive investigations was conducted by the Bureau of Justice Statistics (2006b). It scrutinized information drawn from a variety of independent data sources, including national surveys of students, teachers, and principals, as well as data from federal departments and agencies, such as the Federal Bureau of Investigation and the Centers for Disease Control and Prevention. From these sources, the Bureau of Justice Statistics summarized the research and established a series of indicators of the current state of school crime and safety across the United States.

Due to effective interventions in helping young people whose lives are marked by a propensity for violence, school shootings and suicides have dramatically decreased. In fact, youth between the ages of 5 and 18 are more than 50 times more likely to be murdered and almost 150 times more likely to commit suicide when they are *away* from school than at school. Figure 6.17 displays the number of homicides and suicides of youth between the ages of 5 and 18 by location, while Figure 6.18 charts

FIGURE 6.17
Number of Homicides and Suicides of Youth Ages 5–18, by Location, 2003–2004

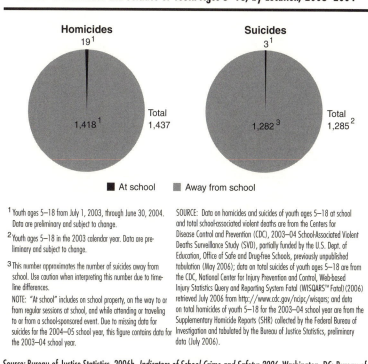

¹ Youth ages 5–18 from July 1, 2003, through June 30, 2004. Data are preliminary and subject to change.

² Youth ages 5–18 in the 2003 calendar year. Data are preliminary and subject to change.

³ This number approximates the number of suicides away from school. Use caution when interpreting this number due to time-line differences.

NOTE: "At school" includes on school property, on the way to or from regular sessions at school, and while attending or traveling to or from a school-sponsored event. Due to missing data for suicides for the 2004–05 school year, this figure contains data for the 2003–04 school year.

SOURCE: Data on homicides and suicides of youth ages 5–18 at school and total school-associated violent deaths are from the Centers for Disease Control and Prevention (CDC), 2003–04 School-Associated Violent Deaths Surveillance Study (SVD), partially funded by the U.S. Dept. of Education, Office of Safe and Drug-free Schools, previously unpublished tabulation (May 2006); data on total suicides of youth ages 5–18 are from the CDC, National Center for Injury Prevention and Control, Web-based Injury Statistics Query and Reporting System Fatal (WISQARS™ Fatal) (2006) retrieved July 2006 from http://www.cdc.gov/ncipc/wisqars; and data on total homicides of youth 5–18 for the 2003–04 school year are from the Supplementary Homicide Reports (SHR) collected by the Federal Bureau of Investigation and tabulated by the Bureau of Justice Statistics, preliminary data (July 2006).

Source: Bureau of Justice Statistics. 2006b. *Indicators of School Crime and Safety: 2006.* Washington, DC: Bureau of Justice Statistics.

the number of homicides and suicides of youth between the years 1992 and 2005.

Although the victimization rates for students age 12 to 18 have generally declined both at school and away from school, theft and violence are still prevalent, exposing victims to a disruptive and threatening environment, physical injury, emotional stress, and interference to their academic success. (Theft includes purse snatching, pickpocketing, all burglaries, attempted forcible entry, and all attempted and completed thefts except motor vehicle thefts. Theft does not include robbery in which threat or use of force is involved. Violent crimes include such serious offenses as rape, sexual assault, robbery, and aggravated assault.) Students age 12 to 18 are more likely to be victims of theft at school than away from school, while rates of serious violent crime tend to be lower at school than away from school.

FIGURE 6.18
Number of Homicides and Suicides of Youth Ages 5–18 at School: 1992–2005

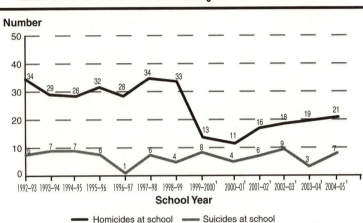

Number

Homicides at school ▬▬▬ Suicides at school ▬▬▬

¹ Data are preliminary and subject to change.

NOTE: Includes homicides and suicides of youth ages 5–18 at school from July 1, 1992, through June 30, 2005. "At school" includes on school property, on the way to or from regular sessions at school, and while attending or traveling to or from a school-sponsored event.

SOURCE: Centers for Disease Control and Prevention (CDC), 1992–2005 School-Associated Violent Deaths Surveillance Study (SAVD), partially funded by the U.S. Department of Education, Office of Safe and Drug-Free Schools, previously unpublished tabulation (May 2006).

Source: Bureau of Justice Statistics. 2006b. *Indicators of School Crime and Safety: 2006.* Washington, DC: Bureau of Justice Statistics.

According to the Bureau of Justice Statistics (2006b), victimization rates for students age 12 to 18 vary according to certain characteristics. To illustrate, older students (age 15 to 18) are less likely than younger students (age 12 to 14) to be victims of crime at school, but the opposite tends to be true for the likelihood of crime away from school. Females tend to have a lower rate of violent victimization at school and a lower rate of serious violent victimization away from school than males, but there appear to be no measurable gender differences in the rates of theft at and away from school.

It is not an uncommon occurrence for students to be threatened or injured with a weapon while they are on school property. The likelihood of being threatened or injured with a weapon on school property tends to vary by student characteristics. A consistent theme in the literature is that males are more likely than females to report being threatened or injured with a weapon on school property (see Figure 6.19). Also, students in lower grades

FIGURE 6.19

Percentage of Students in Grades 9–12 Who Reported Being Threatened or Injured with a Weapon on School Property from 1993–2005

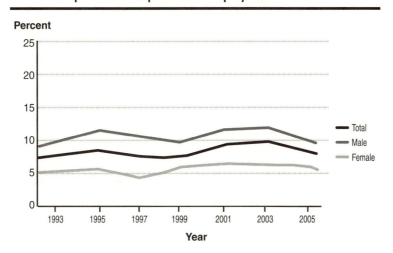

NOTE: "On school property" was not defined for survey respondents. Population sizes from the *Digest of Education Statistics, 2005* (NCES 2006-030) for students in grades 9 to 12 are 13,093,000 students in 1993; 13,697,000 in 1995; 14,272,000 in 1997; 14,623,000 in 1999; 15,061,000 in 2001; 15,723,000 in 2003; and 16,286,000 (projected) in 2005.

SOURCE: Centers for Disease Control and Prevention, National Center for Chronic Disease Prevention and Health Promotion, Youth Risk Behavior Surveillance System (YRBSS), various years, 1993 through 2005.

Source: Bureau of Justice Statistics. 2006b. *Indicators of School Crime and Safety: 2006.* Washington, DC: Bureau of Justice Statistics.

are generally more likely to report being threatened or injured with a weapon on school property than those in higher grades. Finally, the likelihood of being threatened or injured with a weapon on school property appears to vary by race/ethnicity. For example, Hispanic students are more likely than white students to report being threatened or injured with a weapon on school property. However, the literature tends to report no measurable differences in the percentages of black and white students or black and Hispanic students who reported being threatened or injured in this way.

Teachers are not immune to intimidation or violence in the school setting. On the contrary, teachers are on the receiving end of threats and physical attacks from their students. Certain trends related to teacher attacks have been identified by the Bureau of Justice Statistics (2006b). For instance, teachers in central-city schools tend to be threatened with injury or physically attacked more than those educators in rural schools. Gender differences in victimization can also be identified. Although more male than female teachers tend to be threatened with injury, female teachers are more likely to be victims of a physical attack. Finally, secondary school teachers are more apt than elementary school teachers to have been threatened with injury by a student. But elementary school teachers are more likely than secondary school teachers to be physically attacked.

Gangs within the school setting can be disruptive to the student population, since they are often connected to violence, drugs, and weapons trafficking. The Bureau of Justice Statistics (2006b) reports that the presence of a school gang may create fear among students and contribute to increased outbreaks of school violence. Students in urban settings are more apt to report the presence of school gangs than their suburban and rural counterparts. Regarding racial/ethnic variations, Hispanic and black students are more likely than white students to report the presence of gangs in their schools (a trend evident in both urban and suburban settings). Public school students tend to report the presence of gangs more than private school students (regardless of the school's location). No significant difference appears to exist in the extent to which males and females report the presence of school gangs (see Figure 6.20).

As we learned in Chapter 3, bullying by social groups and individuals is often connected to school shootings and other forms of school violence. The Bureau of Justice Statistics (2006b) concurs with this assessment, adding that being bullied at school is associated with key violence-related behaviors, including carrying weapons, fighting, and sustaining injuries from fighting. Citing fairly recent research, the Bureau of Justice Statistics (2006b) shares that almost 30 percent of students report being bullied at school. A wide range of bullying behaviors can be identified: being made fun of; being the subject of rumors; or being pushed, shoved, tripped, or spit on (see Figure 6.21). Most bullying takes place inside the school and, to a lesser degree, outside on school grounds (see Figure 6.22).

White and black students are more apt than Hispanic students to report being bullied. White students are also more likely

FIGURE 6.20

Percentage of Students Ages 12–18 Who Reported That Gangs Were Present at School during the Previous 6 Months, by Urbanicity and Race/Ethnicity: 2005

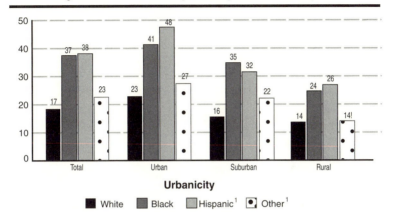

Urbanicity

■ White   ■ Black   ■ Hispanic[1]   ▣ Other[1]

[1] Interpret data with caution

[1] Other includes American Indian, Alaska Native, Asian or Pacific Islander, and more than one race. For this report, non-Hispanic students who identified themselves as more than one race were included in the Other category. Respondents who identified themselves as being of Hispanic origin are classified as Hispanic, regardless of their race.

NOTE: All gangs, whether or not they are involved in violent or illegal activity, are included. "At School" includes the school building, on school property, on a school bus, or going to and from school. In 2005, the unit response rate for this survey did not meet NCES statistical standards; therefore, interpret the data with caution. For more information, please see appendix A. Population size for students ages 12–18 is 25,811,000 in 2005.

SOURCE: U.S. Department of Justice, Bureau of Justice Statistics, School Crime Supplement (SCS) for the National Crime Victimization Survey, 2005.

Source: Bureau of Justice Statistics. 2006b. *Indicators of School Crime and Safety: 2006.* Washington, DC: Bureau of Justice Statistics.

than other racial/ethnic groups to report being bullied and to report that they were the subject of rumors than were Hispanic students and students of racial/ethnic groups. The Bureau of Justice Statistics (2006b) also reports that, generally speaking, grade level is inversely related to students' likelihood of being bullied: As grade level increases, students' likelihood of being bullied tends to diminish. Public school students are more likely to be bullied than those in private schools. Finally, while no measurable gender differences appear to exist in students' reporting a bullying incident, males are more likely than females to report being injured during such an episode.

The Bureau of Justice Statistics (2006b) analyzed data that focused on school fighting and student possession of weapons. Males are much more likely than females to engage in a fight anywhere, including on school property. However, in recent years,

FIGURE 6.21
Percentage of Students Ages 12–18 Who Reported Selected Bullying Problems at School during the Previous 6 Months, by Type of Bullying: 2005

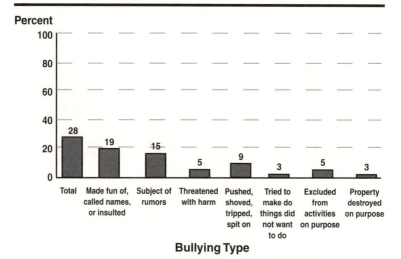

NOTE: "At School" includes the school building, on school property, on a school bus, or going to and from school. Types of bullying do not sum to total because students could have experienced more than one type of bullying. In 2005, the unit response rate for this survey did not meet NCES statistical standards; therefore, interpret the data with caution. For more information, please see appendix A. Population size for students ages 12–18 is 25,811,000 in 2005.
SOURCE: U.S. Department of Justice, Bureau of Justice Statistics, School Crime Supplement (SCS) to the National Crime Victimization Survey, 2005.

Source: Bureau of Justice Statistics. 2006b. *Indicators of School Crime and Safety: 2006.* Washington, DC: Bureau of Justice Statistics.

incidents of female fighting have been on the upswing (see Figure 6.23). For both male and female students, students in lower grades are more apt to engage in fights than students in higher grades. Also, fighting in school varies, depending on students' race/ethnicity. More specifically, Asian students are less likely than students from all other racial/ethnic groups to fight anywhere, including on school property. In recent years, an increase has been seen in the number of Hispanic students choosing to engage in fighting on school grounds and elsewhere.

Males are twice as likely as females to carry a weapon, both on school property and at other locations. Regarding racial/ethnic composition, Asian students are less likely than students from all

FIGURE 6.22
Percentage of Students Ages 12–18 Who Reported Being Bullied at School during the Previous 6 Months, by Location of Bullying and Injury: 2005

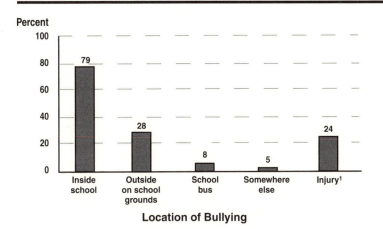

Location of Bullying

[1] Injury includes bruises or swelling: cuts, scratches, or scrapes; black eye or bloody nose; teeth chipped or knocked out; broken bones or internal injuries; knocked unconscious; or other injuries. Only students who reported that their bullying incident constituted being pushed, shoved, tripped, or spit on were asked if they suffered injuries as a result of the incident.

NOTE: "At School" includes the school building, on school property, on a school bus, or going to and from school. In 2005, the unit response rate for this survey did not meet NCES statistical standards, therefore, interpret the data with caution. For more information, please see appendix A. Population size for students ages 12–18 is 25,811,000 in 2005. Location totals may sum to more than 100 because students could have been bullied in more than one location.

SOURCE: U.S. Department of Justice, Bureau of Justice Statistics, School Crime Supplement (SCS) to the National Crime Victimization Survey, 2005.

Source: Bureau of Justice Statistics. 2006b. *Indicators of School Crime and Safety: 2006.* Washington, DC: Bureau of Justice Statistics.

other racial/ethnic groups, with the exception of Pacific Islanders, to carry a weapon anywhere. No discernable differences in weapon possession anywhere appear to exist among white, black, and Hispanic students. Asian students are less likely than students from all other racial/ethnic groups, except for blacks, to carry a weapon on school property. On the other hand, no differences appear to exist among white, black, and American Indian students. Finally, recent research suggests that Hispanic students are more likely than black students to report carrying a weapon during the previous 30 days on school property. Figure 6.24 displays more detail regarding racial/ethnic differences among students carrying weapons.

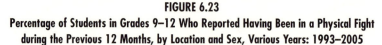

FIGURE 6.23
Percentage of Students in Grades 9–12 Who Reported Having Been in a Physical Fight during the Previous 12 Months, by Location and Sex, Various Years: 1993–2005

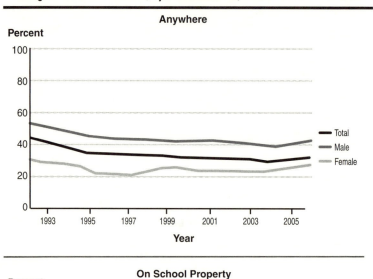

NOTE: "On school property" was not defined for survey respondents. The term "anywhere" is not used in the YRBS questionnaire; students are simply asked how many times in the past 12 months had they been in a physical fight. Population sizes from the *Digest of Education Statistics, 2005* (NCES 2006-030) for students in grades 9 to 12 are 13,093,000 students in 1993; 13,697,000 in 1995; 14,272,000 in 1997; 14,623,000 in 1999; 15,061,000 in 2001; 15,723,000 in 2003; and 16,286,000 (projected) in 2005.

SOURCE: Centers for Disease Control and Prevention, National Center for Chronic Disease Prevention and Health Promotion, Youth Risk Behavior Surveillance System (YRBSS), various years, 1993 through 2005.

Source: Bureau of Justice Statistics. 2006b. *Indicators of School Crime and Safety: 2006.* Washington, DC: Bureau of Justice Statistics.

FIGURE 6.24

Percentage of Students in Grades 9–12 Who Reported Carrying a Weapon at Least 1 Day during the Previous 30 Days, by Location and Race/Ethnicity: 2005

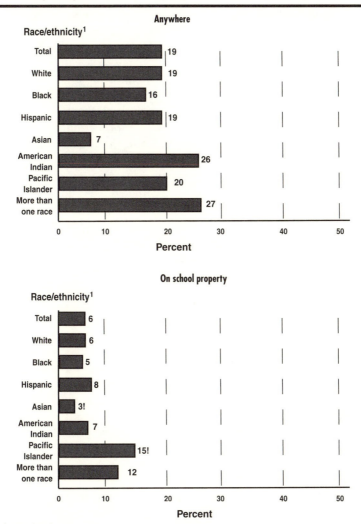

[1] American Indian includes Alaska Native, Black includes African American, Pacific Islander includes Native Hawaiian, and Hispanic includes Latino. Respondents who identified themselves as being of Hispanic origin are classified as Hispanic, regardless of their race.

NOTE: "On school property" was not defined for survey respondents. The term "anywhere" is not used in the YRBS questionnaire; students are simply asked how many days they carried a weapon during the past 30 days. Population size from the *Digest of Education Statistics*, 2005 (NCES 2006-030) for students in grades 9–12 is 16,286,000 (projected) in 2005.

Source: Centers for Disease Control and Prevention, National Center for Chronic Disease Prevention and Health Promotion, Youth Risk Behavior Surveillance System (YRBSS), 2005.

Source: Bureau of Justice Statistics. 2006b. *Indicators of School Crime and Safety: 2006.* Washington, DC: Bureau of Justice Statistics.

Natural Disasters

The National Oceanic and Atmospheric Administration (NOAA) is a branch of the U.S. Department of Commerce. Among its functions, NOAA provides information to citizens, planners, emergency managers, and other decision makers on weather forecasts, severe storm warnings, and climate monitoring. It also provides statistical information on fatalities, injuries, and damages caused by weather-related hazards, including natural disasters.

NOAA's analysis of natural disasters occurring during 2006 illustrates the kinds of data gathered and made available by the organization (National Oceanic and Atmospheric Administration 2006). Consider some of the statistical information on fatalities, injuries, and damages caused by weather-related hazards. After the United States experienced extreme losses—1,836 lives—in 2005, mostly due to Hurricane Katrina, weather-related deaths dipped to 566 in 2006. This total was beneath the 10-year average (1997–2006) of 649. Heat was the most deadly weather hazard in 2006, taking 253 lives, followed by flooding, with 76 victims, and tornadoes, responsible for 67 deaths.

Of the 567 weather-related fatalities, males accounted for more than twice as many deaths (378) as females (181) (the gender of the remaining 7 individuals who died was unknown). Males were more apt to be victims in all age brackets with the exception of the 90+ category. This exception likely reflects the fact that fewer males than females live into their 90s. Tables 6.6 and 6.7 and Figure 6.25 provide more detail on the weather-related fatalities of 2006.

Although weather-related deaths decreased in 2006, injuries sustained from weather events were on the upswing. To illustrate, 3,489 weather-related injuries occurred in 2006, a significant increase from 1,834 in 2005 and the 2,428 that occurred in 2004. Extreme heat was responsible for most of the injuries (1,513), while thunderstorms and high winds caused 380 injuries. Lightning was the fourth-leading cause of injuries (246).

In 2006, July and August claimed the most lives. July recorded the biggest toll, with extreme heat claiming the most lives (160). August was next (144 victims), with extreme heat again being the cause. Regarding geographic location, California recorded the most fatalities (79), 65 being heat related. New York, Pennsylvania, and Illinois were next with 48, 46, and 45 fatalities, respectively.

TABLE 6.6
Summary of Weather Events, Fatalities, Injuries, and Damage Costs: 2006

Weather Event	Fatalities	Injuries	Amount of Property Damage (M)	Amount of Crop Damage (M)	Total Prop/Crop Damage (M)
Convection					
Lightning	48	246	$63.8	$0.0	$63.8
Tornado	67	990	752.3	6.7	759.0
Tstm Wind	14	249	408.0	31.1	439.1
Hail	0	18	1,569.4	132.9	1,702.3
Extreme Temperatures					
Cold	2	5	0.0	11.9	11.9
Heat	253	1,513	0.2	492.5	492.7
Flood					
Flash Flood	59 ⎫	18 ⎫	2,136.6	104.9	2,241.5
River Flood	17 ⎬ 76	5 ⎬ 23	1,631.1	95.2	1,726.3
Small Stream/ Urban Flood	0 ⎭	0 ⎭	0.0	0.0	0.0
Marine					
Coastal Storm	7	16	55.1	0.0	55.1
Tsunami	0	0	0.0	0.0	0.0
Rip Current	23	24	0.0	0.0	0.0
Tropical Cyclones					
Tropical Storm/ Hurricane	0	1	2.4	43.3	45.7
Winter					
Winter Storm	17	109	571.0	0.0	571.0
Ice	0	0	0.0	0.0	0.0
Avalanche	11	6	0.0	0.0	0.0
Other					
Drought	0	4	138.0	2,498.1	2,636.1
Dust Storm	2	22	0.7	2.3	3.0
Dust Devil	0	1	0.0	0.0	0.0
Rain	1	4	52.4	49.7	102.1
Fog	0	0	0.0	0.0	0.0
High Wind	26	133	195.0	15.2	210.2
Waterspout	0	0	0.0	0.0	0.0
Fire Weather	0	0	192.4	0.0	192.4
Mud Slide	3	2	58.9	20.0	78.9
Volcanic Ash	0	0	0.0	0.0	0.0
Miscellaneous	17	126	157.3	232.7	390.0
TOTALS	567	3,492	$7,984.6M	$3,736.5M	$11,721.1M

Source: National Oceanic and Atmospheric Administration, U.S. Department of Commerce. 2006. *Natural Hazard Statistics, 2006.* Washington, DC: U.S. Government Printing Office.

TABLE 6.7
Summary of Fatalities for All Natural Disasters, by Age: 2006

Fatalities	Female	Male	Unknown	Total	Percent
0 to 9	9	17	0	26	5
10 to 19	10	28	0	38	7
20 to 29	18	30	0	48	8
30 to 39	9	39	0	48	8
40 to 49	24	58	0	82	14
50 to 59	27	67	0	94	17
60 to 69	20	51	0	71	13
70 to 79	26	29	0	55	10
80 to 89	26	34	0	60	11
90 to –	9	7	0	16	3
UNKNOWN	3	18	7	28	5
TOTAL	181	378	7	566	100
PERCENT	32	67	1	100	

Source: National Oceanic and Atmospheric Administration, U.S. Department of Commerce. 2006. *Natural Hazard Statistics, 2006.* Washington, DC: U.S. Government Printing Office.

FIGURE 6.25
Monthly Weather-Related Fatalities: 2006

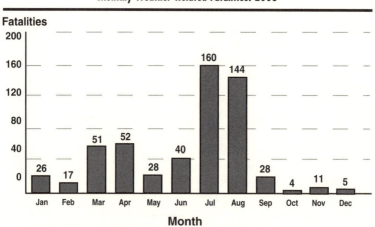

Source: U.S. Department of Commerce, National Oceanic and Atmospheric Administration. 2006. *Natural Hazard Statistics, 2006.* Washington, DC: U.S. Government Printing Office.

New York and Illinois each lost 42 residents to extreme heat, while Pennsylvania numbered 29 heat victims and 9 flood deaths. Forty lives were lost in Tennessee, 34 from tornadoes.

As far as property damage was concerned, severe weather left its mark. Total damages amounted to an estimated $11.72 billion in 2006. Property damages topped $7.98 billion, down from $96.7 billion in 2005. Compared with the previous two years, when hurricanes were the most damaging natural disasters, flooding caused the most property damage in 2006 (an estimated $3.97 billion in claims). Hail was responsible for $1.7 billion in losses, and tornadoes caused another $759 million in damages.

Finally, crop damages in 2006 created a loss of $3.7 billion. Drought was the leading cause, costing farmers $2.5 billion in lost crops. The hardest-hit states were Texas, which lost $2.43 billion in crop damage, and California, which suffered losses of $706 million.

Deployed Military Families

For this section, we will turn to an important demographic account of America's military population, a research investigation coauthored by David Segal and Mady Wechsler Segal (2004) of the Population Reference Bureau. The Population Reference Bureau is an organization seeking to inform the general public about various population trends and transitions, making available objective, applied, and up-to-date demographic research.

This particular analysis of America's military population focused on the approximately 1.4 million active-duty uniformed personnel serving in the four military branches of the armed forces, as well as their 1.9 million dependents. Segal and Segal's (2004) research examines the size, distribution, and composition of this population, analyzing deployment and other separations, marriage and family dynamics, and other lifestyle considerations.

Segal and Segal (2004) inform us that not until the last quarter of the 20th century did the armed forces emerge as a major piece in America's occupational and labor force. Of course, the pattern of surge and decline in the size of the armed forces changes when the United States mobilizes for war. Looking beyond the 1.4 million active-duty uniformed personnel today, it is easy to see how military service has impacted most families in the United States. About 26 million Americans living today have served in the armed forces—24 million of these are veterans, and 12 million are over age 60.

In Chapter 3, it was noted that war-related fatalities and injuries pose complex adjustments for both the veteran and the family. The largest number of combat fatalities (about 300,000) was associated with World War II, the largest military mobilization in U.S. history. The second-largest number (more than 50,000) is linked to America's second-largest mobilization, World War I. As this book goes to press, Operation Iraqi Freedom and Operation Enduring Freedom (in and around Afghanistan) continue to take their toll. To date, more than 4,000 service men and women have been killed and more than 16,600 service men and women have been wounded in action in Iraq, and more than 400 killed and 1,180 wounded in action in Operation Enduring Freedom (DefenseLink Casualty Statistics 2008).

We also mentioned in Chapter 3 that growing numbers of women in the military are deployed and sent overseas for military duty. Segal and Segal (2004) report that while women represented only 1.9 percent of military personnel in 1972, a shift occurred in 1973 with the introduction of an all-voluntary military. Faced with a shortage of qualified male volunteers, the military looked to female volunteers to fill the void. As a result, the percentage of female military personnel spiked, reaching 8.4 percent by 1980 and 15 percent by 2002. Along with this surge came increased job opportunities for enlisted women. Additionally, legal and regulatory changes removed many of the military's gender-based restrictions on the assignment of women to various jobs and positions. For example, in 1991, Congress repealed the provisions of a 1948 law that prohibited women from flying aircraft on combat missions. Starting in 1994, women are allowed to serve on U.S. Navy surface combatant ships.

However, women are still excluded from military units that engage in direct ground combat. This restriction means that women are legally barred from serving in approximately 20 percent of all military positions. To illustrate some of the restrictions, the U.S. Army prohibits females from serving in the fields of special forces, infantry, and armor. In the navy, females are permitted to serve in more than 90 percent of its ranks but are excluded from special forces (SEALS), submarines, and coastal patrol boats, among others. The U.S. Air Force, which has the largest percentage of females of all military branches, poses few restrictions on occupations and positions (approximately 99 percent of the assignments are not gender based). But women are not assigned to ground combat units, pararescue, and tactical air command and control. The U.S. Marine Corps has the smallest percentage of women (about 6 percent both of officers and enlisted personnel) and imposes the most restrictions. Women are excluded from infantry, armor, and artillery assignments, as well as a number of other ground combat units.

Women's occupational distributions within the military vary by rank. Most officers are in support jobs, usually health care and administrative specialties. Combined, these two assignments account for 55 percent of women, compared with only 20 percent of men. However, about 50 percent of female officers and enlisted women are in fields that are not traditional for military women. To illustrate, about 11 percent of female officers are in engineering and maintenance (about the same as for men), and 9 percent are in tactical operations occupations (compared with 42 percent of males). Among enlisted personnel, females are about as likely as men to be in service and supply specialties or intelligence and communication specialties, areas that extend beyond traditional female jobs. Furthermore, enlisted women's concentration in these nontraditional specialties has increased over time.

The research of Segal and Segal (2004) also reveals a statistical portrait of military families. At one time, the U.S. armed forces were composed of young single men. Those females who served in the armed forces who had children were not permitted to remain in the ranks, and men needed their commanding officer's permission to get married. However, trends have changed. Since the draft ended in 1973, the numbers of married military personnel have increased, due for the most part to the military's determination to retain trained and experienced personnel and reduce turnover.

Today, approximately half of U.S. military personnel are married, and nearly three-quarters have children. About 1.4 million active-duty service members have 1.9 million family members, including spouses, children, and adult dependents (such as siblings or parents). This means that America's armed forces have more family members than personnel in uniform. As far as demographics are concerned, more military men than military women are likely to be married or to have children. In many military marriages, both husband and wife are in the service, accounting for approximately 12 percent of all military marriages.

Although most of today's dual-military couples do not have children, the numbers who do are on the upswing.

Similar to demographic trends among civilians, the share of young military adults who are single (because they never married or are divorced or separated) has risen since 1990. Furthermore, a growing percentage of single military personnel have children. Although military women are more likely than men to be single parents, the much larger proportion of men in the armed forces means that there are more single fathers than single mothers. Within the enlisted and officer categories, higher-ranking personnel are more apt to be married than single, since rank and age are closely related. Only lower-ranking enlisted personnel are more apt to be single than married. Men are more likely than women to be married, except in the lowest enlisted ranks. Segal and Segal (2004) point out that the large gender differences among senior enlisted personnel and officers mirror the difficulty for women of juggling work and family life in the military, especially those women with youngsters.

Demographic differences in marriage and family life also exist in the four branches of the armed forces. For instance, air force personnel are more apt to be married than their cohorts in the other branches. This statistic might reflect the fact that those in the air force are the most likely to be viewing military service as a career. Although marine corps enlisted personnel on the whole are younger and less apt to be married than their counterparts in the other branches of the armed forces, enlisted women in the navy are less likely to be married than other enlisted women. Along the same lines, female officers in the navy and marine corps are less likely to be married than women officers in the army and the air force.

In each branch of the military, men are more likely to be married than their female peers, especially among officers. And among married military women, substantial proportions are married to military men. Across all branches, almost half of married enlisted women have established dual-service marriages. Most dual-service marriages are in the marine corps, followed by the air force. Higher-ranking (and therefore older) personnel are more likely than junior personnel to be married.

Finally, Segal and Segal (2004) illuminate racial differences in married military life. Black military women are less likely than other women to be single and childless, and more likely to be single parents. They are also more apt than other servicewomen to be in dual-service marriages with children and less likely to be in dual-military marriages without children. Such differences may be explained—at least in part—by the higher ranks of black women, who tend to remain in service longer than white women. Like black women in the armed forces, black military men are less likely than other men to be single and childless. They are also more likely than Asian/Pacific Islander, white, and Hispanic men to be single parents.

Segal and Segal (2004) note that with the passage of time, the military has been pressured to respond to the increases in the proportion of personnel with spouses and/or children, in single parents, in dual-service couples, and in spouse employment desires. With more frequent deployments and more dangerous missions, the military has been under pressure to respond to greater service member and family dissatisfaction with the military lifestyle and consequent difficulty in retaining experienced personnel. Whether the armed forces becomes more family friendly and eases the burdens borne by the military lifestyle remains to be seen.

Adolescent Suicide

We approach the topic of adolescent suicide by drawing reference to research conducted in 2006 by the Office of Applied Studies (OAS) in the Substance Abuse and Mental Health Services Administration. A branch of the government's Department of Health and Human Services, OAS gathers, analyzes, and makes available important public health information. To this end, OAS utilized two national surveys that probed such areas as suicidal ideation and attempts and, in particular, drug-related suicide attempts. The two surveys were the National Survey on Drug Use and Health and the Drug Abuse Warning Network. Within this section, information is drawn from findings gathered from these surveys (U.S. Department of Health and Human Services 2006b).

In the research design, subjects age 18 or older were asked questions to assess lifetime and past-year major depressive episodes (MDEs). (An MDE is a mental condition that persists for two or more weeks and causes a depressed mood or a loss of interest, as well as such symptoms as sleep problems, loss of appetite, or reduced energy levels.) Suicide-related questions were administered to respondents who reported being depressed for two weeks or longer. These survey items asked, among other questions, whether respondents had ever thought of ending their lives, whether the act of suicide was seen as a solution to their conditions, and whether they had made suicide plans or suicide attempts. Because mental illness and substance use often co-occur, respondents were also asked about their use of alcohol and illicit drugs during the 12 months prior to the interview.

Before turning to some of the major findings of the OAS investigation, the reader is reminded (see Chapter 3) of the high incidence rate of adolescent suicide. By 2004, suicide was the third-leading cause of death for children between the ages of 5 and 14 (10.9 per 100,000 young people in this age group) and for adolescents and young adults between the ages of 15 and 24 (10.3 per 1,000). Gender differences in suicide were also found in these two age groupings. Almost four times as many males as females age 15 to 19 died by suicide, and more than six times as many males as females age 20 to 24 died by suicide. As in the general population, young people were much more likely to use firearms, suffocation, and poisoning than other methods of suicide overall. However, while adolescents and young adults were more likely to use firearms than suffocation, children were dramatically more likely to use suffocation. Although suicide death rates are high for young people, note the disproportionate death rates for older Americans. Table 6.8 displays U.S. suicide death rates between 1950 and 2004; the shaded area highlights adolescence and the young adult years.

The OAS investigation's findings reveal that 14.5 percent of respondents age 18 or older (31.2 million adults) experienced at least one MDE in their lifetime, and 7.6 percent (16.4 million adults) experienced an MDE within the past year. Females were almost twice as likely as males to have experienced a past-year MDE (9.8 vs. 5.4 percent). Rates of past-year MDE varied by age group; people in late adolescence (age 18–20) were more likely to have had a past-year MDE, while adults age 55 or older were least likely to have had a past-year MDE (see Figure 6.26).

Among persons age 18 or older with a past-year MDE, 14.5 percent made suicide plans during their worst or most recent MDEs. Also, 10.4 percent (1.7 million adults) made suicide attempts during such episodes. No significant differences were found between males and females in attempting suicide, but males were more likely than females to have made suicide plans

TABLE 6.8
Death Rates for Suicide, by Age: United States, 1950–2004
(deaths per 100,000 resident population)

Age	1950	1960	1970	1980	1990	2000	2003	2004
All ages	13.2	12.5	13.1	12.2	12.5	10.4	10.8	10.9
5–14 years	0.2	0.3	0.3	0.4	0.8	0.7	0.6	0.7
15–24 years	4.5	5.2	8.8	12.3	13.2	10.2	9.7	10.3
15–19 years	2.7	3.6	5.9	8.5	11.1	8.0	7.3	8.2
20–24 years	6.2	7.1	12.2	16.1	15.1	12.5	12.1	12.5
25–44 years	11.6	12.2	15.4	15.6	15.2	13.4	13.8	13.9
25–34 years	9.1	10.0	14.1	16.0	15.2	12.0	12.7	12.7
35–44 years	14.3	14.2	16.9	15.4	15.3	14.5	14.9	15.0
45–64 years	23.5	22.0	20.6	15.9	15.3	13.5	15.0	15.4
45–54 years	20.9	20.7	20.0	15.9	14.8	14.4	15.9	16.6
55–64 years	26.8	23.7	21.4	15.9	16.0	12.1	13.8	13.8
65 years and over	30.0	24.5	20.8	17.6	20.5	15.2	14.6	14.3
65–74 years	29.6	23.0	20.8	16.9	17.9	12.5	12.7	12.3
75–84 years	31.1	27.9	21.2	19.1	24.9	17.6	16.4	16.3
85 years and over	28.8	26.0	19.0	19.2	22.2	19.6	16.9	16.4

Source: U.S. Department of Health and Human Services. 2007a. *Health, United States, 2006.* Washington, DC: U.S. Government Printing Office.

FIGURE 6.26
Percentages of Adults Age 18 or Older Reporting a Past-Year Major Depressive Episode, by Age Group

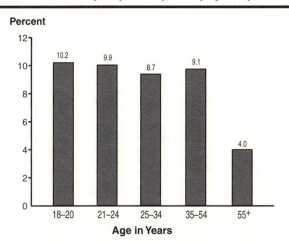

Source: U.S. Department of Health and Human Services. 2006b. *Suicidal Thoughts, Suicide Attempts, Major Depressive Episode, and Substance Use among Adults.* Office of Applied Studies. Washington, DC: U.S. Government Printing Office.

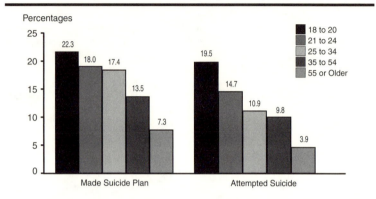

FIGURE 6.27
Percentages Reporting Suicide Plans and Attempts among Adults Age 18 or Older with Past-Year Major Depressive Episodes

Source: U.S. Department of Health and Human Services. 2006b. *Suicidal Thoughts, Suicide Attempts, Major Depressive Episode, and Substance Use among Adults.* Office of Applied Studies. Washington, DC: U.S. Government Printing Office.

(17.9 percent vs. 12.7 percent). Also seen were a few differences by age. Adults age 18 to 20 were more likely than adults in all other age groups to have attempted suicide, and adults age 55 or older with past-year MDEs were less likely to have made suicide plans (see Figure 6.27).

Adolescents age 18 or older who reported having used illicit drugs during the past month were also more likely to report past-year MDEs than adults who had not used illicit drugs during the past month (14.2 percent vs. 7.1 percent). Rates of past-year suicidal thoughts and suicide attempts were also higher among adults with past-year MDEs who had used illicit drugs during the past month than adults with past-year MDEs who had not used illicit drugs.

Finally, the OAS (U.S. Department of Health and Human Services 2006b) investigation explored characteristics of patients involved in emergency department visits for drug-related suicide attempts. In 2004, 106,079 emergency department visits were connected to drug-related suicide attempts by individuals 18 years of age or older. Females had a higher rate of attempts (57 visits per 100,000 population), while adults 55 years of age and older had the lowest rate (10 visits per 100,000). Once again, adolescents and young adults led all age groupings with the most

TABLE 6.9
Demographic Characteristics of Patients Age 18 or Older Treated in Emergency
Departments (EDs) for Drug-Related Suicide Attempts

Demographic Characteristics	Population (in millions)	Estimated ED Visits	ED Visits per 100,000 Population
Gender			
Male	144.5	41,430	39
Female	149.1	64,632	57
Age in Years			
18–20	12.4	11,145	90
21–24	16.9	13,180	78
25–34	40.0	30,076	75
35–54	85.7	45,111	53
55 or Older	65.4	6,568	10

Source: U.S. Department of Health and Human Services. 2006b. *Suicidal Thoughts, Suicide Attempts, Major Depressive Episode, and Substance Use among Adults.* Office of Applied Studies. Washington, DC: U.S. Government Printing Office.

emergency department visits (see Table 6.9). In 41 percent of the drug-related suicide attempts, a psychiatric condition was diagnosed; the most frequent diagnosis was depression, accounting for 36 percent of the total visits.

References

Bureau of Justice Statistics. 2006a. *Intimate Partner Violence in the United States.* Washington, DC: Bureau of Justice Statistics.

Bureau of Justice Statistics. 2006b. *Indicators of School Crime and Safety: 2006.* Washington, DC: Bureau of Justice Statistics.

Cooper, T. J. 2007. *Marriage, Divorce, Remarriage.* Longwood, FL: Xulon Press.

DefenseLink Casualty Report. 2008. "U.S. Military Casualty Update." [Online information; retrieved 5/5/08.] www.defenselink.mil/news/casualty.

Lebey, B. 2005. *Remarried with Children: Ten Secrets for Successfully Blending and Extending Your Family.* New York: Bantam.

Marsolini, M. 2006. *Raising Children in Blended Families: Helpful Insights, Expert Opinions, and True Stories.* Grand Rapids, MI: Kregel.

National Oceanic and Atmospheric Administration, U.S. Department of Commerce. 2006. *Natural Hazard Statistics, 2006.* Washington, DC: U.S. Government Printing Office.

Popkin, M. H., and E. Einstein. 2007. *Active Parenting for Stepfamilies.* Kennesaw, GA: Active Parenting Publishers.

Segal, D. R., and M. W. Segal. 2004. "America's Military Population." *Population Bulletin* 59 (4), 1–40. Washington, DC: Population Reference Bureau.

Stewart, S. D. 2007. *Brave New Stepfamilies.* Thousand Oaks, CA: Sage.

U.S. Census Bureau. 2008. *Statistical Abstract of the United States,* 127th ed. Washington, DC: U.S. Government Printing Office.

U.S. Department of Health and Human Services. 2006a. *Results from the 2006 National Survey on Drug Use and Health: National Findings.* Office of Applied Studies. Washington, DC: U.S. Government Printing Office.

U.S. Department of Health and Human Services. 2006b. *Suicidal Thoughts, Suicide Attempts, Major Depressive Episode, and Substance Use among Adults.* Office of Applied Studies. Washington, DC: U.S. Government Printing Office.

U.S. Department of Health and Human Services. 2007a. *Health, United States, 2006.* Washington, DC: U.S. Government Printing Office.

U.S. Department of Health and Human Services. 2007b. *A Profile of Older Americans: 2007.* Washington, DC: U.S. Government Printing Office.

U.S. Department of Health and Human Services. 2007c. *America's Children: Key National Indicators of Well-Being, 2007.* Washington, DC: U.S. Government Printing Office.

7

Directory of Organizations

This chapter contains a comprehensive listing of organizations, associations, and agencies related to the study of family stress and crises. Web site and e-mail contact information are included for further study. For the dual purpose of convenience and organization, the presentation of these sources is organized according to the sequence of problems, controversies, and solutions presented in Chapters 2 and 3. Readers will recall that Chapter 2 focuses on seven key family crises: addiction, adolescent runaways, unemployment, infidelity, divorce, chronic illness and disease, and caring for aging family members. Chapter 3 examines five problems plaguing families in the United States today: domestic violence, school violence, natural disasters, deployed military families, and adolescent suicide.

Addiction

Addiction Resource Guide
Web site: http://www.addictionresourceguide.com/aboutthisguide.html

A Web site whose mission is to help locate resources on addiction, it provides much information on topics such as self-help groups, addictive problems, and residential treatment resources. The directory of resources listed is organized and explained in simple and understandable terms and concepts. The Web site includes a section on government and intervention resources.

American Society of Addiction Medicine
Web site: http://www.asam.org

This organization seeks to improve the quality of addiction treatment with a particular emphasis on promoting the role of the physician treating the patient facing addiction issues. Readers will discover that this Web site is an excellent resource shedding light on treatment options for those suffering from alcoholism or other addictions. The Web site also offers professional information on licensed physicians in the area of addiction medicine.

Center for Alcohol and Addiction Studies
Web site: http://www.caas.brown.edu/Content/research/projects.html

Located at Brown University in Providence, Rhode Island, the center seeks to promote the identification, prevention, and effective treatment of alcoholism and other addictions through research, education, and policy advocacy. The Web site contains a number of useful links, including links to services and organizations located at Brown University, as well as national organizations specializing in the prevention of addictive behaviors.

Center for Education and Drug Abuse Research (CEDAR)
Web site: http://www.pitt.edu/~cedar/

The Center for Education and Drug Abuse Research, established in 1989, is sponsored by the University of Pittsburgh and funded by the National Institute on Drug Abuse. Its primary focus is to conduct research studies investigating the origins of substance abuse and substance use disorders. Visitors to this Web site will discover a plethora of research investigations and valuable links to other resources.

Community Anti-Drug Coalitions of America (CADCA)
Web site: http://www.cadca.org/

Founded in 1992 under the leadership of Alvah Chapman, this organization seeks to promote safe, healthy, and drug-free communities. Using various components of the community, from parents and businesses to health providers and social service agencies, CADCA works on behalf of more than 5,000 community coalitions in the United States. A particular strength of its programming is providing members with antidrug training opportunities, including specialized workshops and conferences.

National Clearinghouse for Alcohol &
Drug Information (NCADI)
Web site: http://ncadi.samhsa.gov/about/

The National Clearinghouse for Alcohol and Drug Information is sponsored by the U.S. Department of Health and Human Services and the Substance Abuse and Mental Health Services Administration. NCADI's mission is to build resilience and facilitate recovery for people with or at risk for mental or substance use disorders. The organization believes that substance abuse disorders and mental illnesses in general can be reduced by prevention and early intervention with carefully planned research-based services and community supports. This Web site contains a wealth of research studies, books, and pamphlets, as well as referrals to other organizations.

National Council on Alcoholism and Drug Dependence
Web site: http://www.ncadd.org

The National Council on Alcoholism and Drug Dependence was founded in 1944 by Marty Mann. The organization advocates the prevention and treatment of alcoholism and substance abuse through a nationwide network of affiliates. It provides comprehensive and informative publications on all drugs, as well as an exhaustive listing of links and resources. This is one of the more popular Web sites on the topic.

Adolescent Runaways

Child Find of America
Web site: http://www.childfindofamerica.org

Child Find of America was founded in 1980 by the mother of a missing child in upstate New York. Since its establishment, this national, not-for-profit organization has offered the general public information on how to prevent and resolve all cases of missing, abducted, and runaway children and teenagers. As the agency evolved over the years, Child Find of America has broadened its programming and now includes education, mediation, conflict resolution, and referral support services, among other specialties. Each year, the agency receives more than 15,000 calls for help from searching parents and law enforcement officials and brings more than 400 youngsters to a safe environment.

Child Quest International
Web site: http://www.childquest.org/

Readers seeking information on the prevention and recovery of missing, abused, and exploited children will find it at this Web site. Since its founding in 1990, Child Quest International has assisted in the recovery of more than 3,000 children and teenagers. Because the organization is funded through private and corporate donations, grants, and fund-raising, Child Quest never charges a fee to law enforcement or searching families. At the heart of its programming is the provision of safety education to children, teens, preteens, and parents in the war against child victimization. The organization provides extensive Internet resources and safety resources.

Child Welfare League of America (CWLA)
Web site: http://www.cwla.org/

The Child Welfare League of America was founded in 1920 as a means to share ideas and offer mutually supportive ways to promote the welfare and well-being of America's younger generations. Today, CWLA boasts a membership of nearly 800 public and private nonprofit agencies that extend their services each year. Among the targeted populations are runaway children and teenagers.

Family and Youth Services Bureau (FYSB)
Web site: http://www.acf.hhs.gov/programs/fysb/

Established in 1977 by the U.S. Department of Health and Human services, this organization seeks to monitor and improve social services support for the nation's children and families. It offers a variety of programming, including that related to adoption and foster care, child abuse and neglect, child support, disabilities, and child care. Visitors to this Web site will find a generous assortment of fact sheets, agency publications, policy and legislative documents, updates on conferences and events, and grant awards.

National Center for Missing and Exploited Children (NCMEC)
Web site: http://www.missingkids.com/

Established in 1984 as a private, nonprofit organization, the National Center for Missing and Exploited Children provides services designed to combat abduction and the sexual exploitation of children and teenagers. Since its inception, NCMEC has served as a national clearinghouse of information related to missing and exploited younger generations. It also offers a variety of training programs to law enforcement and social service professionals. Readers searching for more information on these topics will find a valuable listing of publications, including such topics as runaways, abduction, Internet safety, basic safety tips for teenagers, child protection, and sexual exploitation.

National Runaway Switchboard (NRS)
Web site: http://www.1800runaway.org/

The National Runaway Switchboard is one of America's most visible and active organizations to keep runaway and at-risk youth safe and off the streets. NRS was founded in 1971 by a group of Chicago agencies to address a growing need for comprehensive crisis intervention for youngsters in the area. In 1974, NRS received a federal demonstration grant to establish a national hotline and supportive services, which served to define the agency's mission and future. The 1-800-RUNAWAY hotline now handles more than 100,000 calls each year. The hotline is available 24 hours a day throughout the United States and its territories, including Puerto Rico, the U.S. Virgin Islands, and Guam.

Vanished Children's Alliance (VCA)
Web site: http://www.vca.org

The Vanished Children's Alliance was formed in 1980 by Georgia K. Hilgeman (VCA's current executive director) and other professionals and victims to address the growing problem of runaway and abducted children and adolescents. At the foundation of VCA's outreach efforts is a strong desire to educate public officials and professionals—as well as the community at large—about America's at-risk children and teens. Since its inception, the VCA has assisted in more than 30,000 cases of missing and abducted children. Of these, more than 90 percent have been found. The VCA does not charge for its services, instead preferring to spread its mission: a dedication to keeping children safe and bringing missing children home.

Unemployment

Bureau of Labor Statistics (BLS)
Web site: http://stats.bls.gov/

The Bureau of Labor Statistics is a branch of the U.S. Department of Labor and exists as a fact-finding agency for the United States in the areas of labor economics and statistics. BLS produces impartial, timely, and accurate data relevant to America's labor force and its families, including unemployment. Regarding the latter, this Web site provides up-to-date information on unemployment rates, employment by occupation, and job openings and labor turnover.

Careermag.com
Web site: http://www.careermag.com

This self-help Web site provides visitors with industry-specific career opportunities along with abundant information to assist individuals tailoring their information to career goals. Among the topics available to explore at this Web site are career consultation, resume building, continuing education, job descriptions, salary reports, franchise opportunities, and industry publications.

Employment Development Department (EDD)
Web site: http://www.edd.ca.gov/aboutedd.htm

Sponsored by the state of California, the Employment Development Department seeks to connect job seekers and employers. The EDD offers a variety of services, including an online job and resume bank, information on filing for unemployment insurance or disability insurance claims, labor market tools to help the unemployed make educated and calculated vocational decisions, information related to employment tax information and forms, and a variety of other vocational and training services.

Employment Guide
Web site: http://www.employmentguide.com

One of the more popular Web sites available to job seekers, Employment Guide makes available a wide range of vocational opportunities, from large franchise opportunities to working from home. Visitors will discover a number of worthwhile topics to investigate, such as educational opportunities and job fairs. The Web site is quite user friendly.

Employment Spot
Web site: http://www.employmentspot.com/

This Web site captures the pulse of today's employment world, including listings of jobs by city, state, or industry. Offering added appeal to this Web site is an extensive library of employment articles on the following timely topics: criteria for choosing an ideal career, employment tips to earn a promotion, minority job and career resources, interviewing dos and don'ts, fastest growing occupations in the United States today, and keys to successful networking.

Michigan eLibrary (MeL)
Web site: http://www.mel.org/SPT—BrowseResources NewMeL.php

This is the official state of Michigan Web site, and it is one of the best of its kind on the Internet. Among its many prominent features are recommended Web sites for specialized topics, databases, and books and journals. More than 45 databases are available to the user, making this an ideal source for students and other readers researching topics related to unemployment. The databases contain full-text articles from magazines, journals, and newspapers as well as digital books.

Monthly Labor Review Online
Web site: http://stats.bls.gov/opub/mlr/welcome.htm

This online resource provides users with complete access to the *Monthly Labor Review*. The *Monthly Labor Review,* founded in 1915, is an authoritative journal of research and analysis from the Bureau of Labor Statistics, drawing upon the collective expertise of economists, statisticians, and other labor force specialists within the private and public sectors. It provides a wide scope of data on employment, including trends in the labor force, inflation, wages, and occupational illnesses and injuries. This online resource makes available access to related Bureau of Labor Statistics programs, as well as valuable links and other resources. This is a highly recommended Web site.

Occupational Outlook Handbook (*OOH*)
Web site: http://www.bls.gov/OCO/

The *Occupational Outlook Handbook* is a must stop for anyone exploring the labor market in these modern times. Published by the U.S. Department of Labor, the *OOH* offers a detailed analysis of hundreds of different types of vocations, offering insight into earnings, anticipated job prospects, job descriptions, working conditions, and training and education needed. The *OOH* is widely known as a valuable and comprehensive career resource, and its user-friendly design allows visitors to this Web site easy access to important sources of vocational information.

Quintessential Careers
Web site: http://www.quintcareers.com/

Attracting more than 1 million visitors each month, this Web site is widely respected in the career world. Visitors will discover a variety of job hunting tips, from developing effective resumes to filing for unemployment benefits. The Web site offers more than 3,500 pages of free college, career, and job-search content and provides visitors with help in writing cover letters, networking, interviewing, and negotiating salaries. The Web site also offers tips, links, and expert advice about undergraduate and graduate college degrees, financial aid, and distance learning.

Infidelity

Affairs-Help
Web site: http://www.affairs-help.com/

This Web site features the expertise of Emily M. Brown, LCSW, director of Key Bridge Therapy and Mediation Center in Arlington, Virginia. She offers her assistance to couples, individuals, and families regarding the underlying issues in marriage, divorce, and betrayal. Her Web site offers a variety of resources to visitors, including publication, consultation services, self-assessment exercises, and links to other Web sites.

**American Association for Marriage and
Family Therapy (AAMFT)**
Web site: http://www.aamft.org/families/consumer_updates/
infidelity.asp

The American Association for Marriage and Family Therapy is a
highly respected professional organization representing marriage
and family therapists. In addition to information about infidelity,
this Web site offers references and resources on the topic, as well
as links to other Web sites.

American Counseling Association (ACA)
Web site: http://www.counseling.org/

Established in 1952, the American Counseling Association is an
organization dedicated to the growth and visibility of the counseling profession. ACA has the distinction of being the world's
largest association representing professional counselors in various practice settings. Members will find an abundance of information here on the topics of marriage and infidelity, along with
myriad topics designed to enhance the quality of life.

Center for Internet Addiction Recovery
Web site: http://www.netaddiction.com/

This Web site was established in 1995 by Kimberly Young, PhD, an
accomplished author and professor at St. Bonaventure University
in New York. The Web site leaves no stone unturned addressing
the many issues surrounding Internet addiction, including cyber-
sex pornography, online affairs, online gambling, online gaming,
compulsive surfing, and eBay addiction. The Web site also offers
valuable articles, books, tapes, and a referral directory of therapists.

Infidelity.com
Web site: http://www.infidelity.com/

Another Web site providing visitors with information on how to
best deal with an unfaithful partner, infidelity.com offers an extensive and comprehensive array of services, in-depth information, and wide-ranging support, including advice from divorce
attorneys, therapists, mediators, arbitrators, and child custody
experts. Another strength is the provision of useful articles and
books on such topics as spotting the signs of infidelity, emotional
infidelity, and ways to survive infidelity.

Infidelity Help
Web site: http://infidelityhelp.com/

This Web site features the insights of Don-David Lusterman, PhD, a licensed psychologist and nationally certified provider of psychological services specializing in infidelity, couples, and family therapy. He sheds light on a number of issues related to infidelity, from what to do if your partner is having an affair to what to do if your parent is being unfaithful. The Web site lists many available books and resources.

The Kinsey Institute
Web site: http://www.kinseyinstitute.org/resources/FAQ.html

The Kinsey Institute, founded in 1947 and located at Indiana University, promotes interdisciplinary research and scholarship in the fields of human sexuality, gender, and reproduction. This is an excellent Web site for students and other readers wanting to research topics related to all aspects of human sexuality, including infidelity. Visitors to this Web site will discover a rich assortment of articles, books, and book chapters representing the work of researchers during their affiliation with The Kinsey Institute. This Web site is highly recommended.

Divorce

Academy of Family Mediators (AFM)
Web site: http://www.mediate.com/people/personprofile.cfm?auid=724

Founded in 1981, the Academy of Family Mediators is the largest family mediation organization in the United States. Its membership consists of mediators in many different sectors, such as the government, schools, courts, and private practice. The Web site contains an impressive listing of mediators at local, state, national, and international levels. It also provides users with a listing of resources, including recently published articles and books.

American Bar Association, Section of Family Law
Web site: http://www.abanet.org/family

The American Bar Association's Section of Family Law boasts a membership of more than 10,000 lawyers, associates, and law students across the United States and abroad. The membership serves the field of family law in such areas as divorce, child custody, adoption, and elder law. The Web site provides visitors with a number of diverse publications to meet educational and informational needs, as well as a generous listing of general public and legal resources. For students undertaking research on the topic of family law, this is a valuable Web site.

DivorceSource
Web site: http://www.divorcesource.com/

A unique Web site offering information on virtually every aspect of separation and divorce, DivorceSource is user friendly as well as supportive in its guidance and advice. Among the divorce topics and services available to visitors are divorce laws by state, state resources, children and divorce, child support, property division, and child custody.

National Conflict Resolution Center (NCRC)
Web site: http://www.ncrconline.com/index.shtml

Founded in 1983, the National Conflict Resolution Center was established by the University of San Diego Law Center and the San Diego County Bar Association. An international leader in mediation and conflict resolution, NCRC operates as a private, nonprofit corporation. The mediation process is handled by family law attorneys, who assist couples in reaching their own agreements on all family law issues, including division of assets and debts and child custody. Since its inception, NCRC has managed thousands of cases, serving clients from public agencies, private industry, the courts, and community and local governments. Services offered by NCRC include conflict resolution, mediation training, community mediation, divorce mediation, and coaching.

National Family Resiliency Center, Inc. (NFRC)
Web site: http://www.divorceabc.com/

This is one of the better Web sites offering supportive advice to families experiencing separation, divorce, and remarriage. Its central theme is helping partners and children to better understand and accept the realities of relationship dissolution with programs and resources. Particular strengths are the provision of articles related to divorce and separation, resources for professionals, and listings of educational seminars and support groups.

Oregon Mediation Center, Inc.
Web site: http://www.to-agree.com

The Oregon Mediation Center was founded in 1983 by Jim Melamed. Through its practice of mediation, the center seeks to offer supportive guidance to the parties involved, assist partners to most capably work together, and help each participant to achieve the greatest available satisfaction. The Web site contains a number of excellent family mediation articles.

Rainbows
Web site: http://www.rainbows.org/mission.html

Rainbows was established in 1983, its vision being to reach out to youngsters grieving a loss from a life-altering crisis. Rainbows is headed by Suzy Yehl Marta and was inaugurated in Chicago. Today, Rainbows has been implemented in 49 of the United States as well as Australia, England, New Zealand, and Switzerland. An estimated 1.6 million participants have benefited from the assistance provided by Rainbows. Visitors to this Web site will discover a host of materials related to programs and training, as well as links to useful resources.

Support Guidelines
Web site: http://www.supportguidelines.com

This Web site will prove invaluable for those readers looking for more information on the interpretation and application of child support guidelines in the United States. Among the contents are a comprehensive overview of the history of child support guidelines as well as child support guidelines for all 50 states and the District of Columbia. An extensive library of articles and books is complemented by a well-rounded listing of resources and links.

Chronic Illness and Disease

American Chronic Pain Association
Web site: http://www.theacpa.org/

The American Chronic Pain Association is one of the more active and visible organizations in this area. It seeks to supply information and support to chronic pain sufferers and their families and to educate the general public about issues related to chronic pain. It offers an extensive news archive that keeps visitors aware of up-to-date developments in pain management.

National Center for Chronic Disease Prevention and Health Promotion
Web site: http://www.cdc.gov/nccdphp/index.htm

Sponsored by the Centers for Disease Control and Prevention, this government Web site is a good information source for chronic illnesses and physical disabilities. The center's programming revolves around three components: preventing death and disability from chronic diseases; promoting health and optimal well-being across the lifespan; and developing partnerships with health and education agencies, major voluntary associations, the private sector, and other federal agencies. The Web site offers access to a data warehouse containing information on all chronic diseases and illnesses as well as health facts for all ages.

National Dissemination Center for Children with Disabilities
Web site: http://www.nichcy.org/

The National Dissemination Center for Children with Disabilities is a comprehensive and detailed source of information on disabilities in infants, toddlers, children, and youth. The Web site contains current issues in research and practice as well as road maps to future research possibilities. This organization also provides disability-related resources in each state as well as very useful state resource sheets. The latter enable visitors to locate organizations and agencies within their states that address disability-related issues.

National Institute on Disability and Rehabilitation Research (NIDRR)
Web site: http://www.ed.gov/about/offices/list/osers/nidrr/index.html?src=mr

The National Institute on Disability and Rehabilitation Research offers a comprehensive program of research related to the rehabilitation of individuals with disabilities. Established in 1978, NIDRR is dedicated to educating the general public about disability and research and to expanding society's capacity to provide full opportunities and accommodations for its disabled citizens, from birth through adulthood.

New Health Partnerships
Web site: http://www.newhealthpartnerships.org/

New Health Partnerships is sponsored by the Robert Wood Johnson Foundation and is geared toward offering information and support to enhance the care and health of individuals afflicted with long-term medical conditions. The organization maintains that patients and families can forge important and needed partnerships with health care providers, in the process creating optimal health care. At this Web site visitors will discover such topics as communicating about health, helping people change, connecting with the community, helping systems change, and using technology. Each of these topics is accompanied by many different links and resources.

WebMD
Web site: http://www.webmd.com/

WebMD provides a wealth of medical information, including tools for managing one's health and supportive guidance to those who are seeking information. The mission of WebMD is to provide users with important and timely health information. It regularly offers in-depth medical news, reference material, features, and online community programs. In addition, the Web site includes newsletters and message boards, the latter enabling users to share their conditions and experiences with others and obtain relevant health information. The content of WebMD is not intended to replace professional medical advice, diagnosis, or treatment.

Caring for Aging Family Members

Aging Parents and Elder Care
Web site: http://www.aging-parents-and-elder-care.com/

This is a highly recommended Web site to those searching for information on elder care. The Web site's mission is to offer the best possible information for caring for aging parents, regardless of whether you are managing the care of aged family members in the home or offering assistance from a distant location. One of its strongest features is information directed to new caregivers, particularly tips to ease the transition. The Web site provides many articles on the topic as well as support groups on elder care.

Caregivers Home Companion
Web site: http://www.caregivershome.com/

The Caregivers Home Companion is a Web site designed to provide the general public with practical guidance, information, advice, and resources for family caregivers. Another important function of this organization is helping caregivers take care of themselves and safeguarding their well-being. In addition to archived articles, the Web site offers a caregiver's hotline and forums. One of the unique features of this organization is that it offers specialized information on the topic, including spousal, professional, spiritual, and family caregiving.

Children of Aging Parents (CAPS)
Web site: http://www.caps4caregivers.org/

Established in 1977 in Levittown, Pennsylvania, this nonprofit, charitable organization offers assistance to caregivers of the aged or chronically ill with timely information, referrals, and support. Driving this mission is the organization's desire to heighten public awareness of caregiving and the many challenges providers face. The Web site is well stocked with valuable links and resources. CAPS is one of the more visible, active, and respected resources of its kind.

Family Caregiver Alliance (FCA)
Web site: http://www.caregiver.org/

Another good resource for those seeking information on caregiving for aging parents, the Family Caregiver Alliance was founded in 1977 in San Francisco. Its mission has remained steady over the years: to address the needs of families and loved ones faced with providing long-term care at home. Since its founding, the organization has mushroomed and now offers programs at the local, state, and national levels. The extensive listing of fact sheets, research publications, newsletters, and support groups makes this Web site well worth the visit.

National Caregivers Library
Web site: http://www.caregiverslibrary.org/

Anyone doing research on the topic of caregiving will find this Web site valuable. It contains hundreds of articles, books, and links to topic-specific resources. Located in Richmond, Virginia, the National Caregivers Library has as its mission to seek to help caregivers find supportive assistance. Among the available topics are types of care facilities, disabilities, diseases, and end-of life issues. The Web site also offers a listing of government resources, legal issues, and long-distance care options.

National Family Caregivers Association (NFCA)
Web site: http://www.nfcacares.org/

The National Family Caregivers Association was created in 1993 by Suzanne Mintz and Cindy Fowler, both of whom at the time were caring for aging family members. Their vision was to supply information and resources to caregivers and to let them know they were not alone and without support. This vision has stood unwavering over the years, the organization empowering family caregivers to act on behalf of their loved ones and removing or minimizing barriers to health and well being. Among its resources, NFCA offers hundreds of caregiving Web sites and resources for such important topics as insurance, training, respite, disease-specific information, and Medicare.

Domestic Violence

Administration for Children & Families (ACF)
Web site: www.acf.hhs.gov/

The Administration for Children & Families is a branch of the U.S. Department of Health and Human Services, which exists to protect the health of all Americans and provide supportive programming, especially to those who are incapable of helping themselves. ACF seeks to empower families to increase their economic independence and build healthy and supportive communities. The organization is committed to curbing all forms of domestic violence and offers a variety of resources, including related links, hotlines, fact sheets, and other important information.

Child Abuse Prevention Network
Web site: www.child-abuse.com/

The Child Abuse Prevention Network Web site offers visitors detailed and practical information on all aspects of child maltreatment, including physical abuse, psychological maltreatment, sexual abuse, and emotional abuse and neglect. The Web site is one of the most thorough of its kind on the Internet, with a diversity of available topics, including tools to support the identification, investigation, treatment, adjudication, and prevention of child maltreatment. The Web site also provides child abuse reporting hotlines, state by state.

Domestic Violence and Violence Related Research Resources
Web site: www.growing.com/nonviolent/research/dvlinks.htm

For those undertaking research in child abuse or domestic violence in general, this is a must stop in your literature review. The Web site provides an exhaustive listing of links, articles, books, and other valuable resources. Among the multitude of available topics are cross-cultural variations in domestic violence; associations, commissions, foundations, institutes, and societies; batterers' intervention resources; books, videos, and publications; child trauma; Bureau of Justice statistics; Children's Bureau resources; and legal issues in domestic violence.

Family Violence Prevention Fund (FVPF)
Web site: www.endabuse.org/

The Family Violence Prevention Fund is an organization whose mission is to prevent violence within the home by reaching out to help those whose lives have been impacted by violence. Additionally, FVPF seeks to reach out to communities to ensure that antiviolence programming remains intact, seeking to change the way employers, health care providers, police, and judges address violence. Visitors to this Web site will also learn how FVPF has extended itself to organizations around the globe, sharing strategies designed to stop violence against women and children. The organization has established partnerships in Russia, India, China, and Mexico.

National Clearinghouse on Families & Youth (NCFY)
Web site: www.ncfy.com/

The National Clearinghouse on Families & Youth was established by the Family and Youth Services Bureau (FYSB) and the U.S. Department of Health and Human Services. Its primary purpose is to distribute free information to individuals, organizations, and communities interested in developing new strategies for supporting youngsters and their families. In the area of domestic abuse, NCFY offers an array of important resources, including a literature database, which contains publications related to family violence prevention. FYSB also awards grants for the provision of shelter, emergency transportation, and child care to victims of family violence and their dependents.

National Organization for Women (NOW)
Web site: http://www.now.org/

The National Organization for Women is the largest organization of feminist activists in the United States. Founded in 1966, NOW has as its vision to bring about equality for all women. The organization seeks to end harassment and discrimination in the labor force, educational sector, justice system, and all other segments of society. A visit to the NOW Web site will enable readers to learn more about the organization's efforts to end all acts of violence against women. The Web site provides facts and statistics about violence against women, progress made against domestic violence, news updates, research, and links to related resources.

Violence Against Women and Family Violence Program
Web site: www.ojp.usdoj.gov/nij/vawprog/pubs.html

The Violence Against Women and Family Violence Program promotes the safety and well-being of women and family members and seeks to increase the efficiency of the criminal justice system's response to domestic violence. The Web site contains research reports as well as information on program grants and workshops. Related content at the Web site addresses intimate partner violence, child abuse and maltreatment, elder abuse, human trafficking, rape and sexual violence, and victims and victimization.

School Violence

American Academy of Child and Adolescent Psychiatry (AACAP)
Web site: http://www.aacap.org

The American Academy of Child and Adolescent Psychiatry, established in 1953, is a nonprofit medical association dedicated to improving the quality of life for children and adolescents. It offers many services to its members, including how to help youngsters cope with school and community violence, in the process strengthening their resiliency. The AACAP Web site is rich with resources, including fact sheets, directories for therapists, videos, and policy statements. Visitors will also discover a number of topics related to school violence: understanding violent behavior in children and adolescents, posttraumatic stress disorder, helping children after a disaster, children and firearms, and bullying.

Center for the Prevention of School Violence (CPSV)
Web site: http://www.ncdjjdp.org/cpsv

The Center for the Prevention of School Violence was established in 1993 and is part of North Carolina's Department of Juvenile Justice and Delinquency Prevention. Its mission is to make schools safe and nonviolent, free of fear, and conducive to learning. Central to its mission is developing an awareness and understanding of school violence, then proposing strategies to eliminate it. The center offers a number of valuable resources, including background readings on school shootings, resource documents and sites, school violence statistics, research bulletins, and parent resources.

International Bullying Prevention Association (IBPA)
Web site: http://www.stopbullyingworld.org/

The International Bullying Prevention Association is an organization that strives to promote and share bullying prevention principles and practices in order to achieve a safe school climate, healthy work surroundings, good citizenship, and civic responsibility. Members/trainers of IBPA seek to exemplify the highest ethical standards in providing and supporting sound, research-based bullying prevention training. Four principles rest at the foundation of the IBPA: ethical teaching practices, ethical conduct toward practices and performance, ethical conduct toward professional colleagues, and ethical conduct toward one's community. This Web site contains an abundance of articles, books, materials for bullying prevention programs, links, videos, and policy guidelines.

National Association of School Psychologists (NASP)
Web site: http://www.nasponline.org

The National Association of School Psychologists is a professional organization seeking to optimize the learning and mental health of school children, including their safety and well-being. One of the many strengths of this Web site is the variety of topics unavailable at other Web sites: vulnerability to violence among gay, lesbian, and bisexual youth; aggression, antisocial behavior, and violence among girls; best practices in school violence prevention; how bullying can lead to violent behavior; and principles for identifying early warning signs of school violence.

National Center for Children Exposed to Violence (NCCEV)
Web site: http://www.healthfinder.gov/orgs/HR3712.htm

The National Center for Children Exposed to Violence is part of the U.S. Department of Health and Human Services. Its mission is to help communities deal with all kinds of violence through public awareness programming and to train the specialists who provide intervention and support. NCCEV publishes educational materials and offers an extensive resource center for visitors. It contains a diverse collection of materials on children's exposure to violence within homes, schools, and communities. A database contains an online library of citations to fact sheets, research briefs, articles, books, chapters, and curricula. For the person doing research on school violence, the database is a good starting point.

National School Safety Center (NSSC)
Web site: http://www.schoolsafety.us

The National School Safety Center focuses its energy on helping institutions of higher education develop safety and crisis management plans. More specifically, NSSC offers the training tools and strategies specific to the culture and safety needs of a particular institution. Once the plan is in place, it is anticipated that heightened levels of campus security and preparedness will have been achieved. A number of resources are available at this Web site, including books, articles, videos, school safety updates, and school crime and violence statistics. Browsers will also find some interesting territory to explore: bullying, schools and readiness, creating a safe school system, national alert systems, and schools and terrorism.

Virginia Youth Violence Project
Web site: http://youthviolence.edschool.virginia.edu/home.html

The Virginia Youth Violence Project is sponsored by the Curry School of Clinical and School Psychology at the University of Virginia. The project seeks to identify effective methods and programming for youth violence prevention, particularly within the school setting. The project conducts and distributes research on the understanding and reduction of youth violence, and it provides education, consultation, and training for teachers, psychologists, and other human services practitioners. The Web site is one of the best of its kind on the Internet, providing visitors with resources on such topics as responding to student threats of violence, reducing the risks of gun violence, school violence myths, threat assessment training, juvenile homicide, and bullying. The Web site also contains extensive reading lists, links to other resources, research reports, and conference presentations.

Wellesley Centers for Women (WCW)
Web site: http://www.wcwonline.org/bullying/index.html

Since 1974, the Wellesley Centers for Women, located at Wellesley (Massachusetts) College, has launched a number of interdisciplinary studies on issues such as sexual harassment in schools, gender violence, and adolescent development. Its ongoing project on teasing and bullying seeks to explore and counteract the effects of child and adolescent bullying. WCW delves into the topic by raising public awareness about bullying and by exploring the connections among bullying, other forms of aggression, and violence. Combining research, action, and advocacy, WCW seeks to better understand the impact of societal messages about gender and gender roles on the development of aggressive and violent behavior. The WCW Web page titled "Teasing and Bullying" contains, among other topics, facts and statistics on bullying, research references, training programs, and related publications.

Natural Disasters

American Academy of Pediatrics (AAP)
Web site: http://www.aap.org/new/disasterresources.htm

The American Academy of Pediatrics is a medical organization whose mission is to promote the well-being of all children and teenagers. It offers many different child health resources and programs, including intervention in the wake of natural disasters. Among the resources at this Web site are how to prepare for natural disasters, psychosocial issues for parents and children involved in natural disasters, and responding to children's emotional needs during crisis situations. Among the more specific and recent topics are the roles of government agencies in planning for and responding to disasters and bioterrorism; health risks of children from wildfires; the care of infants and children during pandemic influenza; and infant nutrition during a natural disaster.

American Psychological Association Help Center
Web site: http://www.apahelpcenter.org/about/

The American Psychological Association Help Center is an online resource center for brochures, guidelines, and articles on the psychological issues that affect a person's physical and emotional well-being. The resources at this Web site are designed to help both young and old cope more effectively with the disruption and upheaval that natural disasters bring. Coverage is given to such topics as managing traumatic stress originating from natural disasters; tornadoes, hurricanes, and children's needs; and achieving resiliency following a natural disaster. The Web site includes guidelines for locating a psychologist and ordering reprints of articles.

American Red Cross Disaster Services
Web site: http://www.redcross.org/services/disaster/
0,1082,0_501_,00.html

The American Red Cross was established in 1905 and is focused on meeting people's immediate emergency disaster-caused needs. When a disaster strikes, the Red Cross provides food, shelter, and health services to address basic human needs. It also feeds emergency workers, responds to inquiries from concerned family members living outside the disaster region, provides blood and blood products to disaster victims, and assists those impacted by disaster to access other available resources. The Web site offers information on all types of natural disasters as well as a range of related topics, including health and safety services, community services, youth services, biomedical services, and international services. Visitors also find press releases, assorted publications, media contacts, and a video library.

Center for Catastrophe Preparedness & Response (CCPR)
Web site: http://www.nyu.edu/ccpr/

The Center for Catastrophe Preparedness and Response was established in 2002 and is located at New York University. It serves as a resource center to enhance preparedness and response capabilities to natural disasters and other catastrophic events and public health emergencies. Its mission is fivefold: to increase America's knowledge base on emergency preparedness; to conduct research addressing the many issues that surround preparedness and response; to provide a forum for public- and private-sector officials to exchange best practices; to serve as a model academic center that is responsive to a critical national need; and to offer support for academic-based research and training and educational opportunities for faculty and students. Published research produced by the center, its projects, and research fellows is available at the Web site.

Centers for Disease Control and Prevention (CDC)
Emergency Preparedness & Response
Web site: http://www.bt.cdc.gov/disasters/

The Centers for Disease Control and Prevention was founded in 1946 and is located in Atlanta. CDC has been a world leader in public health since its inception, promoting health and quality of life by preventing and controlling disease, injury, and disability. At the Emergency Preparedness & Response Web site, visitors will find coverage on virtually every type of natural disaster, from earthquakes and hurricanes to volcanoes and tsunamis. The Web site also offers a considerable amount of information on disaster preparedness, including tips for staying safe, information for evacuation centers and evacuees, protecting pets, power outages, and cleanup. Additionally, readers will discover a wealth of links, surveillance reports, and news releases from CDC.

Disaster Training International
Web site: http://www.disastertraining.org/

Disaster Training International is an organization whose vision is to help adults help children who are faced with the threat, existence, and aftermath of natural disasters or other devastating trauma. More specifically, the organization provides emergency preparedness training, assists with the lessening of hazards at schools, teaches staff how to respond to disasters so that children are safe and can heal, and shows how schools can forge partnerships with families that always keep children at the forefront. The Web site offers an excellent selection of written materials and links to other important sites. Given the organization's mission, this Web site should have significant appeal to teachers, administrators, parents, child care providers, family life specialists, and social workers.

Federal Emergency Management Agency (FEMA)
Web site: http://www.fema.gov/

The Federal Emergency Management Agency is a government-sponsored organization charged with building and supporting America's emergency management system. In 2003, FEMA became part of the U.S. Department of Homeland Security. From a broad perspective, FEMA prepares for disasters and emergencies, such as natural and man-made disasters, and helps people recover from them, reduce the risk of loss, and prevent similar emergencies from recurring. Headquartered in Washington, D.C., FEMA works in partnership with other national organizations and agencies instrumental in America's emergency management system. Among the partners are local and state emergency management agencies, federal agencies, and the American Red Cross.

National Child Traumatic Stress Network (NCTSN)
Web site: http://www.nctsnet.org

The National Child Traumatic Stress Network was established by the U.S. Congress in 2000. Coordinated by Duke University and the University of California at Los Angeles, NCTSN is a unique collaboration of academic and community-based social services. Its mission is to upgrade the standard of care and access to services for America's traumatized children and their families. Visitors to this Web site will find an outstanding assortment of resources related to natural disasters and how they impact children and adolescents. Each type of natural disaster is indexed according to a description of it, guidelines for readiness, responses during the disaster, and eventual recovery. Print materials are indexed according to intended audience: parents and caregivers, medical and mental health professionals, educators, and relief workers.

Deployed Military Families

America Supports You
Web site: http://www.americasupportsyou.mil

America Supports You was established in 2004 by the U.S. Department of Defense. Its mission is to provide opportunities for citizens, organizations, and companies to show their support for the armed forces, both home and abroad. America Supports You home front groups demonstrate their support in a number of ways, including sending care packages, writing letters and e-mails, and offering scholarships and helping the wounded when they return home. The Web site details how individuals and family members can show their support or send messages to troops. It also contains recent news, press releases, corporate supporters, and upcoming events.

Military Child Education Coalition (MCEC)
Web site: http://www.militarychild.org/

The Military Child Education Coalition is a nonprofit, worldwide organization that identifies the challenges that face the military child, increases understanding of these challenges in military and educational communities, and implements programs to successfully address the challenges. The coalition assists schools and military installations in delivering programming and materials that address the transitioning needs of military children and their families. The Web site offers information on such topics as checklists for transferring students, deployment/separation issues, educational partnerships for military families, parent and school support, and student enrichment. Links to other important sources are also available, including those related to school and family, school scholarships, and military organizations. The Web site also has newsletters, information related to training workshops, and various publications and printed materials.

Military Family Research Institute (MFRI)
Web site: http://www.cfs.purdue.edu/mfri/

The Military Family Research Institute is a research program located at Purdue University in Indiana. It is funded by the Lilly Endowment and the Department of Defense, Office of Military Community and Family Policy. The institute conducts outreach programming and activities that assist military families in Indiana and also executes research studies that provide insight into the military quality of life. The Web site is both interesting and informative. Visitors are afforded the opportunity to examine the kinds of research conducted by the MFRI, including research program focus, current projects, and reports. Also available are deployment support resources, including a listing of valuable links to key programs and organizations. The Web site contains a listing of organizations making significant contributions to the success of MFRI.

Military HOMEFRONT
Web site: http://www.militaryhomefront.dod.mil/

Military HOMEFRONT is a military organization that provides accurate and up-to-date information about Department of Defense programs serving troops and their families. A particular emphasis is placed on providing a service that enhances the quality of life, one that supports military members, their families, and retirees across the life cycle. The Web site is extensive in its coverage of military family topics, including deployment, casualty assistance, counseling, education for service personnel and their families, legal assistance, new parent support, financial management, and moving. Links to other resources are provided along with a directory of military installations, including locations of all installation programs and services, maps, and directions.

National Military Family Association (NMFA)
Web site: www.nmfa.org

The National Military Family Association is a nonprofit organization that was founded in 1969. At that time the organization was named the National Military Wives Association by a group of wives and widows. It was renamed the National Military Family Association in 1984 to capture the wider scope of the entire family system. Its mission is to advocate for improvements in the quality of military family life. NMFA has significant support at top levels of the Department of Defense and works regularly on important issues and concerns with other military-related associations. The Web site contains a variety of topics and accompanying resources such as predeployment checklists for military families, advancing the health of the family left behind, and returning to family life after military deployment. An impressive list of links is also available, including deployment support sites, service Web sites, Department of Defense Web sites, legislative and government agency sites, and family assistance sites.

Adolescent Suicide

American Association of Suicidology (AAS)
Web site: http://www.suicidology.org/

The American Association of Suicidology was founded in 1968 by clinical psychologist Edwin S. Shneidman. AAS is a nonprofit organization whose membership consists of mental health practitioners, crisis center volunteers, public health professionals, survivors of suicide, and those persons who have an interest in suicide prevention. The mission of AAS is to conduct and promote research, public awareness programs, public education, and training for professionals and volunteers. Additionally, AAS serves as a national clearinghouse for information on suicide. The Web site offers more detail on the organization, including conferences and training, publications, survivor support services, accreditation, and certification. Also available at the Web site are links of interest as well as a directory of support groups in the United States.

American Foundation for Suicide Prevention (AFSP)
Web site: http://www.afsp.org

The American Foundation for Suicide Prevention was founded in 1987 and devotes itself to understanding and preventing suicide through research and education and to reaching out to people with mood disorders and those impacted by suicide. Its mission consists of six components: funding scientific research; offering educational programs for professionals; educating the general public about mood disorders and suicide prevention; promoting policies and legislation that impact suicide and prevention; providing programs and resources for survivors of suicide loss; and providing programs and resources for people with mood disorders and their families. Features of the Web site include educational resources that embrace the AFSP mission, suicide prevention projects, grants, AFSP news releases, and advocacy and public policy.

National Council for Suicide Prevention (NCSP)
Web site: http://www.ncsp.org/

The National Council for Suicide Prevention, founded in 1999, is an organization promoting suicide prevention through collaborative information sharing and activities with other affiliations. The organization is dedicated to working within the private and public sectors to promote the *National Strategy for Suicide Prevention: Goals and Objectives for Action,* a visionary document encouraging the convergence of allied professionals to collectively curb this alarming social problem. The document was drafted by the Department of Health and Human Services under the direction of the Substance Abuse and Mental Health Services Administration, Center for Mental Health, and the Office of the Surgeon General. NCSP helped shape and release this document to the public sector in 2001.

National Institute of Mental Health (NIMH)
Web site: http://www.nimh.nih.gov/

The National Institute of Mental Health is the largest scientific organization in the world. Located in Bethesda, Maryland, NIMH is dedicated to research focused on the understanding, treatment, and prevention of mental disorders and the promotion of optimal mental health. A visit to this Web site reveals an abundance of information on suicide and suicide prevention. For example, NIMH offers statistics, research findings, press releases, and links to other important resources on the topic. Among the more recent topics on suicide available at the Web site are suicidal thinking during antidepressant treatment, data on suicidal behaviors in black Americans, reporting on suicides, recommendations for the media, and risk factors for suicide.

National Organization for People of Color Against Suicide (NOPCAS)
Web site: http://www.nopcas.org/

The National Organization for People of Color Against Suicide seeks to halt the epidemic of suicide in minority communities. The organization's mission is to develop intervention designed to instill hope, improve health and opportunity, and save lives in communities of color. Among other strategies, it seeks to implement community-based programming to prevent suicide as well as the related problems of violence and depression. An emphasis is also placed on developing corporate partnerships to expand opportunity and forge alliances in inner cities. Visitors to this Web site will discover an impressive array of national statistics, suicide research including articles and publications, guidelines for defining a culturally competent program, and an African American bibliography.

Samaritans USA
Web site: http://www.ncsp.org/samaritans.html

Samaritans USA was established in 1974 and seeks to understand, treat, and prevent suicidal behaviors. It consists of a coalition of 11 nonprofit, nonreligious suicide prevention centers in the United States. Its mission is to befriend individuals who are depressed and offer volunteer-staffed crisis response hotlines, public education programs, and suicide survivor support groups. Since its inception, Samaritans USA has responded to approximately 25,000 calls annually. Volunteers who staff the phones are taught important communication skills, including utilizing the Samaritans' "befriending" model, which emphasizes active listening and the provision of unconditional emotional support. Samaritans USA is a member of the oldest and largest suicide prevention network in the world and has about 400 centers located in 40 nations.

Suicide Awareness Voices of Education (SAVE)
Web site: http://www.save.org

Suicide Awareness Voices of Education is a nonprofit organization incorporated in 1990 and a cofounding member of the National Council for Suicide Prevention. Its mission is to prevent suicide through public education and serve as a resource for those touched by suicide. Central themes of this organization are that suicide should not be considered a hushed or taboo topic and that public awareness of it will save lives. Visitors to the Web site will find information on depression and suicide, an extensive and well-rounded reading list, guidelines on how to talk with children about suicide, tips on responding to survivors, and better understanding the grief that accompanies suicide. Also available are a community action kit and public awareness materials, a suicide prevention education program, and SAVE news and events.

Suicide Prevention Action Network USA (SPAN USA)
Web site: http://www.spanusa.org/

The Suicide Prevention Action Network USA seeks to prevent suicide through public education and awareness; community engagement; and federal, state, and local grassroots advocacy. The network consists of individuals who have been touched by suicide: those who have attempted to end their lives or have been consumed with suicidal thoughts, survivors, professionals involved in suicide intervention and its aftermath, and concerned citizens. The vision of the organization is to create a society in which suicide prevention is embraced as a public priority, where those impacted by suicide are supported and embraced, and where awareness converges with action to save lives.

Suicide Prevention Research Center (SPRC)
Web site: http://www.cdc.gov/ncipc/dvp/suinevada.htm

The Suicide Prevention Research Center is sponsored by the Centers for Disease Control and Prevention (CDC) and is CDC's largest national program in suicide prevention research and training, intervention development, and evaluation. SPRC is located at the Trauma Institute of the University of Nevada School of Medicine. The center consists of four components or areas of activity: administration and program and policy development; methodology development and program evaluation; research; and education and distribution of findings and other printed materials. The ultimate goal of SPRC is the development of a suicide surveillance system linking all available sources of information within this region. Information obtained from the system will be used to develop and implement programming interventions. The Web site contains very useful fact sheets on suicide, scientific data and statistics, and publications.

8

Selected Print and Nonprint Resources

This chapter contains a comprehensive listing of books, research journals, and nonprint resources. Keeping with the format utilized throughout this reference manual, the resources are organized according to the sequence of family crises presented in Chapters 2 and 3. Readers will recall that Chapter 2 addressed seven key problems plaguing modern-day families:

- Addiction
- Adolescent runaways
- Unemployment
- Infidelity
- Divorce
- Chronic illness and disease
- Caring for aging family members

In Chapter 3, attention was focused on five problems particularly prevalent in modern American society:

- Domestic violence
- School violence
- Natural disasters
- Deployed military families
- Adolescent suicide

Books

Addiction

Aue, P. W., ed. 2006. *Teen Drug Abuse.* Detroit: Thomson/Gale.

This book explores whether or not teen drug abuse is on the increase, the core causes, the role of the media in promoting cigarette and alcohol use, and abuse prevention. Charts aid in the presentation of the material, and the book provides contact information for related organizations.

Balkin, K., ed. 2004. *Alcohol: Opposing Viewpoints.* San Diego: Greenhaven Press.

This book contains a wealth of conflicting viewpoints on alcohol's harms and benefits, the marketing of alcohol, different treatment programs (Alcoholics Anonymous, Children of Adult Alcoholics, and others), and various prevention programs.

Brick, J., ed. 2004. *Handbook of the Medical Consequences of Alcohol and Drug Abuse.* New York: Haworth Press.

Brick's handbook is an important contribution to the literature on alcohol and drug abuse. It includes coverage of the relationship between alcohol and accidental injuries, alcohol's effect on skeletal and major organ systems, and its effect on risk factors for certain cancers.

Carson-DeWitt, R. 2001. *Encyclopedia of Drugs, Alcohol and Addictive Behavior.* New York: Macmillan.

This encyclopedia includes a vast amount of information about substance abuse and addiction. It contains material on addictive behaviors not associated with substance abuse, such as gambling and eating disorders. The encyclopedia is a technical work that is accessible to lay readers.

DiClemente, C. 2003. *Addiction and Change: How Addictions Develop and Addicted People Recover.* New York: Guilford Press.

A practical guide designed to help people better understand how addictions can best be prevented and treated. DiClemente provides a clear and detailed picture not only of how people recover but also how they develop addiction.

Dodes, L. M. 2002. *The Heart of Addiction.* **New York: Harper-Collins.**

Dodes reexamines common myths and provides a world of new recommendations aimed at helping anyone with an addiction, be it to gambling, alcohol, or prescription medications. Rather than focusing on the specific object of addiction, he chooses instead to look at the common desires and emotions present in anyone with addiction issues.

Gahlinger, P. 2004. *Illegal Drugs: A Complete Guide to Their History, Chemistry, Use, and Abuse.* **New York: Penguin.**

The author has written a comprehensive reference book that offers timely, pertinent information on every drug currently prohibited by law in the United States. It includes their histories, chemical properties and effects, medical uses and recreational abuses, and associated health problems, as well as addiction and treatment information.

Gwinnell, E., and C. Adamec. 2006. *The Encyclopedia of Addictions and Addictive Behaviors.* **New York: Facts on File.**

The authors provide coverage of the symptoms, possible causes, treatment, rate of occurrence, social and ethnic influences, and emergency treatment of addictions. Useful appendixes provide information on state mental health agencies, rates of substance abuse by teenagers, and demographics of people who have received treatment for substance abuse. Numerous tables and graphs effectively convey statistical data.

Kesten, D. 2004. *Addiction, Progression and Recovery: Understanding the Stages of Change on the Addiction Recovery Learning Curve.* **Eau Claire, WI: PESI Healthcare.**

This engaging and practical book explores how harmful addictions often develop gradually, with many identifiable signs and symptoms emerging over time in a series of progressively worsening stages. It also describes the lifelong learning processes normally followed by people who successfully make the difficult transition from active progression into permanent recovery.

Wekerle, C., and A. M. Wall, eds. 2001. *The Violence and Addiction Equation: Theoretical and Clinical Issues in Substance Abuse and Relationship Violence.* **New York: Brunner-Routledge.**

The authors provide an excellent overview of current information on the overlap between violence and substance abuse. The book is comprehensive, is highly readable, and brings clarity to the often complex issues surrounding the relationship between violence and addictions. In addition to enhancing our understanding of what is known currently about the violence–substance abuse connections, the book identifies areas of controversy and directions for future research.

Adolescent Runaways

Bolnick, J. P. 2000. *Living at the Edge of the World: A Teenager's Survival in the Tunnels of Grand Central Station.* **New York: St. Martin's Press.**

A fascinating and disturbing true account of a teenager who lived for four years in the train tunnels of Grand Central Station amidst the homeless, runaways, and the drug addicted. This is must reading for anyone interested in pursuing a career working with troubled adolescents.

Fitzpatrick, S. 2000. *Young Homeless People.* **New York: Palgrave Macmillan.**

Although politicians, researchers, and the media often focus on the more visible runaways and homeless, this work emphasizes the same population hidden in local communities. Fitzpatrick places their experiences in the context of their biographies as a whole and makes policy and practice recommendations.

Flowers, B. 2001. *Runaway Kids and Teenage Prostitution.* **Westport, CT: Greenwood Press.**

A look at the correlations between runaway children and teenage prostitution in the United States from a criminological, sociological, and psychological perspective. Flowers describes the differences between youth who run away from home and those who leave institutional settings and distinguishes the difference between runaway and throwaway children.

Mickelson, R. A., ed. 2000. *Children on the Streets of the Americas: Globalization, Homelessness and Education in the United States, Brazil and Cuba.* **New York: Routledge.**

A compelling narrative that shows us the face of runaways and homelessness in Brazil, Cuba, and the United States. Mickelson offers the reader a comparative analysis of education for the least privileged children in the context of globalization. It is frightening to imagine that the number of street children in developed and developing nations is rising, often in the midst of prosperity. This book offers special appeal to students working with troubled teens and to social workers who are looking to connect the education of children with larger-scale social processes.

Nunez, R. D. 2004. *A Shelter Is Not a Home . . . Or Is It? Lessons in Family Homelessness in New York City.* **New York: White Tiger Press.**

A sobering but realistic investigation of the New York City shelter system as it exists today, including teenage runaway inhabitants. Nunez maintains that by harnessing the power to foster change within shelters themselves, a blueprint can be developed to successfully move families from homelessness to permanent independent living.

Slesnick, N. 1988. *Our Runaway and Homeless Youth: A Guide to Understanding.* **Westport, CT: Greenwood Press.**

In addition to describing the scope of this problem, Slesnick explains different types of runaway and homeless youths and why they leave home by choice or are asked to leave. Slesnick also explains some of the factors common to these children and their families, as well as what happens to the youths when they leave home.

Staller, K. M. 2006. *Runaways: How the Sixties Counterculture Shaped Today's Practices and Policies.* **New York: Columbia University Press.**

An informative and interesting account of the history of service development and media construction of runaway youth in the United States. Staller's work will be a valuable resource for anyone working with runaway youth. She succeeds in penning a readable, compelling demonstration that ideas matter in forming public policy.

Unemployment

Busse, R. C. 2005. *Fired, Laid Off or Forced Out: A Complete Guide to Severance, Benefits and Your Rights when Starting Over.* **Naperville, IL: Sourcebooks.**

The author seeks to take the fear out of the possibility of losing one's job and replaces it with specific guidelines workers can use to protect their rights. This highly readable and practical book applies to all facets of the work environment, from the factory worker to the professional, the salesperson to upper management.

Endress, D. R., and R. Venckus. 2007. *Why Shouldn't We Hire You?* **Lafayette, IN: Writers' Café Press.**

This book emphasizes how prospective employees can better market themselves by developing effective interviewing skills. Analysis and knowledge of oneself and the prospective company are key, and the authors guide the reader through this critical process of discovery, including ways to perfect the presentation.

Freedman, M. 2007. *Encore: Finding Work that Matters in the Second Half of Life.* **Jackson, TN: Perseus.**

Freedman focuses on the baby boom generation and its implications for the vocational arena. He looks at the dynamics of retirement for middle-agers, including those who eagerly anticipate it, those who wish to keep punching the clock, and those switching interests and pursuing different careers.

Hornby, M. 2007. *Working at 50+: Getting and Keeping a Job in Mid-Life.* **Upper Saddle River, NJ: Prentice Hall.**

This is a valuable book that is loaded with practical advice for anyone looking for a job. Hornby supplies strategies for setting career and life goals as well as creating an effective resume and letters of application.

Kane, A. 2002. *You're Fired: How to Turn a Pink Slip into a Golden Opportunity.* **Boulder, CO: Paladin Press.**

This book is a survival guide that offers practical and inventive suggestions for finding another job. Kane tells readers, among other tips, how to get one's foot in the door, create a resume that will get noticed, network, and evaluate job offers.

Marling, S., and J. Pfaff-Waterbury. 2006. *Boomers' Job Search Guide.* **New York: Life Transition Consulting.**

This book is aimed at the ever-expanding audience of men and women who, for one reason or another, are not ready or willing to climb into the rocking chair following retirement. The rise of "gray labor" is a result of many reasons: the recent economic downturn, increasing life expectancy, corporate downsizing, additional financial pressures, and loss of benefits and increasing entrepreneurial interests. The authors provide a highly readable and easy-to-follow path for mature workers in a job search.

Sack, S. M. 2000. *Getting Fired: What to Do if You're Fired, Downsized, Laid Off, Restructured, Discharged, Terminated, or Forced to Resign.* **Minneapolis, MN: Grand Central.**

This book reaches out to those going through one of the most vulnerable times of their lives. It tells you when to call a lawyer if you are fired and gives an overview of U.S. laws protecting employees from discrimination and unfair dismissal. From sample letters to a list of relevant government agencies, it is designed for the let-go, downsized, or dismissed.

Simerson, B. K., and M. D. McCormick. 2003. *Fired, Laid Off, Out of a Job: A Manual for Understanding, Coping, Surviving.* **Westport, CT: Greenwood Press.**

Simerson and McCormick's perspectives on the job search process provide an insightful, practical, and proactive approach to anyone who may be facing a change in their employment. This is a worthwhile read, not only for those who have been laid off but also for those who have the unpleasant task of delivering the pink slip.

Tatro, W. L. 2002. *The One Hour Survival Guide for the Downsized: What You Need to Know When You're Let Go.* **Sanford, FL: DC Press.**

This is a book that reaches out to people on the receiving end of employment termination. Tatro offers guidance on how to take control of the situation, including what questions to ask human resources representatives about final paychecks and severance pay.

Infidelity

Browne, M. H., and M. M. Browne. 2007. *You Can't Have Him, He's Mine.* **Avon, MA: Adams Media.**

A psychotherapist and family law attorney team up to share insights, including what makes a woman's partner susceptible to sexual advances from another female and what can be done to stop such advances. It includes a chapter focusing on how to assess one's partner as well as the quality of one's relationship and home life for "infidelity vulnerability."

Farbman, S., M. Williamson, and B. Farbman. 2004. *Back from Betrayal: Saving a Marriage, a Family, a Life.* **South Boardman, MI: Crofton Creek Press.**

This book explores the many sides to marital infidelity and the long journey back to reconciliation. It is aimed at those couples who want to repair broken marriages and also guides those in healthy partnerships to a deeper level of commitment and self-awareness. The authors succeed in enhancing our understanding of infidelity and, more important, revealing a process that can lead to healing and renewal.

Glass, S. P., and J. C. Staeheli. 2004. *Not "Just Friends": Rebuilding Trust and Recovering Your Sanity after Infidelity.* **New York: Simon and Schuster.**

The authors contend that even "good" people in "good" marriages can be swept away in a flurry of emotional and sexual intimacy. This book explores affairs and offers well-defined guidelines, including tips for determining how vulnerable individuals and relationships are to temptation, and prescriptions for keeping relationships "safe." Also receiving attention is how partners can repair betrayal-induced damages and recover from the trauma.

Kinnett, L. N. 2001. *Beyond the Affair: The Healing of a Marriage.* **Bangor, ME: BookLocker.**

Kinnett explores the pain of infidelity and the many emotions it triggers. The book offers suggestions regarding feelings of distrust, jealousy, fear, guilt, and, finally, hope and forgiveness.

Neuman, M. G. 2002. *Emotional Infidelity.* **New York: Crown.**

Neuman maintains that one need not have sex with someone other than one's spouse to be considered unfaithful. Rather, Neuman argues that when a marital partner invests emotional energy into an opposite sex coworker or friend—instead of focusing on one's spouse—infidelity has occurred. His viewpoints are both persuasive and challenging, especially the values and strategies he offers to those reexamining their relationships.

Ortega, A., and M. Fleming. 2005. *The Dance of Restoration: Rebuilding Marriage after Infidelity.* **Chattanooga, TN: AMG.**

Couples traumatized by affairs will find this book helpful in rebuilding their marriages. It is written in a simple, straightforward style that seeks to guide couples along the often treacherous path toward reconciliation.

Peluso, P. R. 2007. *Infidelity.* **New York: Routledge.**

Peluso's premise is that relatively little professional literature is devoted to understanding and "treating" infidelity. To fill this void, Peluso has assembled the works of contributors from a range of disciplines and backgrounds, including marital therapy, family therapy, evolutionary psychology, marriage research, and cyber studies.

Spring, J. A. 2005. *How Can I Forgive You?* **New York: HarperCollins.**

Spring supplies concrete, step-by-step instructions for both the hurt party and the offender. She brings to light strategies to help change the way we think about forgiveness, regardless of whether or not the offending party is willing to apologize.

Weil, B. 2003. *Adultery: The Forgivable Sin,* **2nd ed. Poughkeepsie, NY: Vivisphere.**

Weil proposes that infidelity is a cry for help in stabilizing a dysfunctional marriage and that many adulterers are themselves the children of adulterers. Weil describes how knowledge of family intimacy patterns can be used to develop insight, understanding, and forgiveness in a relationship stressed by infidelity.

Divorce

Anderson, K., and R. MacSkimming. 2007. *On Your Own Again.* Toronto: McClelland and Stewart.

Providing down-to-earth help for readers seeking to survive shattered relationships and build new lives, this book shares practical advice that can be used by male or female readers, young or middle aged, straight or gay, in or recently out of troubled relationships, to help cope with the loss and move toward a speedy recovery.

Bailey, J. L. 2007. *The Parental Peace Accord.* Bloomington, IN: AuthorHouse.

Bailey describes a unique process that allows divorced and divorcing parents the opportunity to shift their focus from their own emotional turmoil to the needs and best interests of their children. In so doing, parents learn that while they may no longer be husband and wife, they can and will be "parenting partners."

Baksh, N., and L. Murphy. 2007. *In the Best Interest of the Child.* Gardena, CA: Hohm Press.

This book was written to help parents save their children unnecessary anguish and pressure throughout the divorce process. The book details what adults can expect from a custody battle; what they will encounter in themselves and in their children (emotionally, physically, mentally) during divorce; how parents can make sense out of children's questions; how to make decisions for themselves and their children; and the ultimate importance of putting the children's needs first.

Clarke-Stewart, A., and C. Brentano. 2007 *Divorce: Causes and Consequences.* New Haven, CT: Yale University Press.

This comprehensive book provides a balanced overview of the current research on divorce. The authors examine the scientific evidence to uncover what can be said with certainty about divorce and what remains to be learned about this socially and politically charged issue. The authors convey the real-life consequences of divorce with excerpts from autobiographies by young people, and they also include guidelines for social policies that would help to diminish the detrimental effects of divorce.

Grabenstein, C. C. 2007. *Divorced Parents Challenge: Eight Lessons to Teach Children Love and Forgiveness.* **Calverton, MD: Collier.**

The lessons presented by Grabenstein give parents the opportunity to help their children learn about love and forgiveness by helping to maximize the love in their lives. The advice is simple, straightforward, and nonjudgmental. It seems that all parents would benefit from reading this book, but the message is especially helpful to divorced and remarried couples.

Hansen, D. 2007. *Broken Strings: Wisdom for Divorced and Separated Families.* **Bloomington, IN: AuthorHouse.**

Hansen supplies guidance and direction to families who are currently navigating a divorce or separation. She also seeks to help those who made the trip previously and are now finding that it is never really finished. Hansen regards separation as a life-altering experience for everyone involved, today and into the future of each family. To ease the journey, she offers coping strategies that can help mend the wounds and strengthen resiliency.

Leman, K. 2007. *Step-parenting 101.* **Nashville, TN: Thomas Nelson.**

This book has appeal for those who are just starting out as a step-family or have been battling to unify two families for years. It contains much practical advice conveyed in a clear and convincing writing style.

Smoke, J. 2007. *Growing through Divorce.* **Eugene, OR: Harvest House.**

The author captures how many people going through divorce are left with little hope for the future and even less energy for daily living. Many are forced to accept drastic changes, make lifestyle-altering decisions, and develop new coping skills. This book addresses these and other issues, including helping children adjust, seeking legal advice, and contemplating remarriage.

Stahl, P. M. 2007. *Parenting after Divorce: Resolving Conflicts and Meeting Your Children's Needs.* **Atascadero, CA: Impact.**

This is one of the better books available on the topic. Stahl has penned a very practical guide and an easy read for all parents who are separated or divorced. Stahl's strength is his ability to help parents take a look at what they are doing to create problems so they do not just blame the other parents or, even worse, the children.

Steadman, L. 2007. *It's a Breakup, Not a Breakdown.* **Prince Albert, Canada: Polka Dot Press.**

A survival guide designed to help the reader see his or her divorce not as a breakdown but as an opportunity to break up with a relationship that is no longer working and move on, this book offers many helpful suggestions and guidance along the way.

Chronic Illness and Disease

Bouvard, M. G. 2007. *Healing: A Life with Chronic Illness.* **Lebanon, NH: University Press of New England.**

This memoir tells the story of a woman who came to create a rich and full life despite debilitating physical conditions. Bouvard addresses key issues such as the importance of speaking clearly to the broader society about illness, learning to deal with pain, and learning how to manage relations with physicians. She shares how the meditation and reflection she turned to because of her curtailed activities actually enabled her to cultivate inner strength, flexibility, and adaptability.

Bumagin, V., and K. Hirn. 2006. *Caregiving: A Guide for Those Who Give Care and Those Who Receive It.* **New York: Springer.**

A book having appeal to caregivers of all age groups, from young children to the frail elderly, it is clearly written and loaded with descriptive case examples. Its strength is focusing on the various facets of the caregiving experience—from the caregivers' perspective to that of those who are receiving the care.

Cline, F. W., and L. C. Greene. 2007. *Parenting Children with Health Issues: Essential Tools, Tips, and Tactics for Raising Kids with Chronic Illness, Medical Conditions and Special Healthcare Needs.* **Golden, CO: Love and Logic Institute.**

This book provides helpful guidance to parents when their children struggle with health issues, from weight problems to diabetes and cancer. Readers will discover the essential parenting skills they need to help their children comply with medical requirements, cope with health challenges, and live a hope-filled life.

Davis, N. 2007. *Lean on Me: Ten Powerful Steps to Moving beyond Your Diagnosis and Taking Back Your Life.* **New York: Simon and Schuster.**

The author, a woman diagnosed with multiple sclerosis at age 33, recounts her journey to help others traveling similar paths. She provides readers with an informed overview of how to negotiate the health care system, understand legislation, and navigate Web resources. This book is a valuable contribution to the literature since it represents a practical, methodical plan for dealing with devastating illnesses.

Martz, E., and H. Livneh. 2007. *Coping with Chronic Illness and Disability: Theoretical, Empirical, and Clinical Aspects.* **New York: Springer-Verlag.**

The first part of this informative book provides readers with the major theories and conceptual perspectives on coping, with special emphasis on social aspects and models of coping with different types of chronic illness and disease. The second part offers an array of specific medical conditions, including clinical descriptions; current empirical findings on coping; effective medical, physical, and psychological interventions; employment issues; and social concerns.

Natelson, B. H. 2007. *Your Symptoms Are Real: What to Do When Your Doctor Says Nothing Is Wrong.* **New York: Wiley.**

This book is for the millions of people who suffer from debilitating pain or chronic fatigue that has gone undiagnosed. Natelson, a medical practitioner, draws on his 18 years of dedicated research into "invisible illnesses" that defy medical explanation to reassure readers that their symptoms are real and empower them to take charge of their health with a step-by-step blueprint to wellness. The author explains how to talk with doctors, offers dietary, medicinal, and gentle physical conditioning programs that can gradually help relieve symptoms, and presents the cutting-edge research and promising treatments that are on the horizon.

Schwartz, D. 2007. *Disease Management Directory and Guidebook.* Northboro, MA: HCPro.

This reference manual is must reading for anyone pursuing a career in disease management. Its eight comprehensive sections are loaded with valuable information and advice to help make sure a disease management program succeeds. In-depth case studies of the most successful disease management programs cover a wide range of chronic illnesses.

Thomas, C. 2007. *Sociologies of Disability and Illness.* New York: Palgrave Macmillan.

Thomas cuts across a disciplinary divide and critically reviews and compares the conflicting perspectives on disability and chronic illness found in disability studies and medical sociology. She skillfully outlines the historical development of both these approaches, providing readers with a solid understanding of the overlaps and divergences between the two fields.

Caring for Aging Family Members

Abramson, A., and M. A. Dunkin. 2004. *Caregiver's Survival Handbook: How to Care for Your Aging Parent without Losing Yourself.* New York: Perigee Press.

The authors contend that today's caregivers often feel trapped between the needs of their elderly relatives and their young families. They frequently feel invisible, their own needs unobserved and unappreciated by those around them. This book offers practical caregiving advice for these women, and seeks to help them deal with the emotional concerns they face, such as fostering aging parents' independence; getting help from siblings and other family members; and balancing work, family, and caregiving duties.

Barg, G. 2001. *The Fearless Caregiver: How to Get the Best Care for Your Loved One and Still Have a Life of Your Own.* **Herndon, VA: Capital.**

Barg's book contains a number of valuable articles, helpful hints, and thoughtful commentaries on the difficult task of caring for a loved one. The chapters are easy to read and, most important, address real-life situations. The book guides the reader through the maze of caregiving and is as motivating as it is empowering.

Berman, C. 2001. *Caring for Yourself while Caring for Your Aging Parents: How to Help, How to Survive.* **New York: Henry Holt.**

Berman provides a valuable guide to adult children caring for elderly parents, directing her attention to the emotional, practical, and financial aspects of the chore. Drawing from personal experience, she examines such specific areas as financing, sharing the care among siblings, and coping with loss. The book includes a listing of helpful resources and a suggested bibliography.

Brody, E. 2006. *Women in the Middle: Their Parent Care Years.* **New York: Springer.**

A leading researcher in the field describes and discusses the caregiving woman's subjective feelings, experiences, and problems. She addresses the effects of caregiving on female caregivers' mental and physical well-being, lifestyles, family relationships, and vocational activities. The book features case studies and narratives.

Bumagin, V., and K. Hirn. 2006. *Caregiving: A Guide for Those Who Give Care and Those Who Receive It.* **New York: Springer.**

This book focuses on the various facets of the caregiving experience and the ways in which caregiving is affected by the conditions, personalities, capabilities, and wishes of the caregivers and the care recipients. It explores the range of care receivers and the difference in styles and options that exist. The book includes a number of case examples.

McLeod, B. W., ed. 2003. *And Thou Shalt Honor: The Caregiver's Companion.* **New York: Rodale.**

Throughout this comprehensive resource book, actual caregivers tell their stories, acknowledging their vast range of experiences and emotional reactions alongside a gamut of action plans, checklists, and medical and support networking information. This book is highly recommended.

Nerenberg, L. 2007. *Elder Abuse Prevention*. New York: Springer.

Nerenberg provides a comprehensive look at elder abuse prevention trends and strategies. Drawing from existing models and research, she outlines approaches to intervention that consider victims and perpetrators and engage communities and service systems. She also offers meaningful responses to the many challenges endemic to elder abuse work.

Rubenson, A. F. 2000. *When Aging Parents Can't Live Alone*. Lincolnwood, IL: Lowell House.

Written for those affected by an elderly parent's inability to continue living autonomously, Rubenson provides comprehensive information on in-house help, retirement communities, assisted living options, and nursing facilities. Financial, medical, and emotional considerations are also discussed, enabling families to make healthy decisions about this sometimes delicate and emotional situation.

Szinovacz, M. E., and A. Davey. 2007. *Caregiving Contexts*. New York: Springer.

This book explores the ways in which demographic change will influence the availability of caregivers and how the welfare system will affect care among family members and between family and formal care systems. The authors also discuss the differences in experience between spousal and adult child caregivers, special circumstances such as child or adolescent caregivers, and government and workplace policies that are available to support caregivers in the United States and in some European countries.

Domestic Violence

Bancroft, L., and J. G. Silverman. 2002. *The Batterer as Parent: Addressing the Impact of Domestic Violence on Family Dynamics*. Thousand Oaks, CA: Sage.

This book exposes the world in which batterers live and raise their children. The authors shed considerable light on the many problems batterers exhibit as parents, how these behaviors affect children, and what needs to be done in terms of intervention. This is an excellent resource book for students majoring in psychology, sociology, and family studies.

Barnett, O. W., C. L. Miller-Perrin, and R. D. Perrin. 2005. *Family Violence across the Lifespan: An Introduction.* **Thousand Oaks, CA: Sage.**

Chapters in this book cover child physical, sexual, and emotional abuse; courtship violence and date rape; spouse abuse, battered women, and batterers; and elder abuse. The book also includes a chapter on future directions for research as well as appendixes with a thorough guide to resources.

Flannery, D. J. 2006. *Violence and Mental Health in Everyday Life: Prevention and Intervention Strategies for Children and Adolescents.* **Lanham, MD: Rowman and Littlefield.**

Flannery reveals the impact of violence and victimization in the lives of children and adolescents from a developmental perspective. He explores how young people experience violence in their everyday lives and how this exposure impacts their mental health and ability to cope with challenges and crises. Flannery provides the reader with lists of professional resources, including Web sites and readings related to violence and mental health.

Hines, D. A., and K. Malley-Morrison. 2005. *Family Violence in the United States: Defining, Understanding, and Combating Abuse.* **Thousand Oaks, CA: Sage.**

This book examines all types of family aggression. It is designed to stimulate readers into questioning assumptions, evaluating information, formulating hypotheses, and designing solutions to problems of family violence in the United States. The authors probe the most well-recognized forms of maltreatment in families, but also less understood and more controversial issues such as husband abuse, parent abuse, and gay/lesbian abuse.

Jaffe, P. G., L. L. Baker, and A. J. Cunningham. 2004. *Protecting Children from Domestic Violence: Strategies for Community Intervention.* **New York: Guilford.**

This text provides the reader with a broad background on domestic violence. Well written and engaging, it conveys how children are impacted by domestic violence and the types of intervention that are needed, at both the individual and community levels.

Kurst-Swanger, K., and J. L. Petcosky. 2003. *Violence in the Home: Multidisciplinary Perspectives.* **New York: Oxford University Press.**

The authors review the most current theoretical explanations of family violence and then link theory to practice. The book examines the systems and institutions that interact with families that are mandated to provide protection and services, and it explores the current debates surrounding family violence and public policy. In addition, the authors explore the role of power in abusive relationships and consider the short- and long-term consequences of abuse.

Loseke, D. R., R. J. Gelles, and M. M. Cavanaugh. 2005. *Current Controversies on Family Violence.* **Thousand Oaks, CA: Sage.**

This important book contains thoughtful discussions that highlight the most current controversies, research, and policy directions in family violence. It includes chapters by academic and public policy researchers, therapists, lawyers, victim advocates, and educators. The writing is clear and understandable.

Roberts, A. R., and B. S. Roberts. 2005. *Ending Intimate Abuse: Practical Guidance and Survival Strategies.* **New York: Oxford University Press.**

This book is based on more than 500 interviews with battered women. Among other topics, it teaches how to recognize the warning signs of a dangerous relationship and urges women who have been battered in a dating, cohabiting, or marital relationship to end it quickly. The book includes a national directory of domestic violence hotlines and intervention programs and a detailed glossary of key terms.

Schewe, P. A. 2002. *Preventing Violence in Relationships: Interventions across the Life Span.* **Washington, DC: American Psychological Association.**

Each chapter of this book covers relationship violence at a different stage of life and in different relationships, from child and partner abuse through rape and elder abuse. Empirical research is blended with practical guidance for day-to-day interventions in the lives of children and adults.

Shipway, L. 2004. *Domestic Violence: A Handbook for Health Professionals.* **New York: Routledge.**

This is a clearly written handbook on the major issues surrounding domestic violence, one that is interspersed with much practical advice on possible interventions. Focusing on improving the care of clients, the book explores the causes of domestic violence, professional issues for the practitioner, the process of intervention (in specific settings and with children), multiagency approaches, and education.

School Violence

Dawn, J. 2007. *Managing Violence in Schools.* **Thousand Oaks, CA: Sage.**

Dawn covers preventive methods and strategies for strengthening school culture, such as peer support and cooperative group work. This book also provides guidance for implementing a needs analysis, formulating a cycle of change for handling bullying and violence, and creating a shared understanding of the issue. Each strategy for preventive and integrative practice is illustrated with real-life case studies and relevant experiential exercises.

Denmark, F. L., ed. 2005. *Violence in Schools: Cross-National and Cross-Cultural Perspectives.* **New York: Springer.**

This collection of articles provides both a broad overview of violence in schools and offers specific descriptions of models that have been used successfully within school settings to prevent violent crime from occurring. It explores the history of school violence and delineates what constitutes violence. Regarding the latter, the focus is not only on physical assault but also on the neglect and abusive behavior that contribute to its occurrence.

Hardy, G. V., and T. A. Laszloffy. 2006. *Teens Who Hurt: Clinical Interventions to Break the Cycle of Adolescent Violence.* **New York: Guilford.**

This book presents an overarching framework and many specific strategies for working with violent youth and their families. The authors shed light on the complex interplay of individual, family, community, and societal forces that lead some adolescents to hurt others or themselves. The book provides essential guidance on connecting with aggressive teens and their parents and managing difficult situations that are likely to arise.

Larkin, R. W. 2007. *Comprehending Columbine.* **Philadelphia: Temple University Press.**

This title is as compelling as it is intriguing. Larkin offers one of the first serious, impartial investigations into the cultural, environmental, and psychological causes of the Columbine High School shooting in Littleton, Colorado. Rather than simply looking at Columbine as a crucible for all school violence, Larkin places the tragedy in its proper context and, in doing so, examines its causes and meaning. Using firsthand interviews and a review of the relevant literature, Larkin examines the numerous factors that led the two young men to plan and carry out their massacre.

Lieberman, J. 2006. *The Shooting Game: The Making of School Shooters.* **Santa Ana, CA: Seven Locks Press.**

This book provides an overview of the 30-year school shooting phenomenon, one that sheds light on the rampage shooters: their motivations, their mentality, and contributing community factors. This book is one that no parent, educator, administrator, law official, or counselor can afford not to read.

Rivers, I., V. Besaq, and N. Duncan. 2007. *Bullying: A Handbook for Educators and Parents.* **Westport, CT: Greenwood Press.**

This book offers insights into the immediate and long-term impact bullying can have upon the lives of students, their families, and teachers. It provides parents and guardians with useful tips on working proactively with school administrators to resolve bullying issues and provides teachers with materials that facili-

tate a better understanding of the social dynamics of the classroom, hallways, and playground. The book also includes a guide
to recent directives and legislation relating to bullying.

Thomas, R. M. 2006. *Violence in America's Schools: Understanding, Prevention, and Responses.* **Westport, CT: Greenwood Press.**

According to Thomas, violence in American schools is persistent
and includes fighting, sexual abuse, carrying weapons to school,
vandalism, and assorted other crimes. These crimes take place in
elementary, middle, and high school settings across the country
and have caused violent victimization and death, not to mention
the disruption of learning and fear among student bodies and
teaching staffs. Thomas provides a foundation for understanding
why violence occurs, as well as how we can prevent it from happening. This book is highly recommended.

Wilde, J. 2002. *Anger Management in School: Alternatives to
Student Violence,* **2nd ed. Lanham, MD: Scarecrow Press.**

Wilde shares how anger is directly linked to violence, health
problems, and interpersonal difficulty. Because of such negative
effects, it is imperative that we teach children to control their
anger. Wilde shows how teachers and counselors can encourage
students to acknowledge and change feelings that are causing
problems in their lives without the use of anger.

Zins, J. E., M. J. Elias, and C. A. Maher, eds. 2007. *Bullying, Victimization, and Peer Harassment: A Handbook of Prevention
and Intervention.* **New York: Haworth.**

Zins, Elias, and Maher integrate emerging research, theory, and
effective practice on this subject into this book. It targets the complex problems of victimization, peer harassment, and bullying
and advocates intervention on an individual level as well as
broad, systems-level change within schools and communities.
The challenge of prevention is also explored, using the latest
studies as a conceptual foundation. Suggestions are provided de-
tailing effective strategies to make changes in the culture within
schools while offering directions for future research.

Natural Disasters

Alexander, D. 2000. *Confronting Catastrophe: New Perspectives on Natural Disasters.* New York: Oxford University Press.

This book provides a comprehensive overview of the physical, technological, and social components of natural disaster. The relationship between disasters and society is examined with respect to a wide variety of themes, including damage assessment and prevention, hazard mapping, emergency preparedness, the provision of shelter, and the nature of reconstruction.

Bradford, M., and R. S. Carmichael. 2001. *Natural Disasters.* Pasadena, CA: Salem Press.

This is an excellent reference source for the student. It covers virtually all kinds of natural disasters: blizzards, epidemics, explosions, famines, floods, hurricanes, and tornadoes. Each topic is introduced with an overview of the phenomenon along with a definition and the regions affected. The authors supply maps, charts, and photographs throughout the book.

Bryant, E. 2001. *Tsunami: The Underrated Hazard.* New York: Cambridge University Press.

Bryant has authored a book that fully describes the nature and process of tsunami; outlines field evidence for detecting the presence of past events; and describes particular events linked to earthquakes, volcanoes, submarine landslides, and meteorite impacts. Although technical aspects are covered, much of the text can be read by anyone with a high school education. The book will appeal to students and researchers in earth and environmental science, as well as those involved in emergency planning.

Faidley, W. 2006. *The Ultimate Storm Survival Handbook.* Nashville, TN: Thomas Nelson.

This practical book provides the information you need to prepare to survive any major storm. It covers all forms of severe weather, including snowstorms, tornadoes, ice storms, hurricanes, and firestorms. In addition to practical advice on preparing your home, avoiding dangers, and creating action plans, it features special chapters on pet care, poststorm dangers, children, and phobias.

Halpern, J., and M. Tramontin. 2007. *Disaster Mental Health.* **Belmont, CA: Thomson Learning.**

The authors have prepared a valuable resource tool in disaster preparedness and planning. This book presents a theoretical integration and context for what disaster mental health is and what it is not. A practical discussion of a range of mental health interventions appropriate in the wake of a disaster helps the reader effectively prepare to respond to a disaster of any kind.

Hansen, A., and C. Gibson. 2007. *Extreme Natural Disasters.* **New York: HarperCollins.**

For those wanting to study natural disasters up close and personally, this is the book for them. It features catastrophic events such as volcanic eruptions, earthquakes, hurricanes, floods, and other extreme acts of nature. The reader will discover facts on the worst and deadliest of these events, including the scientific explanations behind them.

Hyndman, D., and D. Hyndman. 2005. *Natural Hazards and Disasters.* **Monterey, CA: Brooks/Cole.**

This book emphasizes earth and atmospheric hazards that appear suddenly or rapidly, without significant warning. It discusses ways to prevent or mitigate the damage caused by natural hazards, providing readers with the latest scientific research about these topics. The authors reinforce the need to become informed citizens and make educated living decisions. Readers will find a balanced coverage of North American natural hazards, including earthquakes, hurricanes, floods, and volcanic eruptions. These hazards are illustrated using numerous four-color photos and diagrams.

Smith, K. 2007. *Environmental Hazards: Assessing Risk and Reducing Disaster,* **3rd ed. New York: Taylor and Francis.**

This book is an objective, up-to-date, and thoughtful introduction to important findings from the natural social sciences. Smith provides much information on disaster databases, El Niño events, sea-level rise and coastal flooding, mega-cities and sustainability, epidemics, storms, and other natural disaster issues.

Torrence, R., and J. Grattan. 2002. *Natural Disasters and Cultural Change.* New York: Routledge.

This book contains comprehensive coverage of natural disasters, with a particular emphasis on the role they play in influencing cultural change. The authors describe how tsunamis, earthquakes, volcanic eruptions, flooding, and other natural disasters wreak havoc on human life and communities.

Deployed Military Families

Doell, S. 2006. *Mom's Field Guide: What You Need to Know to Make It through Your Loved One's Military Deployment.* New York: Warrior Angel Press.

Supportive advice for deployed military families does not come any more personal than this book. When the author's son was deployed to Iraq in 2004, she felt overwhelmed with fear and anxiety and could not help but worry. She put her thoughts into action and penned this book, full of support and guidance for others like her to follow. The end result is a book filled with compassion and practical advice.

Dumler, E. G. 2007. *I'm Already Home Again: Keeping Your Family Close while on Assignment or Deployment.* Cambridge, MA: Frankly Speaking.

This is another good sourcebook designed to keep service men and women connected to their families while they are on assignment or deployment. Dumler provides countess sources of available aid and guidance for readers, whether they are preparing for active-duty training or are about to be deployed.

Hosek, J. R., L. Miller, and J. Kavanagh. 2006. *How Deployments Affect Service Members.* Santa Monica, CA: Rand.

The authors provide a readable and understandable book covering the complexities of military families experiencing deployment. The book offers insights into the challenges faced by active-duty service members deployed to Iraq and Afghanistan, the resiliency they and their families have shown in coping with these challenges, and the adequacy of defense manpower policy in assisting members and families.

Kay, E. 2002. *Heroes at Home: Help and Encouragement for America's Military Families.* Minneapolis, MN: Bethany House.

This is another book authored by a military wife whose husband has been deployed into hostile territory. It is also one of the best. Using her firsthand knowledge, the author shares practical ideas for military families, including dealing with multiple moves, pre-deployment readiness, and staying in touch when families are separated.

Neven, T., and C. C. Krulak. 2006. *On the Frontline: A Personal Guidebook for the Physical, Emotional, and Spiritual Challenges of Military Life.* Colorado Springs, CO: WaterBrook Press.

The authors maintain that the demands of military life can be staggering. Soldiers, sailors, air personnel, and marines face pressures and temptations that civilians will never know. This book offers supportive assistance designed to help deployed military families face their many challenges. Among the topics covered are how to manage financial affairs, how to build and maintain friendships, and how to deal with the threat of injury or pain. Underlying themes of this book are hope, encouragement, and practical everyday guidance.

Pavlicin, K. M. 2007. *Life after Deployment: Military Families Share Reunion Stories and Advice.* St. Paul, MN: Elva Resa.

This book captures the emotional stories of military families during their reunions. Service members and their spouses, parents, fiancées, and children share the joy and anxiety of homecoming, the adjustments of living together again, and how they coped with anger, depression, posttraumatic stress disorder, injuries, grief, and other challenges.

Schaeffer, F. 2005. *Voices from the Front: Letters Home from America's Military Family.* Cambridge, MA: Da Capo Press.

This is must reading. Schaeffer takes us directly to the often invisible front lines in Iraq and Afghanistan, from first deployment to patrols to combat to field hospitals and eventually returning home. Powerful and moving, this book tells the story of this war in the voices of the Americans who are living—and dying—in it every day.

Westling, L. L. 2006. *When Johnny/Joanie Comes Marching Home: Reuniting Military Families Following Deployment.* **Gainesville, GA: Praxis Press.**

Westling offers insight into the family dynamics of military separations as well as the reunions and restoration of the family circle. This book deals specifically with what combat does to the combatant, to the family, and to the nation, with suggested coping strategies for those involved. A strength of this book is that it includes all of the armed forces and both genders—women as well as men returning to their families from combat.

Adolescent Suicide

Baugher, R., and J. Jordan. 2002. *After Suicide Loss: Coping with Your Grief.* **New York: Routledge.**

This book is organized chronologically around the first days, weeks, and months after a suicide loss. It includes information about psychiatric disorders, where to seek professional help, and practical strategies for coping and healing. This book is one of the better self-help books on the market.

Carlson, T. 2000. *Suicide Survivors' Handbook.* **Duluth, MN: Benline Press.**

A very important book for those grieving the loss of a loved one, it is well written, insightful, and filled with practical guidance. This is a valuable reference source for those who work with teenagers and suicide survivors.

Crook, M. 2004. *Out of the Darkness: Teens Talk about Suicide.* **Vancouver, Canada: Arsenal Pulp Press.**

Based on interviews with teen suicide survivors, parents, and professionals, the author sensitively explores all aspects of teen suicide, in particular the reasons why certain young people are driven to it. The book also examines the history of teen suicide in Western and other cultures, what roles parents and schools can play in suicide prevention, and coping strategies for teens in crisis.

Helen, M. 2002. *Coping with Suicide.* **London: Sheldon Press.**

This book is aimed at those whose loved ones have committed suicide; it will also be useful for people working with the relatives and friends of those who have committed suicide. The book covers the reasons for suicide, emotional and practical issues, and where to go for help.

Myers, M. F., and C. Fine. 2006. *Touched by Suicide: Hope and Healing after Loss.* **New York: Gotham.**

The authors recognize that the loss of a loved one by suicide is as tragic as it is traumatic for survivors. They provide expert guidance and advice to those left behind, conveyed in a compassionate tone designed to support the healing journey.

Robinson, R., and P. Hart. 2001. *Survivors of Suicide.* **Franklin Lakes, NJ: New Page.**

The authors dispel the myths surrounding suicide, based on the latest research and interviews with leading medical experts. The book also contains interviews with family and friends who have survived the suicide deaths of loved ones and who offer support, knowledge, and comfort to other survivors. An informative, applied book, it serves as a good reference guide.

Ross, E. B. 2002. *After Suicide: A Ray of Hope for Those Left Behind.* **Jackson, TN: Perseus.**

Ross takes the reader beyond the silence and shame often associated with suicide and shatters some of the most pervasive myths surrounding this tragedy. Utilizing dozens of real-life case studies, this book offers hope for the survivors and helps them maintain their sanity and poise during this most difficult time. The book also includes a comprehensive resource guide.

Smith, H. 2007. *A Long-Shadowed Grief: Suicide and Its Aftermath.* **Lanham, MD: Cowley.**

In the aftermath of suicide, friends and family face considerable grief and reflection. The author offers a compassionate narrative of the suffering that friends and family endure in the wake of a loved one's suicide. At the heart of the book are true stories of suicide and the words of survivors.

Research Journals

Addiction

Addiction
http://www.blackwellpublishing.com/journal.asp?ref=0965-2140&site=1

Published on behalf of the Society for the Study of Addiction, this journal offers a wide range of articles, commentaries, interviews with leading researchers, and book reviews.

Addiction Research and Theory
http://www.tandf.co.uk/journals/journal.asp?issn=1606-6359&subcategory=PS050000

A cross-disciplinary journal that explores addictive behaviors from a variety of different fields, including anthropological, medical, historical, psychological, and sociological perspectives.

Alcoholism
http://www.blackwellpublishing.com/journal.asp?ref=0145-6008&site=1

Provides readers with current and important findings on alcoholism and drug dependence, including topics focusing on medical topics, clinical research, and health care issues.

American Journal on Addictions
http://www.tandf.co.uk/journals/journal.asp?issn=1055-0496&subcategory=PS050000

As the official publication of the American Academy of Addiction Psychiatry, this journal contains topical issues, including research related to the prevention and treatment of substance abuse.

Adolescent Runaways

Deviant Behavior
http://www.tandf.co.uk/journals/titles/01639625.asp

Readers will discover a diversity of topics covered in this journal, including alcohol abuse, mental illness, crime, sexual deviance, and juvenile delinquency.

Journal of Family Issues
http://www.sagepub.com/journalsProdDesc.nav?prodId=
Journal200912

Sponsored by the National Council on Family Relations, this publication provides a forum on important family topics in modern society and includes articles and commentaries.

Journal of Marital & Family Therapy
http://www.blackwellpublishing.com/journal.asp?ref=
0194-472X&site=1

This is the official publication of the American Association for Marriage and Family Therapy and provides extensive coverage of the major issues and challenges facing families today.

Journal of Research on Adolescence
http://www.blackwellpublishing.com/journal.asp?ref=
1050-8392&site=1

A rigorous exploration into adolescent research, including coverage of the physical, cognitive, social, and emotional domains of the teenage years.

Youth & Society
http://www.sagepub.com/journalsProdDesc.nav?prodId=
Journal200812

A valuable reference source for educators, policy makers, and researchers, especially those seeking information on such topics as adolescent pregnancy, runaways, sexually transmitted diseases, and substance abuse.

Unemployment

Journal of Career Development
http://www.sagepub.com/journalsProdDesc.nav?prodId=
Journal201758

This research journal provides subscribers with the latest in career development theory and practice, including career development across the lifespan, vocational satisfaction, midcareer changes, and unemployment.

Journal of Vocational Behavior
http://www.elsevier.com/wps/find/journaldescription.cws_
home/622908/description#description

One of the leading research journals in the career field today, offering coverage of vocational decision making as well as adjustments and adaptations.

Work & Stress
http://www.tandf.co.uk/journals/journal.asp?issn=
0267-8373&subcategory=PS650000

An international, quarterly publication featuring the psychological, organizational, and social components of work, health, and organizations.

Work, Employment and Society
http://www.sagepub.com/journalsProdDesc.nav?prodId=
Journal201568

In addition to regular coverage of unemployment, this publication features articles on industrial relations, labor economics, and organizational analysis.

Infidelity

American Journal of Family Therapy
http://www.tandf.co.uk/journals/journal.asp?issn=
0192-6187&subcategory=PS350000

This research publication provides subscribers with the latest findings on treating normal and atypical relationships. Topics include research on intimacy and sexuality, alternative relationships, and therapeutic styles of intervention.

Family Journal
http://www.sagepub.com/journalsProdDesc.nav?prodId=
Journal200924

The official journal of the International Association of Marriage and Family Counselors, this publication showcases contemporary research and applied formulation for educators, practitioners, and students.

Journal of Sex & Marital Therapy
http://www.tandf.co.uk/journals/usmt

Readers can expect to find side coverage of special medical and clinical problems, therapeutic intervention for sexual dysfunctions, and the interplay between sexual functioning and marital stability.

Sexual and Relationship Therapy
http://www.tandf.co.uk/journals/titles/14681994.asp

One of the more visible research journals of its kind, offering a forum for review of all sexual and relationship dysfunctions and therapies.

Divorce

Counseling Psychologist
http://www.sagepub.com/journalsProdDesc.nav?prodId=Journal200805

Keeps readers abreast of important topics in the counseling field today, including issues related to divorce, separation, and remarriage. The publication also features information on professional issues as well as coverage of international perspectives.

Family Process
http://www.blackwellpublishing.com/journal.asp?ref=0014-7370&site=1

This is the official publication of the Family Process Institute, an international and multidisciplinary journal offering cutting-edge research in family interaction and therapy.

Family Relations
http://www.blackwellpublishing.com/journal.asp?ref=0197-6664&site=1

One of the more popular and visible research journals of its kind. Its timely and applied articles hold vast appeal to educators, therapists, and family studies researchers.

Journal of Marriage and Family
http://www.blackwellpublishing.com/journal.asp?ref=
0022-2445&site=1

Published on behalf of the National Council on Family Relations, this journal represents the leading research journal in the field. Every serious-minded student in family studies should have access to it.

Chronic Illness and Disease

Chronic Illness
http://www.sagepub.com/journalsProdDesc.nav?prodId=
Journal201862

A forum in which researchers share findings on important issues in chronic illness, with a particular emphasis on the experience and management of long-term medical conditions.

Disability and Rehabilitation
http://www.tandf.co.uk/journals/tf/09638288.html

This publication is the official journal of the International Society of Physical and Rehabilitation Medicine. It seeks to foster a better understanding of all aspects of disability and to promote all phases of rehabilitation.

Disability & Society
http://www.tandf.co.uk/journals/carfax/09687599.html

An international journal focusing on such topics as definitions of disability, discrimination, social policy related to the disabled, and community care and inclusion.

Pain Research & Management
http://www.pulsus.com/journals/journalHome.jsp?origPg=
journalHome.jsp&jnlKy=7&/home.htm&&HCtype=Consumer

This publication is the official journal of the Canadian Pain Society and offers subscribers coverage of all facets of the management of pain.

Caring for Aging Family Members

Gerontologist
http://www.gerontologyjournals.org/

The official publication of the Gerontological Society of America. It offers multidisciplinary perspective on aging, including social policy and program development.

Journal of Aging and Health
http://jah.sagepub.com/

A good resource for the latest findings on such topics as factors influencing life expectancy, disease prevention, health care, diet and nutrition, and social support for the aged.

Journal of Applied Gerontology
http://jag.sagepub.com/

This highly regarded research publication publishes a variety of multidisciplinary articles on aging, including psychological and social investigations of aging and the aged.

Journal of Elder Abuse & Neglect
http://www.haworthpressinc.com/store/product.asp?sku=J084

A quarterly journal offering subscribers the latest advances in research and policy issues involving the abuse and neglect of the elderly.

Domestic Violence

Child Maltreatment
http://www.sagepub.com/journalsProdDesc.nav?prodId=Journal200758

This journal is the official publication of the American Professional Society on the Abuse of Children. It offers research, information, and technical innovations on the topics of child abuse and neglect and has significant appeal to professionals involved in child protection, social work, law enforcement, and psychology.

Journal of Family Violence
http://www.wkap.nl/journalhome.htm/0885-7482

An interdisciplinary journal that publishes research from noted scholars in the field, including those from social work, sociology, psychology, law, and criminology. Covers all forms of domestic abuse.

Journal of Interpersonal Violence
http://jiv.sagepub.com/

This journal provides subscribers with in-depth coverage of child sexual abuse and neglect, intimate partner violence, rape, and other violent crimes. Also included are book reviews exploring key contributions to the field.

Violence against Women
http://www.sagepub.com/journalsProdDesc.nav?prodId=Journal200837

A peer-reviewed research journal that focuses on all facets of violence against women. The journal includes empirical research as well as book reviews from scholars in women's studies.

School Violence

Aggression and Violent Behavior
http://www.elsevier.com/wps/find/journaldescription.cws_home/30843/description#description

Coverage includes child and youth violence, including school shootings, gang violence, and domestic abuse.

Journal of Child & Adolescence Trauma
http://www.haworthpress.com/store/product.asp?sku=J392

Explores the prevention and treatment strategies for dealing with symptoms and disorders related to the psychological effects of trauma, including school shootings and loss. Also offers coverage of school and community violence prevention programs.

Journal of Early Adolescence
http://www.sagepub.com/journalsProdDesc.nav?prodId=Journal200872

A recognized leader among research journals focusing on the teenage years, specifically ages 10 through 14 years of age. Contains original theories and studies, guest editorials, and literature reviews.

Youth Violence and Juvenile Justice
http://www.sagepub.com/journalsProdDesc.nav?prodId=Journal201632

This interdisciplinary research journal is a valuable resource for those exploring research in such areas as youth violence and school safety. It offers considerable appeal to those involved in education, social work, psychology, public health, therapy, and other disciplines.

Natural Disasters

American Journal of Disaster Medicine
http://www.pnpco.com/pn03000.html

Offers readers an important resource on the care and treatment of injuries and other physical trauma suffered in the wake of natural disasters and disease outbreak.

Disasters
http://www.blackwellpublishing.com/journal.asp?ref=0361-3666&site=1

A peer-reviewed quarterly journal that provides coverage of all features of disasters, including intervention, policy, and management issues.

Journal of Emergency Management
http://www.pnpco.com/pn06001.html

A bimonthly research journal designed to educate readers on emergency preparedness for everything from natural disasters to acts of terror, fires, and other catastrophes.

Trauma
http://www.sagepub.com/journalsProdDesc.nav?prodId=Journal201832

Makes available a diverse selection of topics for those involved in the management of trauma patients, including survivors of natural disasters.

Deployed Military Families

American Psychological Association publications
http://www.apa.org/journals/

Readers will find an abundance of research articles on the psychological effects of war, including posttraumatic syndrome.

Armed Forces Journal
http://www.armedforcesjournal.com/

A global newsweekly designed for those seeking information on defense programs, policy, business, and technology.

Armed Forces & Society
http://www.sagepub.com/journalsProdDesc.nav?prodId=Journal201730

A peer-reviewed, international journal offering coverage of such topics as the consequences of war, terrorism, and family and health issues.

Stress, Trauma and Crisis
http://www.counselingarena.com/journals/Stress-Trauma-and-Crisis-1543-4613

Includes coverage of topics such as disequilibrium and instability, stress management, and crisis intervention in a variety of settings such as families dealing with the many sides of military deployment.

Adolescent Suicide

Archives of Suicide Research
http://www.tandf.co.uk/journals/titles/13811118.asp

Offers an examination of suicidal behavior, its causes and effects, and intervention techniques.

Crisis: The Journal of Crisis Intervention and Suicide Prevention
http://www.hhpub.com/journals/crisis/index.html

One of the better research journals on the topic of suicide. It offers timely and important articles as well as reviews of important books, videos, and training programs.

Journal of Loss & Trauma
http://www.counselingarena.com/journals/Journal-of-Loss-and-Trauma-1532-5024

This journal is a forum examining personal losses relating to family and health, including the tragedy of adolescent suicide.

Preventing Suicide
http://www.preventsuicide.net/

In addition to presenting important research, including scientific and medical studies, this journal examines trends and practical information on the topic of suicide prevention.

DVDs/Videotapes

Addiction

Addictions: Chemical and Behavioral (2004)
http://www.films.com/id/11903/Addictions_Chemical_and_Behavioral.htm

An examination of how addictions develop, as well as the interventions that are available.

Alcohol (2001)
http://www.films.com/id/1804/Alcohol.htm

A look at how alcohol impacted the lives of three teenagers.

Constant Craving: The Science of Addiction (2000)
http://www.films.com/id/1284/Constant_Craving_The_Science_of_Addiction.htm

This video sheds considerable light on the biological causes and consequences of addiction.

Young Addicts: Drugs, Alcohol, and America's Future (2006)
http://www.films.com/id/12997/Young_Addicts_Drugs_Alcohol_and_Americas_Future.htm

A troubling look at how young generations are turning to drugs and alcohol, and the dangers that such choices bring.

Adolescent Runaways

Adolescent Family Therapy **(2002)**
http://www.insight-media.com/IMHome.htm

A look at some of the strategies involved in therapeutic intervention for teenagers.

Challenge of Counseling Teens, The **(2004)**
http://www.insight-media.com/IMHome.htm

Helpful information about engaging adolescents in therapy and overcoming resistance.

Teens and Runaways **(2007)**
http://www.cambridgeeducational.com/id/15185/Real_Life_Teens_Teens_and_Runaways.html

Explores why adolescents run away from home and where parents can turn for help.

Unemployment

The Business Cycle **(2000)**
http://www.insight-media.com/IMHome.htm

The various types of unemployment are captured in this video.

Dealing with Job Loss **(2006)**
http://www.jist.com/shop/web

Viewers are taught how to deal with the crisis of unemployment, with a particular emphasis on the steps needed to launch a new job search.

Rebounding from Job Loss **(2000)**
http://www.impactpublications.com/

An insightful look at unemployment and what displaced workers can do to regain stability in their lives.

Infidelity

Couples Therapy for Extramarital Affairs (2000)
http://www.apa.org/videos/4310360.html

A noted psychotherapist explores couple strategies when one partner has had an affair.

The Love Lab: Putting Marriages Back Together (2002)
http://www.insight-media.com/IMHome.htm

An inside look at how marital distress is assessed and the manner in which relational changes are implemented.

Love, Lust and Marriage: Why We Stay and Why We Stray (1997)
http://www.insight-media.com/IMHome.htm

An interesting look at marital fidelity, infidelity, and how modern divorce rates have impacted the notion of love.

Divorce

Changing Families (2007)
http://www.insight-media.com/IMHome.htm

An exploration of the modern-day family, including how divorce rates have affected the family as a social institution.

Child Custody (2006)
http://www.insight-media.com/IMHome.htm

Safeguarding the best interests of the children of divorce rests at the foundation of this program.

Divorce: How It Affects Kids (2002)
http://www.insight-media.com/IMHome.htm

A thoughtful analysis of how divorce affects children and what parents can do to ease the transition.

Effects of Divorce (2000)
http://www.insight-media.com/IMHome.htm

A presentation focusing on the negative effects of divorce and what can be done to minimize the damage.

Working with Couples Considering Divorce (2006)
http://www.insight-media.com/IMHome.htm

Sheds light on the manner in which therapeutic intervention is aimed at couples considering marital dissolution.

Working with Stepfamilies (2004)
http://www.insight-media.com/IMHome.htm

Suggests ways blended families can overcome obstacles and achieve domestic harmony.

Chronic Illness and Disease

A Disease Called Pain (2003)
http://www.fanlight.com/catalog/films/377_adcp.php

An investigation of chronic pain through the lives of patients as well as physicians and researchers seeking to supply relief, comfort, and hope.

Finding Optimism in a Family with Chronic Illness (2006)
http://www.insight-media.com/IMHome.htm

An exploration of the challenges and hardships of families dealing with chronic illness as well as ways to ease the burden.

Not on the Sidelines (2000)
http://www.fanlight.com/catalog/films/280_nos.php

A poignant look at four people whose lives were changed by illness or injury.

Caring for Aging Family Members

Growing Up and Growing Old: Caring for Our Parents (2002)
http://www.fanlight.com/catalog/films/365_gugo.php

Explores the challenges and struggles of grown children caring for aging parents.

Parenting Our Elderly Parents (2004)
http://www.insight-media.com/IMHome.htm

The focus of this program is how to care for aging parents while preserving one's own quality of life.

When Help Was There: Four Stories of Elder Abuse (2000)
http://www.fanlight.com/catalog/films/335_whwt.php

A look at elder abuse, including physical, emotional, and financial consequences.

Domestic Violence

Battered Hearts (2005)
http://www.fanlight.com/catalog/films/430_bh.php

A documentary designed to increase awareness of domestic violence and of programs available to those seeking help.

Breaking the Cycle of Domestic Violence (1998)
http://www.fanlight.com/catalog/films/321_btcodv.php

Excellent overview of the many sides to domestic violence.

Breaking the Silence: Issues of Sexual Abuse (2000)
http://www.insight-media.com/IMHome.htm

An investigation of the long-term consequences of child sexual abuse.

Broken Child: Case Studies of Child Abuse (2000)
http://www.insight-media.com/IMHome.htm

A compelling look at the cycle of child abuse, including causes and consequences.

Child Abuse: How to See It, How to Stop It (2004)
http://www.insight-media.com/IMHome.htm

Explores physical abuse, sexual abuse, emotional abuse, and neglect.

School Violence

Bullied to Death (2000)
http://www.insight-media.com/IMHome.htm

This video explores the effects of bullying and offers intervention strategies for parents as well as teachers.

Bullies and Harassment (2001)
http://www.films.com/id/15168/Real_Life_Teens_Bullies_and_Harassment.htm

Insightful look at bullying and how this growing social problem can be curbed.

Calming the Tempest: Helping Explosive Children (2004)
http://www.insight-media.com/IMHome.htm

Thoughtful analysis of how to reach out and help children having anger management issues.

Killer at Thurston High, The (2000)
http://www.pbs.org/wgbh/pages/frontline/shows/kinkel/

A chronology of school shooter Kip Kinkel's life and the events leading up to the horror of May 20–21, 1998.

Preventing School Violence (2001)
http://www.films.com/id/4614/Preventing_School_Violence.htm

Proposes innovative strategies to reduce school violence among children and teenagers.

School Shootings: America's Tragedy (1999)
http://www.films.com/id/623/School_Shootings_Americas_Tragedy.htm

A penetrating look at the causes and long-term effects of school shootings.

Natural Disasters

Crisis Stabilization for Children: Disaster Mental Health (2006)
http://www.insight-media.com/IMHome.htm

A video focusing on strategies designed to assist and support children after a disaster.

Helping Children Cope with Disaster (2003)
http://www.insight-media.com/IMHome.htm

In addition to describing children's typical reactions to disaster, this program outlines effective coping strategies for easing stress and anxiety.

Killer Hurricane: Anatomy of Katrina (2005)
http://www.films.com/id/12606/Killer_Hurricane_Anatomy_of_Katrina.htm

A detailed look at Hurricane Katrina's effects on infrastructure, economic conditions, and human lives.

Savage Earth (1998)
http://www.pbs.org/wnet/savageearth/

Compelling look at volcanoes, earthquakes, and tsunamis, including their origins and the impact they bring to people's lives.

Deployed Military Families

My War Diary (2005)
http://shopping.discovery.com/product-64821.html
?endecaSID=116164E5C954

A look at combat from the eyes of soldiers on the front line of Iraq as well as from loved ones awaiting reunion.

Talk, Listen, Connect: Helping Families during
Military Deployment (2000)
http://www.militaryonesource.com/skins/MOS/home.aspx

Meeting the needs of children during deployment is the focus of this video.

These Boots: A Spouse's Guide to Stepping Up and Standing
Tall during Deployment (2000)
http://www.militaryonesource.com/skins/MOS/home.aspx

Practical advice for deployed military families to help ensure healthy adjustment.

War Letters (2001)
http://www.shoppbs.org/product/index.jsp?productId=1402920

The connection between soldiers in combat and family on the home front is captured in this heartfelt collection of letters.

Adolescent Suicide

It's Never Too Late: Stopping Teen Suicide **(2005)**
http://hrmvideo.com/

Teaches viewers how to recognize and respond to the risks of adolescent suicide.

Remembering Tom **(1999)**
http://www.fanlight.com/catalog/films/320_rt.php

The trauma of adolescent suicide and its impact on the family system are explored in this video.

Suicide Prevention for Parents and Teachers **(2005)**
http://www.insight-media.com/IMHome.htm

Informative video that explores the risks of suicide as well as the recognition of warning signs.

Links to Additional Resources

Family Health and Well-Being

Administration for Children and Families
http://www.acf.hhs.gov

American Academy of Pediatrics
http://www.aap.org

American Medical Association
http://www.ama-assn.org

American Psychological Association
http://www.apa.org

American School Health Association
http://www.ashaweb.org/

Children's Health Council
http://www.chconline.org

Cross Cultural Health Care Program
http://www.xculture.org

Facts for Health
http://www.factsforhealth.org

Federation of Families for Children's Mental Health
http://www.ffcmh.org

KidsHealth
http://www.kidshealth.org

National Center for Children in Poverty
http://www.nccp.org/

National Center for Education in Maternal and Child Health
http://www.ncemch.org/

National Center for Health Statistics
http://www.cdc.gov/nchs/

National Resource Center for Health and Safety in Child Care
http://nrc.uchsc.edu

National Training Institute for Child Care Health Consultants
http://www.sph.unc.edu/courses/childcare/

Safe Kids Worldwide
http://www.safekids.org

World Health Organization
http://www.who.ch

Family Policy

Advocates for Youth
http://www.advocatesforyouth.org

American Youth Policy Forum
http://www.aypf.org

Center on Budget and Policy Priorities
http://www.cbpp.org

Center for Law and Social Policy
http://www.clasp.org

Child Advocate
http://www.childadvocate.net

Child Welfare League of America
http://www.cwla.org

Children Now
http://www.childrennow.org

Children's Partnership
http://www.childrenspartnership.org

Coalition for America's Families
www.coalition4families.com

Economic Policy Institute
http://www.epinet.org/

Families Worldwide
http://www.fww.org

Human Services Policy Center
http://www.hspc.org/

Insight: Center for Community Development
http://www.insightcced.org/

Institute for Child Health Policy
http://www.ichp.ufl.edu/

Institute for Women's Policy Research
http://www.iwpr.org

National Families in Action
http://www.emory.edu/NFIA

National Women's Law Center
http://www.nwlc.org

Stand for Children
http://www.stand.org

Government Agencies Serving Families

Administration for Children and Families
http://www.acf.hhs.gov

Afterschool.gov
http://www.afterschool.gov

Child Care Bureau
http://www.acf.hhs.gov/programs/ccb/

Division of Violence Prevention
http://www.cdc.gov/ncipc/dvp/dvp.htm

Family and Youth Services Bureau
http://www.acf.hhs.gov/programs/fysb/

Healthy Schools, Healthy Communities
http://www.educationmoney.com/prgm_93.302_hhs.html

National Child Care Information Center
http://www2.nccic.org/index.html

**National Institute of Child Health and
Human Development**
http://www.nichd.nih.gov

National Institutes of Health
http://www.nih.gov

Office of Community Services
http://www.acf.hhs.gov/programs/ocs

Office of Family Assistance
http://www.acf.hhs.gov/programs/ofa

Office of Family Planning
http://www.cdph.ca.gov/programs/ofp/pages/default.aspx

Social Security Administration
http://www.ssa.gov/

U.S. Department of Health and Human Services
http://www.hhs.gov

U.S. Department of Labor Women's Bureau
http://www.dol.gov/dol/wb

U.S. Government Printing Office
http://www.access.gpo.gov/

USA Services
http://www.info.gov/

National Family Organizations

About Our Kids
http://www.aboutourkids.org

Center for the Child Care Workforce
http://www.ccw.org/

Child Care Institute of America
http://www.nccic.org/orgs/ccia.html

Children, Youth and Family Consortium
http://www.cyfc.umn.edu

Children's Defense Fund
http://www.childrensdefense.org

Children's Foundation
http://www.thechildrensfoundationchasi.org/

Council on Contemporary Families
http://www.contemporaryfamilies.org/

Council for Exceptional Children
http://www.cec.sped.org

The Fathers Network
http://www.fathersnetwork.org

FPG Child Development Institute
http://www.fpg.unc.edu

The Future of Children
http://www.futureofchildren.org

Institute for Youth, Education, and Families
http://www.nlc.org/IYEF/index.aspx

National Adoption Information Clearinghouse
http://www.adoption.org/adopt/national-adoption-
information-clearinghouse.php

National Black Child Development Institute
http://www.nbcdi.org

National Council on Family Relations
http://www.ncfr.com

National Dissemination Center for Children with Disabilities
http://www.nichcy.org

National Resource Center for Family Centered Practice
http://www.uiowa.edu/~nrcfcp/

National Youth Development Information Center
http://www.nydic.org

North American Council on Adoptable Children
http://www.nacac.org/

Zero to Three
http://www.zerotothree.org

Family Research Sites

Bureau of Labor Statistics
http://www.bls.gov

Child Trends
http://www.childtrends.org

Children, Youth and Families Education and Research Network
http://www.cyfernet.org

ChildStats.gov
http://www.childstats.gov

Early Childhood Research & Practice
http://www.ecrp.uiuc.edu

Guttmacher Institute
http://www.agi-usa.org

Harvard Medical Library
http://www.med.harvard.edu

Library of Congress
http://www.lcweb.loc.gov/

National Research Council
http://www.nas.edu/nrc/

**Research Forum at the National Center for
Children in Poverty**
http://www.researchforum.org

**Research and Training Center on Family Support and
Children's Mental Health**
http://www.rtc.pdx.edu

U.S. Census Bureau
http://www.census.gov

Glossary

ABCX model   A model of family crisis developed by Reuben Hill. The component parts of the model include the stressor, resources, the family's definition of the stressor, and the actual crisis.

acute stress disorder   A psychological disturbance marked by intrusive and disturbing memories of the crisis, an exaggerated startle response, and a tendency to avoid the situation by withdrawing from it physically and psychologically.

addiction   A dependence on a behavior or substance that a person is powerless to stop.

biochemical stressor   An external condition that creates disequilibrium, such as heat, cold, injury, pollutants, toxicants, or poor nutrition.

blended family   A family that results when a divorced parent with custody of children remarries.

bullying   A form of violence that exposes a person to abusive actions repeatedly over time. It entails unwanted and repeated written, verbal, or physical behavior, including any threatening, insulting, or dehumanizing gesture, by an adult or a student that is severe or pervasive enough to create an intimidating, hostile, or offensive environment.

child abuse   Harm to, or neglect of, a child by another person, whether adult or child.

child sexual abuse   A form of child abuse when the child is used for sexual purposes by an adult or adolescent. It involves exposing a child to any sexual activity or behavior.

chronic illness   A progressive disorder caused by a nonreversible condition that often leaves the person with some type of disability.

codependency   A relationship in which a person exhibits too much, and often inappropriate, caring for addicts who depend on him or her.

community divorce   A divorce process described by Paul Bohannan. It entails how the divorced person's status changes or is altered by one's surrounding neighborhood.

contact addiction   An extension of Internet addiction that is characterized by the obsessive use of cell phones and text messaging.

coparental divorce   In all likelihood, the most difficult of all divorce components described by researcher Paul Bohannan. The coparental divorce focuses on the issue of child custody.

cyclical unemployment   Unemployment caused by a drop in economic activity.

developmental crisis   A state of disequilibrium originating from predictable, developmental changes over the course of the family life cycle. Also called a *normative crisis.*

distress   Negative and unpleasant stress.

divorce from dependency   The last of six divorce processes proposed by researcher Paul Bohannon. The key challenge here is for separating partners to establish psychological autonomy.

domestic violence   An abusive relationship within an intimate relationship where one partner uses a pattern of assault and intimidating acts to assert power and control over the other partner. Also called *intimate partner violence.*

Double ABCX model   A model of family crisis proposed by Hamilton McCubbin and Joan Patterson. The component parts of the model include the pileup of family demands, family adaptive resources, family definition and meaning, and family adaptation balancing.

economic divorce   According to divorce expert Paul Bohannan, one of the six components of the divorce process. The economic divorce entails decisions regarding how to divide money and property.

emotional divorce   According to Paul Bohannan, one of the six processes or components of divorce. The emotional divorce is centered around the deteriorating marriage and the initial motivations for considering a divorce.

endemic stressor   An external condition that creates disequilibrium and is usually long term in scope. An endemic stressor is one that has become so prevalent that the individual has learned to live with it, such as being afflicted with a chronic disease or illness.

eustress   A term referring to positive stress. Eustress occurs when the body's reactive change is put to productive use.

family crisis   A situation that occurs when the family system encounters disruption to its everyday routines and experiences a state of disequilibrium or instability.

family disequilibrium   A family condition marked by upheaval and instability.

family equilibrium　The ability of a system to function smoothly and demonstrate stability and balance, particularly in the face of challenge or change.

family metacognition stage　According to Constance Ahrons, a stage that accompanies marital degeneration. At this time, the entire family system recognizes that the marriage is deteriorating.

family redefinition stage　Final stage of divorce suggested by Constance Ahrons. At this time, the family system must redefine its identity, particularly parent-child relationships.

family reorganization stage　Stage of divorce proposed by Constance Ahrons focusing on the family adjustments required once the divorce is finalized.

frictional unemployment　Temporary unemployment originating from the normal and routine job search process.

individual cognition stage　Stage of divorce proposed by Constance Ahrons. At this time, attention is focused on the individual perceptions and reactions that accompany a deteriorating marriage.

infidelity　Sexual activity with another person without the consent of one's spouse.

Internet addiction　The excessive use of the Internet that causes psychological, social, and physical problems for the user.

multigenerational household　Living arrangements in which older persons are living with adult children and/or grandchildren under the same roof.

natural disaster　An extreme, sudden traumatic crisis caused by environmental factors. A natural disaster can strike at any time, often with little or no warning, and can threaten the lives of people and destroy property.

philosophical stressor　An external condition that creates disequilibrium, such as value-system conflicts, lack of purpose, or lack of direction.

physical disability　An impairment of body structure and function, including mobility impairments, amputations, skeletal deformities, and disfigurements.

primary stressor　A stressor that is responsible for initiating the stress response.

psychological stressor　An external condition that creates disequilibrium, such as worry and anxiety.

psychosocial stressor　An external condition that creates disequilibrium, such as the loss of a job or the death of a friend.

relapse A term often used in connection to addiction; a return to the abused substance or behavioral pattern.

resiliency A family's ability to recover from disruptive change without being overwhelmed or acting in dysfunctional ways.

secondary stressor A condition that results from the first stressor and keeps the stress response activated.

separation stage Stage of divorce proposed by Constance Ahrons. At this time, one parent physically leaves the home and consequently forces adjustments and adaptations on remaining members of the system.

situational crisis A state of disequilibrium that is neither predictable nor normal. Rather, this type of crisis is sudden and abrupt and can occur at any point in the family's development. Also called a *nonnormative crisis*.

social stressor An external condition that creates disequilibrium, such as noise or crowding.

stress The common, nonspecific response of the body to any demand made upon it, be it psychological, sociological, or physiological.

stressor An external event or condition that affects the equilibrium of an organism.

structural unemployment Unemployment resulting from changes in the economy caused by technological progress and shifts in the demand for goods and services.

system A term referring to the family unit and the members comprising it.

systems theory A school of thought proposing that an individual's behavior cannot be understood without reference to the individual's past and present relationships, especially family interactions.

teenage runaway A person under 18 who is away from home or place of legal residence at least one night without the permission of parents, guardians, or custodial authorities.

traumatic crisis A state of disequilibrium that is often life threatening and, due to the circumstances, gives survivors a feeling of extreme helplessness. A traumatic crisis is a highly stressful event.

unemployment rate The percentage of the U.S. labor force that is unemployed. It is calculated by dividing the number of unemployed individuals by the sum of the number of people unemployed and the number of people employed.

Index

Note: italic page number indicates figure; t. indicates table.

About the Author

Jeffrey S. Turner is a full professor in the Human Development and Family Studies Department at Mitchell College in New London, Connecticut. Dr. Turner is the author of many college-level textbooks, including *Dating and Sexuality in America; Families in America; Marriage and Family: Traditions and Transitions; Encyclopedia of Relationships across the Lifespan; Lifespan Development; Contemporary Adulthood; Exploring Child Behavior;* and *Contemporary Human Sexuality.* Dr. Turner's various books have sold more than 260,000 copies and have been used in many colleges and universities in the United States and abroad. He is also the author of articles and studies and has received numerous awards and citations for his distinguished teaching and writing accomplishments.

DATE DUE

Overdue charge is 10 cents per day,
Including Saturdays, Sundays and holidays.